INHERIT MORE

INHERIT MORE

MARTIN M. SHENKMAN

WILEY

JOHN WILEY & SONS, INC.

Published by John Wiley & Sons, Inc., Hoboken, New Jersey.
Published simultaneously in Canada.

For general information on our other products and services please contact our Customer Care Department within the United States at (800) 762-2974, outside the United States at (317) 572-3993 or fax (317) 572-4002.

Wiley also publishes its books in a variety of electronic formats. Some content that appears in print may not be available in electronic books. For more information about Wiley products, visit our web site at www.wiley.com.

Library of Congress Cataloging-in-Publication Data:

Shenkman, Martin M.
    Inherit more / Martin M. Shenkman.
      p. cm.
    Includes index.
    ISBN 0-471-42116-2 (cloth : alk. paper)
    1. Decedents' estates—United States—Popular works. 2. Estate planning—United States—Popular works. 3. Inheritance and succession—United States—Popular works. I. Title.
KF753.Z9 S52 2003
346.7305′2—dc21

                                          2002034323

Printed in the United States of America.

10 9 8 7 6 5 4 3 2 1

To my parents, Jack and Miriam Shenkman, whose legacy has included the values of charity, family, and personal integrity—an inheritance far more valuable than money.

Acknowledgments

I would like to thank a number of people who were of considerable assistance in the preparation of this book:

- Michael Hamilton of John Wiley & Sons, whose support and encouragement were outstanding, as usual.
- Special thanks to Rebecca Gottlieb, a Columbia Law School student at the time of her research and drafting assistance on this book. The book could not have been completed without her able assistance, creative thoughts, research, writing, and other skills.
- Gary Goldberg, host of the *Money Matters* radio show (www.mmfn.com) and of Gary Goldberg Financial Services in Suffern, New York on which some of the ideas for this book have been discussed.
- Dani Koesterich and Neil Goldberg of mastermailings.com for their help in developing the Law Made Easy Press Web site, www.laweasy.com.
- Benjamin Eckman, Esq. for his suggestions and comments on Chapter 10; any mistakes remain mine.
- Nikhil Hanmantgad, a student of Northern Valley-Demarest High School in Demarest, New Jersey, for his research of cases.
- Stanley and Sylvia Teitelbaum, brilliant and insightful psychologists practicing in Teaneck, New Jersey, for their thoughts and comments on the psychology of inheriting more.

- Rosalie Gross and the editorial and publishing staff at the *New Jersey Lawyer* for their openmindedness and willingness to publish articles on religion and the law and all those religious experts who gave of their time.

- Charles Abut, Esq. of Fort Lee, New Jersey, for his professorial insights into matrimonial issues.

Any errors or omissions are my own.

Contents

1   Why Inherit More?   1

2   Talking to Your Parents   15

3   Second (and Later) Spouses Can Destroy
Your Inheritance   47

4   Do Your Parents Have the Right
Insurance Coverage?   69

5   Are Your Parents' Assets Managed and
Invested Appropriately?   85

6   How Do Your Parents Own Their Assets:
Judging a Book by Its Cover   111

7   Jewelry, Vacation Homes, Family Apartments,
and Other Tough-to-Divide Assets   137

8   Identifying Hidden Assets   147

9   Do Not Overlook the Paperwork   163

10   Medicaid Nursing Home Costs   181

11   Estate, Gift, and Other Taxes That Can
Decimate Your Inheritance   189

12   Is Your Mom's Lawyer Billing Excessive
Fees and Expenses?   203

13   Dealing with Will Contests and Lawsuits   215

14   Preventing Your Ex-Spouse from Running
     Off with Your Inherited Assets   237

15   Inherit the Best Way Possible—A Lifetime Trust   249

16   Safeguarding Your Inheritance   255

Index   271

1 WHY INHERIT MORE?

$150 billion a year—that's how much the *Wall Street Journal* estimates baby boomers will inherit. Not in total, but *every* year for the next five years! Now *Inherit More* introduces a new perspective on estate planning. Until now, estate-planning books and seminars have focused on encouraging parents or elder persons to protect their estate for their heirs. This book is written not to help parents plan how to bequeath their estate, but to help those who will inherit it. The unique approach of *Inherit More* empowers you, the potential heir, to assist your parent or other benefactor in planning and to increase the wealth you may receive. You can guide your parents in taking advantage of new trends in estate and related planning practices. Every caring child wants to ensure that parents (other senior family member or other benefactor) are well provided for in their golden years. Every child, after fulfilling that responsibility, also wants to maximize any future inheritance. You can maximize your inheritance while helping your parents live better and achieve their goals. Protecting your inheritance need not be inconsistent with your parents' wishes. If done correctly, both you and your parents should benefit. No parent wants to see lifetime savings dissipated by taxes, nursing home costs, excessive legal fees, and worse.

Why inherit more? We live in a world where a college degree can cost upward of several hundred thousand dollars. If we do not seek out advantages wherever they lie, we may be cheating our own heirs. It is necessary to acknowledge these facts so that you can plan around them, which is what this book will help you do. The

1

coming chapters explain how to maximize your inheritance while protecting your benefactor's interests.

HOW YOU CAN INHERIT MORE

The first chapter of this book is an overview that explains how your active participation not only can maximize your inheritance, but can provide tremendous assistance to your parents or other family member or benefactor. Too often, poor planning dissipates money. Although the proposition may offend some people's sensibilities, you should not feel guilty about planning to maximize your inheritance. Invariably, inadequate planning results in spending significant sums of money on unwarranted legal fees, professional fees, medical costs, and so on. This is not something that any parent would want.

Furthermore, when done properly, maximizing your inheritance will not harm your parents or other benefactors. Rather, it will safeguard their own interests and ensure that asset distribution after their death will reflect their true intent.

Insight: Many people are troubled by the idea of trying to maximize their own inheritance. They may want the money, but it is tied into a lot of guilt and negative feelings. You may have to deal with your own feelings about these issues before you can effectively help your parents. "There are different styles of dealing with this uncomfortable truth," observes Dr. Stanley Teitelbaum, of Teaneck, New Jersey, the truth being that you want to inherit more. But this truth is laden with tremendous emotional issues. If you don't address the emotional issues, you won't achieve your goals.

INHERITANCE PLANNING—MORE THAN ESTATE PLANNING

At some point in your life, you may have an elderly parent, family member, or friend who is likely to leave you a significant inheritance. What steps can you take to secure, safeguard, and assure that you receive the inheritance, and do so in a most advantageous manner? You may have spent months or years caring for an elderly relative or friend, paying bills and providing for the person's needs. In the end, you might discover that medical expenses, a jealous sibling, taxes, legal fees, or other avoidable problems infringe on, or even eliminate, your anticipated inheritance.

Whereas scores of books have been written about estate planning, there are very few about inheritance planning—protecting what you as the heir will receive. Possibly, this is because such planning may appear to be a selfish endeavor. There is nothing morally wrong, however, with maximizing the benefits of somebody's generosity to you. If you don't take practical steps to protect yourself and your benefactor, you may jeopardize what is potentially a once-in-a-lifetime opportunity. Creditors, claimants, greedy family members and friends, the taxman, overreaching attorneys, and hordes of others can intercede if you don't protect your rights.

Although greedy persons can abuse the methods outlined in this book, they are not intended to help you take unfair advantage of the elderly or infirm. They are offered simply to guide you in protecting your rightful inheritance. Few parents, relatives, or friends looking to benefit a favorite child, niece, nephew, or other helper would be pleased to find that most of their assets were decimated by nursing home costs, taxes, unintended beneficiaries, and legal fees. More importantly, no parent or other benefactor wants heirs to end up in a bitter feud over inheritance. These tragic situations can be avoided if you act affirmatively to prevent them.

HOW THE FAMILY INHERITANCE IS OFTEN DESTROYED

The scenarios of destroyed inheritances, family feuds, and tax nightmares often play out along common themes. In one of the most familiar situations, a family member, neighbor, friend, or caregiver provides devoted assistance to an elderly, infirm benefactor for years. When the benefactor seeks to reward the years of goodness, other potential heirs raise an outcry. The following case study, only slightly modified from an actual situation, is typical of thousands of scenarios that play out yearly. Don't prejudge the

caregiver versus the other potential heirs without carefully reviewing each person's perspective.

Case Study: Shirley Masters was a loving and doting niece to her favorite uncle, Albert Jones. For more than seven years, she saw to all of his
needs because as Albert grew older, he became a bit paranoid and uncomfortable with strangers. He thwarted Shirley's efforts to hire nursing
care with angry outbursts. The result was that for many years Shirley visited Albert—initially once a week and then increasing to three or four
times a week—to ensure that his needs were met. She also enlisted a
friendly neighbor to help out when she was unavailable. Shirley paid all of
Uncle Albert's bills, tended to his shopping and, perhaps more important
than anything, read to him providing comfort as his eyesight failed. Her
companionship was priceless to Uncle Albert.

Over the years, Uncle Albert encouraged and directed Shirley to
change the ownership of some of his larger certificates of deposit (CDs)
from his name alone to the two of them jointly. Shirley, at Uncle Albert's
direction, helped him renew maturing certificates of deposit by changing
the ownership (title) to read: "Albert Jones and Shirley Masters, as joint
tenants with the right of survivorship." Thus, on Albert's death, any CD
with that title would pass automatically to Shirley instead of as directed
by Uncle Albert's will.

Uncle Albert directed Shirley to make these changes with full understanding that it meant that the assets would be distributed to her directly
on his death. Neither Uncle Albert nor Shirley focused on Uncle Albert's
will, signed many years before, that distributed all of his assets equally to
his niece and nephews (four nephews and Shirley).

Uncle Albert did not remember having heard from any of the
nephews, with the exception of an occasional birthday or Christmas
card, in many years.

When Uncle Albert died, Shirley and the four uninvolved nephews received a copy of Uncle Albert's will and a statement of assets (an "accounting"). They found, to their shock, that Shirley had inherited more
than half of Uncle Albert's estate directly, instead of the 20 percent they
thought was her rightful share.

The four disenfranchised nephews collectively sued challenging Shirley
for having used undue influence during her time alone with Uncle Albert to coerce him into transferring many of his certificates of deposit to
joint title with her. They contended that she thereby circumvented Uncle
Albert's stated intent under his will of having assets distributed equally.
The nephews, caught up in their own lives, truly believed that they had
been good nephews. They honestly believed that they had called, written,
and inquired after Uncle Albert on a regular basis. They assumed that
Shirley, with a career and family of her own, couldn't possibly have spent
much more time with Uncle Albert than they had. Their conclusion,
which to any uninformed outsider might have appeared reasonable, was
that Shirley was after Uncle Albert's money. No one, other than Shirley
and Uncle Albert, was aware of the hours of reading and companionship
that she had given him.

What was the truth? Did Shirley really spend considerable time being a caregiver and companion to Uncle Albert? Did the nephews really call Uncle Albert regularly? Was Uncle Albert's memory simply faltering in his later years and he didn't remember the calls from his nephews? Did Shirley convince Uncle Albert that the nephews were really uninvolved? The difficulty of proving either scenario, the heated emotions (often exacerbated by an adversarial legal system), the lack of careful planning, the belief by each side (Shirley on one hand, the nephews on the other) of the veracity of their views, led to a long, expensive, and acrimonious legal battle.

What could Shirley do to address the lawsuit? More importantly, what should Shirley have done while Uncle Albert was alive to secure her inheritance? Defending the lawsuit by her well-meaning but misinformed siblings (Uncle Albert's nephews) would easily cost tens of thousands of dollars, or more. Shirley should have taken practical steps before Uncle Albert's death to secure her inheritance. In this case, litigation ended up costing the family collectively over $100,000 in legal fees and resulted in Shirley giving a significant portion of what Uncle Albert intended her to receive, almost $250,000, to siblings to whom she will no longer speak. The nephews didn't fare well either. Their relationship with their sister was irretrievably destroyed. They lost substantial money on otherwise avoidable legal fees. Their lives were consumed for more than a year with acrimonious litigation. Whatever they ultimately received, they believed it to be far less than what their Uncle Albert had intended. The good that Uncle Albert had wanted to bestow on his family became much the opposite.

Uncle Albert truly loved his niece and nephews and believed he was doing what was fair and best for all. The resultant tragedy was that lawyers' fees exceeded what any nephew inherited and family relationships were destroyed. Worse yet, the entire situation was avoidable. This book will show you how.

THE TAXMAN CAN DECIMATE A POORLY PLANNED ESTATE

So you thought that the estate tax was repealed? Well, not yet. It also remains to be seen what a future Congress will do to the favorable changes made to the estate tax in 2001. Will budget deficits entice a future session of Congress to scale back the phaseout of the tax? If the tax is repealed, will it be reenacted? Even if the federal estate tax is ultimately eliminated, how costly will a state's estate or inheritance tax be? To the surprise of many taxpayers, the gift tax and lifetime transfers can undermine your benefactor's wishes and your inheritance. Misunderstandings by a parent or other benefactor over what the taxman can reach can be devastating.

Case Study: Fred Whittaker had a multimillion-dollar estate before he died. It was divided equally between his children, with one exception. Fred wanted to bequeath his vacation home to his favorite nephew Steve, his wife Jane, and their children; the remainder of the estate was to be divided equally between Fred's daughter, Patty, and his son, Harold. The estate was taxable for both federal estate tax purposes and state inheritance tax purposes. When Fred died, the executor reviewed the will and paid taxes. The way that Fred's will was written resulted in Steve and Jane having to pay a pro rata share of the estate tax on the value of the vacation home. Since the vacation home was worth about $300,000, and the tax rate was nearly 50 percent, they had to come up with $150,000 to keep the vacation home. Steve and Jane were forced to sell the house because they did not have the cash. They couldn't afford to mortgage the vacation home and pay the large monthly payments either. Fred's wishes were not met. Steve and his family, instead of having their uncle's vacation home to enjoy for a lifetime, had half that amount in cash. Everyone lost, except the taxman. Sadly, a modicum of advance planning by Fred, or a will drafted to reflect his real intent, would have enabled Steve and Jane to enjoy the vacation home intended for them. Had Steve known how to intercede with his Uncle Fred, it would have helped everyone.

All that Fred had needed to do was to have his lawyer draft his will to assure that Steve and Jane did not have to pay tax on their inheritance, which was Fred's real intent. This approach would have resulted in Fred's children bearing the tax cost on the bequest of the vacation home to Steve and Jane. This would not have been problematic since Patty and Harold each inherited well over a million dollars. However, careful planning could have avoided any tax on anyone. Fred could have made annual gifts of parts of the home to Steve and Jane (and perhaps each of their five children, although there might have been issues if they were minors) for several years before his death. Everyone can gift $11,000 (indexed for inflation) to any number of people per year, with no estate or gift tax cost. About four years of such gifts to Steve, Jane, and their children would have eliminated the entire tax problem. Would this have been a selfish move by Steve and Jane? Encouraging Uncle Fred to make gifts of his assets before he died could be viewed by some as selfish. If Fred's hope, however, was to pass along the vacation home he loved so much to his nephew and the nephew's family, so it could stay in their family for generations, their apparent selfishness would have helped their uncle achieve his goal. Using this plan instead of revising the will also would have saved their cousins the $150,000 in tax they would have had to bear under that scenario. Estate planning is all a matter of perspective. Far from being a bad thing, endeavoring to inherit more would have helped fulfill some of their uncle's final wishes and saved a fortune for everyone but the taxman. This book will guide you in accomplishing this objective.

THE CASE OF THE MISSING FAMILY APARTMENT

Although the heading sounds like the title of a mystery story, it is a common and sad scenario that plays out frequently and destroys many families.

Case Study: John and Jane Wyckoff spent years saving for retirement and providing an inheritance for their three children: Sarah, Tom, and Samantha. Their prized asset, and the hoped-for financial legacy for their children, was a four-unit apartment house. They lived in one unit and rented the other three generating enough income, along with Social Security, to pay for all their expenses through retirement, as well as enough extra to pay for their children's weddings, loan Sarah money to start a business, and so on. On John's death, his wife Jane inherited his entire estate that included his half ownership interest in the apartment house. Jane lived her last years in their apartment, but began to decline physically near the end. Samantha, the only unmarried child, moved into one of the two apartments on the top floor to help care for her mother who lived in the adjacent apartment. When Jane passed away, the family was distraught over their loss and waited more than six months to contact a lawyer to probate Jane's will.

About three months after Jane's death, when all the parents' personal belongings had been divided among the children, Samantha hired a contractor and converted the two top-floor apartments into a single larger unit. Thus, she took over the entire top floor of the building, her apartment and her parents' former apartment.

When the family jointly met with a lawyer six months after Jane's death, Samantha was already comfortably ensconced in her enlarged apartment. The will, the lawyer advised, left the apartment house to all three children equally. There were few other assets. The fact that Samantha was occupying half of the building had to be addressed. If she paid fair rent for the apartment (the same rent the children would receive if the top floor were rented as two separate apartments to unrelated tenants), all would be fair.

> Samantha, however, had financial problems, and Tom and Sarah were quite a bit better off. Their mother's will was unambiguous. But what could Tom and Sarah do? They could demand fair rent from their sister. They could sue to have her evicted but Samantha couldn't afford either to move or to pay fair rent. They could either take it on the chin financially or start an ugly family feud.

Fights over a family vacation home or apartment are common and often devastating. Even if a major legal battle doesn't ensue, the family relationships are often irreconcilably damaged. In the Wyckoff family, the parents might have avoided the entire dilemma by taking a few legal steps. The reality, however, is that neither John and Jane Wyckoff nor the general practice attorney they consulted for their simple wills, understood the potential problem. They saved a few thousand dollars on the cost of their documents, but Tom and Sarah will lose more than that every year for many years to come. Samantha also is in a precarious position. Her relationship with her family has been fractured, and she knows that at any time her siblings could try to have her evicted. If the children had been proactive in their parents' estate planning, they could have avoided these problems. The entire family would have benefited, and the parents' lifelong wish of leaving a financial legacy to their children could have been fulfilled. This book will help those who are in Tom, Sarah, or Samantha's position to approach their parents and pursue planning.

WHAT DOES INHERITING MORE MEAN TO YOU?

A lot! Baby boomers stand to inherit trillions of dollars in the biggest wealth transfer in history. Estimates have been made that the figures could be $150 billion a year.

The median family net worth is estimated to be under $60,000. That includes the equity in your home, the cash value of your life insurance, pension and retirement plans, and everything else. In 2002, the cost of one year of college for one child was upward of $15,000 to $20,000 before factoring in books and living expenses. Law school and medical school now cost more than $30,000 a year, and the cost of one year of dental school is nearing the $50,000 mark. We all want what's best for our children and grandchildren, and taking steps to preserve even a modest inheritance can have a huge impact on your personal financial security and the future of your family members and other loved ones. The techniques described in this book can help you preserve more of your parents' or other benefactors' estate and thus, in turn, provide a better future for both you and your heirs.

Insight: There is a physiological theory that talks about the three approaches people have toward conflict: moving toward, moving away, and moving against. Some move toward conflict and embrace it and tolerate the discomfort they feel about wanting to inherit more. Some move away. They may recognize the importance of planning but their discomfort results in their avoiding the issue. Some are so uncomfortable with the issue of parental mortality that they move against it. They simply dismiss the importance of the entire topic. If you can identify your style it will help you address your ability to inherit more. Those who are immature turn away from it. It takes maturity to address these issues and find a constructive resolution. The goal is to see the task of inheriting more as a worthwhile endeavor. "Deal with it," advises Dr. Stanley Teitelbaum. There are positive outcomes. It is usually in everyone's best interest to approach planning rather than moving away or against the idea. Tell yourself that although you have a vested interest in the outcome, it is a valid and appropriate one. If guilt about wanting your parent's money keeps you away, don't let it. It's okay to be self-protective. Struggle with your guilt. Remember that every conflict has two sides. Planning has to be done so that everyone can benefit. Allow for the reasonable self-protective side to win over the guilt. If you don't deal with your guilt while your parent is alive, you will suffer additional guilt later. You'll feel guilty for having done nothing to help your parent, and you'll feel additional guilt over having not protected yourself.

Action Step: You can't make up what you haven't done before. Approach your guilt proactively, recommends Dr. Stanley Teitelbaum. If you feel you haven't been a good child in the past, you can make up for it now—in the present. If past inactions have you feeling guilty, do something now to remove this feeling. Don't dwell on the past. You can take responsibility today to move forward. If you hadn't been responsive to your parent's difficulties in home care in the past, start today. Visit today. Take your mother shopping. If she can't buy things you know she might need, or enjoy, bring them to her when you visit. Flowers or plants are a beautiful gesture. If one of your siblings has been the primary caretaker, send him or her a gift, a thank-you note, or just call and offer to help. Actions today can help you turn guilt over past inactions into positive feelings. This can help you move forward in your relationships.

Exercise: Develop a self-assessment about how good you've been. Once you've given yourself a report card, you can use it to improve your grades while there is time. Your report card, and the steps to take to get on the "Dean's List" is based on an assessment of how you've helped, and can help, your parents through the process of aging. The following example illustrates steps for nine key categories. You can fill in your own report card and begin feeling better today.

Step	To What Extent Have You Been . . .	Your Grade (Performance)	How to Improve (Future)
1.	Patient	As parents age, they may tend to repeat, belabor a point, or pause during conversations. Being curt because of your life's pressures has hindered open communications.	Resolve to let your parent finish each sentence. Don't say "I have to go" or rush through a conversation. If the timing is bad, call when you can be patient. Time your typical phone call. Resolve to stretch out calls by 50% longer to let your parent feel heard.
2.	Available	You visit your parents once a month. Are you really available to help your parents when *they* need help? As parents age and become frailer, they worry more, they become more insecure. Sometimes having you be there, even if their reason doesn't sound important, may be important to them. Your personal and family situation have limited your time when they need it most.	Call more often, even short calls. Offer to visit if it would be helpful. If you have something that is a priority to you so that you cannot be available, perhaps you can fit in a quick visit of reassurance before or after your appointment.
3.	Giving	You have not assessed what you've given to your parents in years, so that the manner in which you give doesn't conform with their changing needs as they age. Giving of your time to help with errands and chores may be more important than sharing the family vacation or holiday meal as you did when your parents were younger. But you haven't changed. If your parents have financial problems,	Read literature about aging. Talk to your parents and other older relatives about concerns they have. Try to identify ways you can be more giving to your parents. Remember—as your parents age, they need more time and emotional support.

Step	To What Extent Have You Been . . .	Your Grade (Performance)	How to Improve (Future)
		lending assistance in helping them qualify for a government program may be more important than discussing stock tips as in past years, but you haven't inquired.	
4.	Empathic	Your job is in jeopardy and your kids are demanding. Chores and errands have you so worn out you really haven't taken the time to consider how your parents must feel; how aging, health issues, family crises, and other issues have affected them.	To best relate to your parents, and best help them through the aging process so that you can address estate and other planning, try to put yourself in your parents' position and frame of mind.
5.	Sensitive	As your parents age, their temperaments and abilities change. They begin to lose control over matters they took for granted, physical, emotional, and other. Be sensitive to these changes and try to respond accordingly. When your parents were younger, a strained relationship may have been easier to tolerate. As they become conscious of their lives drawing to an end, family friction, for example, is harder to live with because there is less time to rectify it.	Listen actively. Try to read between the lines of what your parent is saying to understand his or her needs.
6.	Caring	You haven't really given your aging father the concern and serious attention that you should, or he feels entitled to after supporting you through college and so many of life's travails. You have assumed responsibility for taking him to the doctor, but haven't addressed any other issues.	Caring for an elderly or infirm parent takes more time and energy than it did before larger health issues and the impact of aging took hold. Review your parents' life status and typical daily and monthly routines. How can you show real caring? What daily functions does your parent need help

(continued)

Step	To What Extent Have You Been . . .	Your Grade (Performance)	How to Improve (Future)
			with? Has carrying grocery packages become so burdensome that they have gone without needed or wanted items?
7.	Attentive	While you've remained polite and courteous to your parent, from your perspective, you haven't been sufficiently observant to notice that your mom doesn't hear as well as she used to. Instead of speaking louder and standing closer when you talk, you've continued to carry on conversations as in the past.	Observe your parent's conduct carefully for clues as to what you can do to be more attentive. If your mom cannot hear well, speak louder, purchase a telephone with adjustable volume controls. If sight is a problem, purchase large print books and audio cassettes. Telephones and remote controls with extra large buttons are available. If your parent's independence has been compromised, discuss installing an alarm with panic buttons.
8.	Nurturing	You've assumed that nurturing is something that you must provide your young children, not an elderly parent.	Everyone, including an elderly parent, needs nurturing. If your parent is participating in an exercise program or adult study program, has a hobby or other activities, ask how they are doing. Show an interest and encourage their continued active involvement. An active life will help your parent achieve a better physical and emotional state.
9.	Helpful	Make up a list of the ways in which you've helped your parent.	Compare the list of what you've done to what your parent needs or wants by way of help. Talk with other family members, friends, and, if applicable, caregivers to divide the tasks. The better the division and the more organized the help the more your parents will receive and the better they will fare.

A NOTE ON STYLE, EXAMPLES, AND CASE STUDIES

Celebrity Case Studies are, to the best of the author's knowledge, accurate portrayals of actual situations gleaned from the Internet. They make it easier for you to identify with many of the issues and planning points in the book. All the other examples, case studies, and illustrations are based on real situations; however, names and facts have been changed to disguise the identity of those involved.

Although this book can help you maximize what you inherit from a mother, father, aunt, uncle, friend, or any other benefactor, the language generally refers to "parent" for simplicity.

This simplicity, however, can mask some potential traps, so caution is in order. A child has a right to inherit under the laws of intestacy (a parent dies without a will so state law governs who inherits). A niece has a similar right, but has a much lower priority on the list of who will inherit. Under state law, a friend has no right to inherit if there is no will. Thus, even though this book refers to "parent," your inheritance rights might vary depending on your familial relationship with your benefactor.

Tax rules can also differ significantly depending on your relationship with your benefactor. Many states have inheritance taxes that vary in their impact depending on your consanguinity to your benefactor. As a son or daughter, you may face no tax or a lower tax rate than as a nephew or friend. The use of the term "parent," may sometimes obfuscate these important nuances. But if you heed the advice of this book and seek expert professional counsel, you can navigate these traps.

There is no intent for this book to reflect any gender bias. Although phrases like "he or she" may be politically correct, they have not been used because they are cumbersome to read. I have attempted instead to use both male and female examples.

LESSONS TO LEARN

Planning for your future and the future of your family is universally recognized as a necessary and admirable endeavor. Included in that plan should be all necessary steps to ensure that there will be as little stress as possible when you are faced with the death of a beloved family member or friend. You cannot avoid the stress inherent in losing someone dear to you, but you can take steps to avoid many pitfalls that add tension to an already emotional situation. Proper planning can preempt many of the problems that arise when settling an estate. Being proactive will help not only in carrying out the final wishes of the deceased, but also in mitigating problems that can excessively shrink an estate and cause irreparable damage to family relationships. Whereas it may seem selfish to the casual observer, learning how to inherit more can result in attaining truly worthy goals for you, your parents, other benefactors, and your entire family.

2 TALKING TO YOUR PARENTS

To inherit more, your first step should be to open a dialogue with your parents (aunt, uncle, or other prospective benefactor). Since much of the planning depends on cooperation from your benefactor, without a dialogue there is often little you can do to maximize your inheritance. If an open discussion is not feasible, you need to focus on the alternative strategies discussed in later chapters of this book. This chapter suggests questions and answers to guide you, describes potential benefits that may encourage your parents or benefactor to pursue planning, and then explains how to plan once you have reached agreement.

OPENING THE DIALOGUE

Choose Discussion Topics That Give Your Parent Comfort

There are as many ways to begin estate-planning discussions as there are parents. The key is to pick the most appropriate topics, times, and approaches for your parents and their circumstances. You could discuss strategies that might give your parents comfort in later years, ways to assure their financial security, your own estate planning, charitable giving, or religious issues. Pick the most feasible approach, move slowly, and be sensitive.

When to Begin

Older people often dislike talking with younger family members about personal finances and their estate. They grew up in a time when discussing money was considered crass, and parents seldom reviewed their financial situation with their children. With that in mind, when should you begin the dialogue? What do you say? How do you say it?

First, begin this process with your parents as soon as possible. Try not to wait until old age and infirmity have set in; start this discussion when the specter of death is not looming. Find a time when your parents are at their leisure, relaxed, and in good health or if they have chronic health problems, at least when they are comfortable.

Show Your Parents That You Want to Protect Them

The objective of your conversation should not be how you can inherit more, but how you can help them. From your perspective, the two may often be synonymous, but from your parents' perspective, one reflects a helpful child and the other a greedy and untrustworthy heir.

Focus on how you can help protect your parents:

- Has an overly aggressive stockbroker undermined your parents' financial security?

Case Study: This series of events occurred in 1999 and was used as a case study (names changed) on a financial talk show. Sid and Freeda Lang had just moved to a retirement community, and Sid had only a few weeks to go before retirement. They were working with a financial planner at one of the largest and best known financial services companies. Other than their new house and a modest checking account, all of their assets were invested in equities. Most of the equities were "hot" stocks. The financial planner completed an analysis of the Langs' financial picture. The planner projected increases in their expenses using a historical rate of 3 percent (without considering how postretirement travel and medical costs would affect this). He increased their assets at an assumed rate (net of tax and costs) of 12 percent. Although 12 percent per year may have seemed conservative in the 1990s, it was completely unrealistic from a historical planning perspective and eventual reality. The planner then convinced the couple to purchase a multimillion-dollar, second-to-die (survivorship) life insurance policy to pay the huge estate tax he projected. Had the attorney for the Langs not objected vigorously to this plan (which was actually a great arrangement for the planner, not the Langs), they could have been ruined financially. Where were the Langs' children, the intended heirs, throughout the planning process?

- Do they have a durable power of attorney so that someone (not necessarily you) can manage their assets in the event they become unable to manage their own affairs? Assuring control over financial decisions and safeguarding life savings are always serious concerns. Happenstance alone will not guarantee this protection. (Don't begin by suggesting they choose you to manage their funds.)

- Ask your parents if they have living wills and health care proxies to address medical issues. Do they understand that medical decisions will be made for them and that they could be kept on life support long after they might wish to be? If your parents have strong religious convictions, a living will should make them known or those criteria may be completely ignored in their treatment.

- Many senior citizens secure financial management and backstop a living will with a revocable living trust to assure that their health care decisions are carried out. When properly done, there is no more comprehensive and valuable tool than a revocable living trust to manage assets during someone's disability. If your parents already have a revocable trust, were accounts set up in the name of the trust and assets transferred to it? If the trust is not funded, it may not be as effective as they wish. Was it a standardized form (boilerplate) or tailored to their needs?

- If your parents are concerned about the costs of nursing homes, have they purchased long-term care insurance? Have they even investigated its availability and cost?

Approach all of these issues with concern for your parents' welfare at the forefront of your mind and always remember that they are older—they are not stupid.

Once you and your parents are comfortably focusing on their welfare (and powers, living wills, and other core steps discussed in this book are in place), you may broach the topics of a will, trusts, and perhaps even tax planning.

If your parents are unwilling even to consider these topics with you, it is often helpful to discuss the plans you have made for your own estate. This will ensure that you make plans for your future and may also serve to open the dialogue with your parents in a non-threatening manner. If you want to address the topic of writing a living will, begin by outlining to your parents the directives in your own. If you have named one of your parents as an agent in your document, or want their input about religious or other personal decisions, seek their counsel. Seeking their advice is a positive and deferential way to open the discussion. And don't discount the knowledge that age and the loss of friends and family has taught them. In your parents' answers, you may also find the key to discussing their own planning.

Once you are actively talking about your planning, it may become a simple matter to segue from a discussion of your living will to a discussion of theirs. You need only to ask if they agree with your decisions and if they are in any way similar to the decisions your parents made when drawing up their living wills.

Keep in mind that you cannot accomplish this kind of discussion at one sitting, or in merely a few hours. There are many issues to address, and every decision will require forethought, planning, and careful attention to details. What constitutes sufficient time will vary by age, gender, religion, size of the estate, health requirements, and other individual needs.

Sometimes it is best to introduce the topic and then wait for your parent to open the discussion again at a later date.

GENDER DIFFERENCES ARE REAL: PLAN FOR THEM

In the Age of Aquarius, Mars and Venus affect estate planning, too! There are basic differences in gender approaches to estate planning. Men and women often look at money and life from vastly different perspectives. As a general rule, men focus on the pragmatic financial aspects of planning, whereas women tend to be more emotional and concerned with the potential impact on interpersonal relationships. While these are not inflexible categories, they provide a starting point in understanding your parents and how to approach planning their estate.

These differing viewpoints are particularly important when you discuss estate planning with your parents or, with their approval, hire an attorney to draft an estate plan. If you ignore these personal and emotional elements, you will compromise achieving yours and their objectives.

Perspectives of Men and Women

Generalizations obviously do not fit every situation, but they provide a touchstone for considering the emotional impact of gender on planning. "Women look at money more as a form of protection," notes Sylvia Teitelbaum, a psychoanalyst. Typically, women earn less than men, and a wife often worries about the impact her husband's death will have on her personal finances. On the other hand, a man may have vastly different concerns regarding continuity of his name and protection from the government of assets he has worked hard to accumulate. Typically, a woman wants a trustee she can trust, whereas a man may prefer a trustee who is an astute investor. A wife may wonder how she will survive if her husband dies and may be overwhelmingly concerned with safety and protection. A husband does not necessarily worry about his financial future in the same way, perhaps because generally he relies less on his wife's income than she does on his. Also, statistically, wives tend to outlive their husbands.

Disclaimer Estate Plans and Gender Perspectives

An important planning area for many wills and estate plans is a concept called a *disclaimer* or *renunciation*. This is a legal procedure in which a person such as a surviving parent (e.g., your mother after your father's death) takes legal action not to directly inherit assets.

This technique has seen increasing use following the 2001 Tax Act. A will might include a provision stating that all assets on one parent's death will be bequeathed directly to the surviving parent. However, if the surviving parent takes legal action not to directly receive those assets, they will instead be distributed to a trust. The trust can minimize or avoid estate tax and safeguard the assets from mismanagement or creditors, not to mention a new spouse. If your parents' estate plan is to rely on disclaimers, it is essential to address their emotional reactions.

For example, if you expect your mother to disclaim the amount of assets necessary to fund a Bypass Trust for you or other potential heirs, this may not happen. The nine months following the loss of a spouse are traumatic for the surviving spouse. "When this is coupled with the general financial insecurity of the widow, she may be reluctant to disclaim assets thus losing some element of control, even if there is a significant future tax advantage," comments Sylvia Teitelbaum.

To Succeed, Consider Male and Female Views

Keep gender differences in the forefront of your mind when mapping out an estate plan that will satisfy both your parents and you as their heir. The main focus of estate planning discussions must be on assuring that your parents' wishes will be carried out. If you focus instead on what you want to get out of them, more likely than not they will reject your suggestions and distrust your offers to assist in managing their estate plan.

APPEAL TO YOUR PARENTS' PERSONAL WISHES

Everyone Has Personal Wishes

Every parent or benefactor has important personal wishes. Too often, professional advisers or the media subvert these hopes. Proper planning is essential to assure parents that what they feel to be important will, to the extent feasible, be addressed. If you can assist your parents in this aspiration, you will build a lot of goodwill toward assuring proper planning to benefit you as well.

Celebrity Case Study: Liberace, the colorful pianist, earned millions during his brilliant career. Although he had been generous with his nieces and nephews during his lifetime, he ignored them in his will. Liberace left the majority of his estate to the Liberace Foundation for the Performing and Creative Arts, a fund to help sustain the music programs of 25 universities around the country. Liberace's relatives contested the will, and the ensuing lawsuits caused the public revelation of his gay lifestyle and the AIDS-related complications that led to his death, in violation of his wishes.

Find Your Parent's Soft Spot

Everyone has soft spots. It might be providing grandchildren with a college education, funding a specific charitable cause, or being the oldest person in their retirement community to take up skydiving. Not only is honoring your parents' wishes in personal matters as important as planning for financial matters, it may encourage your parents to pursue proactive planning on all fronts.

If you fail to help your parents plan for all their needs, or only show interest in monetary decisions, they may exclude you from all of their planning. The legal system rarely pays attention to such personal matters as religious rituals, burial instructions, religious or cultural preferences for the rearing of children or grandchildren, and so on. You have to take the initiative, communicate with your parents about their personal wishes, and insist that the planning and legal documents address their requests. Your parents may want to be buried and you may think they prefer cremation. If you don't find out what they really want, you may unknowingly make the wrong choice.

How Death Will Come

The knowledge that they will die in the manner in which they lived may bring great comfort to your parents in their waning years.

Without communication, you cannot possibly know what your parent or other potential benefactor may wish. The breadth of choices is broad. Many people want to die in the comfort of their own home, unhampered by myriad medical paraphernalia and the heroic, often painful and taxing, procedures that accompany them. The knowledge that they will have the peacefulness of dying at home among family and friends may bring some people comfort. Others will want to prolong their life with every heroic effort modern science can provide. Some will go further and through cryogenics try to assure that they can benefit from medical advances only future knowledge may provide.

Caring enough to ensure that your parents will spend their last days in accordance with their unique wishes may bring you even closer together. Above all, be sensitive to their needs on a spiritual as well as a physical level. Planning that meets both these needs will reassure your parents of your good intentions. The more kindly they view your assistance, the easier it will be for you to help plan their estate and protect your inheritance. This basic step of planning for personal as well as financial needs will go far in convincing your parents that you are trustworthy.

Unusual Requests

Many people have unique requests for their last days, burial, and funeral ceremonies. In identifying your parents' desires, you will give them peace of mind and help strengthen your bond with them. If these wishes are not formally communicated in writing, they may be forgotten or ignored.

Celebrity Case Study: In recent years, a well-known celebrity requested that his ashes be released in space.

Although most requests are more mundane, they are equally important to the individuals requesting them. You can address all of these and other requests when helping loved ones plan their estate. Even burial can be personalized to an individual's wants. Requests of a parent or benefactor have included everything in the following list, and more:

- The number of days a person should lay in state.
- Use or nonuse of pain medications.

Example: With the growth of Buddhism in the United States, especially among several well-known celebrities, Buddhist perspectives on will provisions, death, and dying have assumed greater influence. A key concept is that a person should be conscious at the moment of death. This objective is in dramatic conflict with what most Westerners opt for—maximum pain relief, even at the expense of awareness. If this wish to be conscious isn't communicated (to loved ones and in writing by inclusion in a living will), it may be overlooked.

- The people who should be present at the wake.
- The kind of flowers to be used at the funeral.
- The nature and type of ceremony.
- Location of burial.

Celebrity Case Study: A famous Wall Street executive has a large private farm in New England where he wishes to be buried because the farm has brought him so much peace and solace over the years. Local ordinances restrict burial to designated cemeteries. Absent considerable legal actions, burial on his private property remains prohibited.

- Engraving on headstone.
- Ceremonial requests for the funeral such as naming those people who will eulogize them, or alternatively specifying that there be no funeral service at all.
- The clothing and jewelry they wish to be buried in.
- Whether the funeral will be open casket or closed.
- Pet owners may want the remains (ashes) of their deceased pets placed in the coffin with them.
- Some people prefer cremation while others prefer burial at sea. Needless to say, if the wrong method is used, reversal is usually impossible.
- Many people request burial in a particular state or country. This could be the country that they were born in, or a country with

particular religious significance. In either event, several special problems must be resolved.

Planning Point: If your parent or benefactor's desires are unusual or expensive, you should take several steps. The desires should be communicated to family and noted in the living will, but when they could involve considerable cost (e.g., an expensive casket, transport of the body to another country for internment, cryogenics), the desires should be listed in the will with a directive for the executor to pay for them. Otherwise, where will the funds come from? If you are your benefactor's confidant and only you know of an elaborate funeral request, how will you convince the executor to pay for it or to reimburse you if you advance the funds?

Problems Implementing Requests

Although your first inclination may be to balk at what appears to be a bizarre request, don't be judgmental. Surprisingly, some highly unusual requests often have some basis for them.

Celebrity Case Study: A wealthy industrial magnate died, and the funeral became a veritable circus of celebrities and paparazzi in attendance. The grieving widow was appalled by the frivolous atmosphere and at the hypocrisy of those who had not paid a visit during the last difficult illness but were now showing up to be "seen." To demonstrate her point, her living will specified that she be cremated, any service be a private one for the immediate family, and that her ashes be interred in a Ben & Jerry's Cherry Garcia ice cream container.

Sometimes the special requests have religious underpinnings, many of which are discussed in the following sections. Late in life, people tend to find great solace in returning to the religious roots of their youth, or sometimes to religious roots for the first time in their life. Pain, suffering, and the closing of one's life are all points of reflection. Be sensitive to these changes and in particular to the fears and needs they address.

Other requests are designed to prevent future family strife. This is common in a second or later marriage, or where the family has mixed religious affiliations. A parent may specify a separate burial plot to avoid conflict between children who would have to decide in which cemetery, and next to which spouse, they should bury the parent.

Case Study: Karen Green was married for the second time. She had children from her first marriage and her second marriage. She opted to be buried next to her first husband, the love of her youth, who had died at an early age in a tragic car accident. Her children from her second marriage were devastated that she didn't want to be buried next to their father, her second husband. The conflict resulted in the estrangement of the two sets of children.

Parents may state the religious rites they want to have observed to eliminate quarrels between siblings of different religious persuasions. Often, guiding a parent to a peaceful middle ground is difficult because many people insist on specific requests that they know will offend some key family members. If you can encourage your parents to rethink their choices, you might preserve family unity. But exercise great caution because you also risk alienating and angering the vary person you are trying to help.

Not all requests are reasonable or advisable, and you should discuss potential problems with your parents.

Women have been known to request that expensive jewelry be buried with them. Whether this stems from pure eccentricity or a desire to avoid squabbles between heirs, this plan should never go unchallenged. Burying expensive assets with a body practically begs vandals to try to steal them. Denying any heir particular jewelry will almost always breed anger and resentment. There are many better ways to deal with jewelry issues (see Chapter 7). Whatever the intent behind the request, try to avoid such pitfalls.

Other problems arise if a parent requests the remains of beloved pets be buried with them or that their ashes be scattered in a particular location.

Case Study: Joan Johnson requested that on her death she be buried next to her pet German shepherd, Spike. After a bit of research, it was determined that the only way to adhere to her wishes was to arrange for her and Spike's burial in a special section of a pet cemetery reserved for pet lovers and their pets. These requests were memorialized in her will and living will, as well as in a personal letter of instruction Joan wrote to her family. Following her death, her wishes were made known (and eventually carried out), but her husband's shock at her demands was indescribable.

Health concerns being what they are, legalities may prevent you from carrying out last requests of your loved ones. You can avoid the guilt that attaches to ignoring these requests by discussing them with your parents and checking to see if they are feasible, before writing them into any official documents.

Celebrity Case Study: Before his death, Ted Williams, a Baseball Hall of Famer, requested that his remains be cremated and that there be no large funeral in his honor. When Williams died, however, his son had his body cryogenically frozen. Knowing about her father's preferences, Williams's estranged daughter from a different marriage challenged her half-brother's actions in the international media community. Calling her half-brother an opportunist who was scheming to make money off her father's DNA, Williams's daughter made a public spectacle of her father's death. All of this could have been avoided had Ted Williams formally documented his wishes as part of his estate planning. Months later, the half-brother and sister produced a scrap of paper supposedly signed by Williams stating that he wanted to be frozen. Surely there will be even more legal wrangling before the authenticity of that document is determined. Instead of treating the legendary ballplayer with the same quiet dignity in death that he had displayed in life, his heirs have produced a circus of media frenzy and Ted Williams has been denied his final request . . . that his passing not be marked with any kind of hoopla.

RELIGIOUS ISSUES

Most surveys of the American public find that more than 95 percent believe in a higher being (God). If so, why do only a negligible number of estate plans consider religious issues in any manner? The answer is that too few people insist that their attorneys address religious issues or make the effort to have their priest, rabbi, imam, or other religious leader consult with their attorney to carry out their desires. With only a modicum of effort, you can be instrumental in having your parents' important beliefs respected through their final days and burial.

Religious considerations are vitally important and even comforting for many parents and other potential benefactors, especially toward the end of life. Few informative treatises, legal forms, or other sources are available for addressing these matters. You must be aware of the possible issues in order to raise them with your parents and appropriate advisers, and to understand how to pursue them.

Because it has become so common in today's society for family members to intermarry and/or adopt different faiths, it is no longer feasible to assume "the family knows" the appropriate religious rituals. Too often, they have no idea.

Many religious issues that implicate estate planning are consistent through all major religions. Every religion seeks charitable donations and endorses supporting the community and its religious institutions in death as well as in life. Most major religions also favor living wills. Religious leaders of almost every faith have addressed questions surrounding pain management, the determination of when death actually occurs, and acceptable extraordinary life-sustaining activities. The details and directives may vary, but ignoring these issues when planning with your parents may signal to them that you aren't sincerely trying to be helpful.

The following subsections provide some background about the beliefs of several major religions and how these beliefs may affect your parent's estate planning. Use this information only as a starting point for discussions with your parents, their lawyer, and most importantly, their religious advisers.

Christian (Eastern) Orthodox Issues and Estate Planning

The Orthodox Christian Church (which includes all Eastern Orthodox Churches—Greek, Russian, Antiochian, etc.) has many beliefs that should be considered in estate planning. Living wills and health care proxies ideally should reflect the Church's view of life and death.

A major tenet of the faith is that it is unethical to take a life. Although staying alive is not the highest of all values, believers cannot affirmatively take steps to kill someone. The Church strongly opposes euthanasia and suicide; however, if the patient and medical care providers permit nature to take its course without heroic intervention, God may take the person's life.

The difficulty lies in thinking about these issues in abstraction when they must be resolved in real life on a case-by-case basis. If your parents want to have a priest present at their sickbed, make sure certain language is incorporated in their living wills affirming their affiliation with the Church and its basic values. The presence of a priest is extremely important because of rituals and important differences in managing pain to preserve consciousness for these rituals. Consider the following sample provision:

Sample Provision: My Orthodox Christian beliefs hold that it is un-ethical to take a life. While it is not the highest of all values to preserve life, affirmative steps to cause death, including but not limited to eu-thanasia or suicide, are inappropriate. It can be permissible, and even ap-propriate in some circumstances, to allow nature to take its course without heroic medical intervention, until God determines to take my life. Using heroic medical measures merely to maintain my body's bio-logical functioning is not appropriate since mere biological existence is not considered to be of value. My death, if with dignity and proper ob-servance and respect for the rites and traditions of the Church, can be a victory of faith.

Provisions concerning consciousness and administration of pain relief have special implications for Orthodox Christians, who affirm that the act of suffering provides purification, redemption, and sal-vation. Suffering is not encouraged, however; steps can and should be taken to alleviate it, but never to the extent of actually taking a life. "An Orthodox Christian should make provisions in advance by spec-ifying their wishes in a living will and telling their family," notes Fa-ther Thomas Hopko, dean and professor of theology at St. Vladimir's Orthodox Theological Seminary of the Orthodox Christian Church.

Many ancient rites and customs are associated with death in the Orthodox Church. See to it that your parents request that a priest be present at their deathbed who can provide comfort and perform whatever religious rites may be appropriate. Tell family members exactly what customs surround death in the Orthodox religion and what might be required of them, and explain Church views on pain management and lucidity near death.

The presence of a religious adviser will provide great comfort to your parents and ease their way to a peaceful death. If the family is not present and the living will does not inform the medical care providers to send for an Orthodox priest, the patient's spiritual needs and wishes could be overlooked. Even if the children or other family members are present, they may have different religious beliefs, be unaware of these rites and traditions, or not realize that the parent was faithful and overlook these spiritual needs.

A provision governing pain relief included in many living wills should be modified to reflect the particular religious beliefs of an Orthodox Christian. Consider the following sample provision:

Sample Provision: I wish that all treatment and measures for my comfort, and to alleviate my pain, be provided, so long as they do not rise to the level of constituting euthanasia. In making decisions concerning the administration of pain relief, I request that consideration be given to my Orthodox Christian beliefs, and in particular the importance of my having some level of consciousness prior to death to be able to participate in accepting Holy Communion and making a final confession of my sins, as well as participating in certain prescribed prayer services. I request that my health care agent and medical care providers endeavor to humanely and compassionately balance my desire for pain relief and my desire to participate in these my last religious observances.

Organ donations are not prohibited according to the Orthodox Church. As with most religions, however, they raise a host of issues even implicating the definition of death. There are no theological problems with organ donations so long as those involved are not trafficking in payments for organs or taking a life to obtain the organ. In fact, many pastors encourage organ donations out of compassion for those in need.

The definition of death profoundly implicates the question of organ donation. If it is unethical to take a life to harvest an organ, the definition of death is vital because removing an organ too early could cause death. If the patient would die without life support, harvesting organs at that time generally would not be an ethical problem in the medical field (although it is a gray area from a religious perspective). Ethical experts would probably use the modern medical test of cessation of brain stem activity as a definition of death. Whether or not your parents' religious leaders agree with that definition, it is necessary to include your parents' consent to or refusal of organ donation in their living will.

It is critical that patients have complete information about their condition; otherwise they will never know when to begin the many important religious observances that accompany the process of dying. Your parents should address this issue as well. They might want to include a provision that reads:

Sample Provision: I specifically direct my Agent and all attending medical personnel to fully and completely inform me and my Agent of my medical condition, including but not limited to the fact that I may have a terminal illness and my anticipated life expectancy. This information is vital to my carrying out important religious practices as an Orthodox Christian.

Charitable giving is an important principle of many faiths. The Orthodox Church encourages members to consider charitable bequests as part of their planning. When developing an estate plan, it is customary to consider charitable giving. Your parents will be grateful for the reminder, and it will give you an opportunity to discuss proposed charitable bequests with them. The Orthodox Church, like most religions, believes that it is a religious obligation for people to use what they need and to share with others any excess. There have always been members for whom giving large gifts to the Church was a normal part of their religious life and planning for charitable bequests will allow your parents to continue this practice even after their death.

What about inheritance? As wonderful as charitable bequests may be, there is also a religious obligation to care for family. Apostle Paul in a Letter to Timothy [1 Timothy 5:8] states: "If anyone does not provide for his relatives, and especially for his own family, he has disowned the faith and is worse than an unbeliever." Family then extended to more than just the nuclear family. This directive includes giving consideration to the needs of other relatives as well as the spouse and children.

There are many scriptural provisions concerning responsibilities to family, and, indeed, to the whole human community. This is why Orthodox Christians must reasonably address life insurance needs, write a will, and attend to all aspects of estate planning. The Church preaches to its congregation that they have obligations to their spouses and children, and to their church and society at large after they die. By encouraging your parents to see to their estate and to provide for their heirs, you are assisting them in fulfilling these duties.

Many of the preceding issues apply to all religions. The desire for a priest or religious leader to be on hand when nearing death is true for faithful, and even not so faithful, adherents of any religion. Clauses stipulating administration of pain medication and what information should be relayed to the patient should be in every living will regardless of your parents' religion. Organ donation and the definition of death are also implicated by every faith, as are charitable donations and the necessity of bequeathing assets to one's children and not disinheriting them.

Jewish Issues and Estate Planning

Many points of Jewish law affect financial, estate, and personal planning. How should you handle these when helping your parents, and what are some of the key issues? Every standard secular living will form violates Jewish religious principles. If your parent has any interest or sensitivity to their Jewish heritage, you must discuss this before encouraging them to sign a standard living will. It would be a tragedy for your parent to face the trauma of a severe illness compounded by a document that violates their religious beliefs.

Many people who are not particularly religious find solace in their faith during trying times. Unfortunately, they are not always cognizant of the problems that may arise when they attempt to reconcile modern medical practice and religious directives.

"Jewish Law touches on every aspect of death and dying from time and definition of death to organ donation, life support, and autopsies," notes Rabbi Chaim Jachter, a judge (Dayan) with the Rabbinical Court of Elizabeth, New Jersey, and a professor at Torah Academy of Bergen County. Life support and heroic measures often cannot be withdrawn if the result is to hasten the onset of death. Organ donations are permitted; however, organs cannot be harvested until the patient has died as defined under Jewish law. Some religious authorities believe that a cessation of cardiopulmonary function is necessary for a patient to have died under Jewish law. Under such a definition, most organ donations won't be feasible. Other Jewish authorities believe a cessation of brain stem function is sufficient to constitute the death of a patient. This definition allows the donation of many vital organs, and according to some, this is a necessary and positive step to take under religious law.

Jewish religious authorities are still debating how to resolve this question. The best approach is to advise your parents to consult with their rabbi as to the appropriate approach. Once your parents receive a response, ensure it is codified in their living will.

Jewish parents have other religious concerns besides those pertaining to medical treatment. Jewish law requires surviving children and siblings to recite Kaddish—the prayer for the dead—for a deceased family member. Kaddish is recited daily at each of the three prayer services among a congregation. Generally, the children of the deceased assume this burden. However, parents who doubt their children will recite the prayer, or who have no living sons, might want to request in their will that a particular relative, friend, or the rabbi of the community recite the Kaddish.

Additionally, Jewish law provides a step-by-step guide to prepare a corpse for burial, which must take place within the first day after death. While waiting for burial, the corpse may not be left unattended and autopsies are forbidden except in a few particular circumstances. Rabbinic authorities have addressed every detail of death, burial, and ritual mourning: the kind of shroud to be worn, the kind of coffin to be used (a plain pine box), and the Shiva, a period of intense mourning for surviving relatives in the seven days following the death of a spouse, parent, child, or sibling. If your parents wish these laws to be followed, they must make these wishes known during the estate-planning process.

Islam and Estate Planning

The law of inheritance is the largest, and probably the most important, legal topic in the Koran, the holy book of Islam, and has been one of the most analyzed subjects in Islamic law. Muhammad, the prophet of Islam, was an important social reformer and made major changes in the rules for inheritance under Islamic law.

Muhammad Farooq Malik, chairman of the board of trustees of the Institute of Islamic Knowledge in Houston, Texas gave us some insights into Muslim customs.

There are a number of key issues that a Muslim should consider when planning an estate. Islamic law affects the laws of inheritance, and hence every estate plan. Living wills and health care decisions are affected by Islamic law. Charitable giving is encouraged.

Every Muslim is under the obligation to follow what the Koran states. Sayings of the Prophet Mohammad relate to inheritance based on the Koranic injunctions. Finally, there are decisions, called *Fiqh,* which is analogous to case law in the American legal system. These Fiqhs are jurists' analyses of the issues covered by the Koran and the sayings of the Prophet. If these sources are silent then a decision must be made that is consistent with the spirit of them; for example, in a community property state in the United States. These laws only establish ownership, not the distribution so the Muslims can follow them.

Islam provides for several basic laws of inheritance. Historically, men could inherit but women could not. This issue has been addressed. Women cannot be disinherited. Now any natural born child cannot be prohibited from receiving an inheritance. Males inherit twice the value (shares) that female children inherit. Two-thirds of the estate must be distributed among the heirs as prescribed in the Koran:

Forever parent and relative We have appointed the rightful heirs to inherit what they leave. As for those with whom you have made firm agreements, give them their share. Surely Allah is a Witness to everything. 4:[33]

The distribution in all the following cases shall be after fulfilling the terms of the Will and the payment of Debts.

Allah commands concerning your children: that the share of a boy shall be twice that of a girl. If there are more than two girls, their share will be two thirds of the estate; but if only one girl, her share will be one half of the estate. If the deceased left children, each of

the parents shall get one-sixth of the estate; but if the deceased left
no children and parents are the only heirs, the mother shall get one-
third of the estate; but if the deceased left brothers and sisters, then
the mother will get one-sixth. With regards to your parents and children, Allah issued this ordinance. You shall inherit one-half of your
wive's estates if they leave no child, but if they leave a child, then
you will get one-fourth of the estate . . . Your wife shall inherit one-
fourth if you leave no child, but if you leave a child then the wife
gets one-eighth of your estate . . . If a man or a woman leaves neither
ascendant nor descendant but has left a brother or a sister, each inherit one-sixth; but if more than two, they shall share one-third of
the estate . . . without prejudice to the rights of the heirs. (See
Chapter 4:[11–12].)

    If they ask you for a legal decision **[relating to inheritance in
the case of a childless person],** say: Allah gives you His decision
about those who leave no descendant or ascendant as heirs. . . . Allah
has perfect knowledge of everything. (See Chapter 4:[176].)

It is mandatory for every Muslim to use this dispositive scheme in
their wills. Up to one-third of the estate can be given to anyone the
decedent wishes. This one-third includes charities, non-Muslims,
nonfamily, anyone other than those required as per the above requirements.

There are other issues of inheritance as well. The marital residence cannot be disturbed or distributed for one full year and the
wife must be given the right to live in the house for that time. This
is in addition to any inheritance. If the wife decides not to exercise
this right, it can be avoided. The distributions for all inheritances,
other than maintenance, will be held in abeyance until the child is
born. This approach will help assure protection of an expectant
mother.

Charitable giving is very important in the Islamic faith. Helping
your parents or other benefactor meet these goals will undoubtedly
help give them peace of mind in planning their estate. Charitable
giving is one of the reasons that the one-third discretionary distributions of estate assets are permitted. Giving charity is looked upon
very favorably because it provides the donor rewards after death.
There is no ruling to give any specified amount to charity but such

giving is encouraged where it will be used in perpetuity. This could include a school system that can educate children for many years to come, rather than for a one-time use.

In contrast to the strict requirements for bequests, lifetime gifts by a Muslim are treated differently. There are no restrictions on gifts (lifetime transfers). Thus, any Muslim can convey property as they wish while they are alive.

Health care issues are important to Muslims. Islamic law permits the use of living wills. Decisions concerning health are primarily given to the physicians. If actions enable someone to be restored to health, they should be taken. If the medical decision would merely keep a person alive, they need not be taken. Keeping someone alive on life support is not mandatory under Islamic law, but heroic measures may be continued if the family wishes.

There are a number of ancillary issues that are important to Muslim parents in planning their estates and trusts. The charging of interest has important significance in Islamic law. There are different scholarly views on what constitutes interest or *riba*. If there is no change in form, for example, if money is repaid with interest as money, it may be viewed as *riba*. Other scholars say that some forms of interest, such as a mortgage, is not *riba*. Therefore, care must be exercised in any estate planning transaction based on an interest payment.

Also of importance is how investment clauses in wills and trusts should be handled. The standard language used in many documents may not suffice. Islamic law may make it inappropriate to pay or earn interest based on a prohibition of making a guaranteed profit on capital. Stock mutual funds have also been formed that invest in a manner that conforms with Islamic law by purchasing stocks for investment, while avoiding stocks of companies that engage in businesses involving alcohol, gambling, or pornography. Bank stocks can be problematic for the same reasons.

A sample clause to be used in a will or trust might appear as follows:

Further, the Trustee is authorized and directed, to structure any investments and assets, to the extent feasible, to be in accordance with Islamic religious principles, if the beneficiaries of any Trust formed hereunder request such standard in writing. Such standard may include by way of example, a prohibition against paying or earning interest based on a prohibition of making a guaranteed profit on capital. Stock mutual funds formed which invest in a manner which conforms with Islamic law by purchasing stocks for investment, while avoiding stocks of companies that engage in businesses involving alcohol, gambling, or pornography. Bank stocks may also be prohibited. In the event that there is a conflict between beneficiaries of any Trust as to whether such standard shall apply, then the Trustee shall divide such Trust into separate parts and invest each part accordingly. This limited right of a beneficiary to designate whether or not Islamic investment standards should apply shall not be interpreted as providing any further rights or powers to any beneficiary. In the event of any dispute as to the application of Islamic investment standards the Trustee shall consult the ISNA (the Islamic Society of North America) for further clarification. If such action is not feasible, or not determinative, the Trustee may consult any Islamic scholar or Imam of the Trustee's choice and rely on the determination of same.

Buddhism and Estate Planning

There are significant differences between how the Buddhist philosophy views death and how most Western religions view it, and these differing concepts should be conveyed in the drafting of a living will. "Clearly, no Buddhist would want to suffer unnecessary pain, so provisions authorizing and directing pain relief would be appropriate," noted Richard Baksa of the Chaung Yen Monastery in Carmel, New York, director of the English-speaking program.

However, a Buddhist also wishes to die consciously. "Your state of consciousness at the moment of death is believed to strongly influence your rebirth in the next life," noted The Reverend Guna, senior nun and assistant manager, Chaung Yen Monastery in Carmel, New York. "As a result, it is important that the living will convey your parent's desire for consciousness, since this is a perspective that can differ considerably from how many Westerners might view the process."

Buddhist traditions are sometimes inconsistent among practitioners, so it may be difficult to find any standardized forms to assist Buddhist relatives and friends. Unlike many other religions, Buddhism developed and spread to numerous countries and over the centuries has adopted diverse local customs that are compatible with the original Buddhist philosophy and approach to life. As a result, a Buddhist with origins in Taiwan might have customs distinct from those of a Buddhist whose origins are from Japan or elsewhere.

Regardless of geographic origin, there are many practices and customs that adherents might wish to consider mentioning in their living wills. Many Buddhists are strict vegetarians out of compassion for animals and other living beings. Since this diet differs significantly from mainstream American culture, Buddhists should note it in revocable living trusts and living will health care proxies. Otherwise, caregivers may not be aware of a Buddhist's dietary restrictions, especially when family members are not nearby.

In notable contrast to many other religious faiths, the Buddhist custom is to avoid removing the body from the place of death for at least 7 days. Several rituals or customs are performed following death. The belief is that the spirit of the deceased can remain with the body until rebirth, which will occur within 7 days, so the body should not be moved or tampered with during this 7-day period. Because it is impossible to adhere to these customs in a hospital, Buddhists should endeavor to spend their last days at home, where family members may be able to respect such traditions. Thus, a living will or letter of instruction for Buddhist parents should suggest that, if feasible, they are to be permitted to spend their last days in an appropriate facility or home.

Following the one-week waiting period after death, either cremation or burial is permissible. Since Buddhism does not stipulate a preference for cremation or burial, that decision is usually culturally based. Buddhists also might wish to specify in their living will some details of the type of funeral service they prefer. Although there are common elements among the different Asian traditions, many customs vary from culture to culture and your parent might want to designate the rituals to be performed.

Burning incense is very important to practicing Buddhists. "The burning of incense, in particular, raises considerable difficulties in any medical institution," noted Baksa. "Many hospitals have tried to look the other way for perhaps the burning of a single stick of incense," explained Reverend Guna. "However, this is why the preference would be to spend one's last days at home—so these customs can be adhered to. The general objective is to pursue as natural a death as possible from the Buddhist perspective."

The Buddhist standpoint about the "Do Not Resuscitate" (DNR) order is that it is inappropriate to resuscitate a patient with severe brain damage. "The goal is to die with as clear and calm a mind as possible," explained Reverend Guna. Thus, taking heroic measures could in fact be contrary to a major lifetime objective of a Buddhist patient.

Under Buddhist tradition, organ donation poses problems particular to that religion. "The difficulty with organ donations," explained Baksa, "is that the body is not to be disturbed for 7 days." "On the other hand," he continued, "Buddhism views any selfless act of charity to help another as very admirable. Thus, there is a tremendous incentive to try to assist others in need. There are differences among the cultures in how a Buddhist from any given tradition will view the concept of organ donations in light of the above conflict."

Dana (good deeds), or charitable giving, is a vital component of Buddhism. "There is a Buddhist tradition of giving one-sixth of one's income to the Buddhist temple," notes Reverend Guna. "In death, however, it is generally up to the person to decide how much to give, although the same one-sixth portion remains common." Care should be taken in discussing charitable bequests as charitable giving is handled differently from one Buddhist tradition to another.

Which traditions and customs do you need to discuss when drafting a will? Important considerations for Buddhist parents are choosing trustees who will respect the Buddhist traditions of the heirs, naming guardians sensitive to children's Buddhist beliefs, and fostering the Buddhist religious upbringing and lifestyle in their children, grandchildren, and other heirs. There is no religious imperative for distributing the estate, although where there is wealth, provisions for charity are uniformly encouraged.

Developing the will and estate plan provides an opportunity to encourage actions that minimize or eliminate anger and greed. If a Buddhist parent wants to write somebody out of his will because of resentment or hatred, such a plan is the antithesis of what Buddhism stands for and should be discouraged. On the other hand, if disinheriting a person is done in a way that minimizes bitterness, or is made from the standpoint of compassion and an effort to help the individual in question, then eliminating that person from the will would not be inappropriate.

Hinduism and Estate Planning

If your parents are Hindus, there are some basic faiths and beliefs that the estate-planning professionals advising them should be familiar with. Hindus believe in reincarnation, according to Dr. Venkat Kanumalla, honorary head priest and founder of the Sri Ranganatha Temple in Pomona, New York. All life forms, including humans, go through a recurring cycle of birth, death, and rebirth. The consequences of a person's actions in life determine the form and fate of his or her reincarnation.

There is a tradition to give to charity. Hindus believe that God will take care of everything as long as the believer follows the Hindu laws and does his or her duties. The ancient scriptures of Hindu laws called the *Laws of Manu* set forth the codes by which all Hindus must conduct their day-to-day life. Although some of these laws are not practical, Hindus in general try to follow the Laws of Manu. Charitable giving plays a very significant role in life. Over his lifetime, a Hindu should give *approximately* 6 percent of his life's assets to charity.

Every Hindu religious occasion requires feeding the poor and giving charity to the needy. According to Hindu traditions, on the eleventh day after death, the family donates gold, silver, rice, vegetables, land, cow, umbrella, shoes, and other specified gifts to the poor and needy in memory of the departed. How much should be given will depend on the person's financial ability. It is believed that the blessings from the receivers of the charitable gifts will guide the departed soul in its journey to the next life. The will should direct the executor to purchase these items and give them to a charity for the poor. It is recommended that a certain percentage of the assets be given to the temple or a charity.

Living wills and health care issues raise specific concerns for a Hindu parent. Life support is not permitted. One lives as long as one naturally can and accepts the end when it happens. If a person has suffered severe brain damage and there is no hope of recovery, there is no basis for prolonging life by artificial means. Do Not Resuscitate (DNR) orders are standard for every Hindu. If a bad drug or reaction to a drug were the issue, DNR would still apply. A medical mistake would not be considered as acceptable in altering that person's destiny. Supporting a life by artificial means is not permitted spiritually. A Hindu may not be kept on a respirator because this interferes with the life cycle. Blood transfusion and dialysis are very difficult and personal issues and should be carefully discussed with the persons involved. Pain relief is an important issue to address. Beliefs can differ considerably from those assumed to be natural by many Western faiths. With the cycle of birth and rebirth, deferring death when there is no consciousness is not as critical as it may be from a Western perspective. However, trying to maintain consciousness at the time of death is an important goal for a Hindu. It is necessary to be conscious to perform certain important rituals and chants before and at the time of death.

Euthanasia is not permitted. Killing a person—suicide, euthanasia, abortion—are no different from murder. An elderly person who is suffering and who is given medication to hasten death is considered murdered.

For Hindus, there are important customs prior to death that provide solace. According to Hindu tradition, it is not proper to die in a bed. Within a few hours of death, the person should be laid out on the floor and an oil lamp lit by his head. The family should try to give the person holy water and should chant prayers for the peaceful passing of the soul. Lying on the floor reinforces the belief in the inevitability of death and the futility of materialistic affluence. Because these customs are difficult to perform in a typical hospital setting, a Hindu may prefer to spend his last days at home.

Hindu rituals following death are also important to consider. According to Hindu law, the body should be cremated within 24 hours of death. However, a female child who dies before marriage should be buried and a male child who dies before baptism, which occurs generally at age 8, should be buried and not cremated. Funeral rites are always performed by the oldest male child. If a person does not have a son, it is customary to name a male family member to perform the rites. These are ancient rules and are not followed by all Hindus. The living will is very important.

The mourning or quarantine period is 10 days after death, including the day of death. *On days 11, 12, and 13,* various funeral rites are to be performed for the departed soul to rest in peace and donations and charitable gifts are made.

For the first year after death, every month, on the day the person died, special rituals are performed by the sons. After one year, on the anniversary *day* of death, prayers are offered by the sons for the rest of their lives. Feeding the poor and charitable giving are important parts of these rituals.

After cremation, the ashes should be immersed in the holy river Ganges in India. A will should specify if the ashes should be taken back to India. Ashes should be kept safe and in a dignified manner until this can be done.

Rebirth is an important concept to Hindus and may affect estate planning and living wills. Hindus believe in reincarnation. Human life is a transition point. The results of your actions are reflected in your next life. Through your actions, you can elevate yourself to the level of angels or decline to the level of animals. Humans have a highly developed consciousness to attain salvation; which is freedom from the cycle of repeated births and deaths. Animals and plants do not have this advanced consciousness. Positive actions will be weighed against negative actions and the ultimate salvation may take thousands of births and rebirths to achieve. Provisions in a Hindu will could address this. The goal of Hindu philosophy is to guide a person for spiritual elevation, not material success. The path of desire, or the attractions of worldly success, is ephemeral and seductive. The spiritual way has sanctions for material advancement, but this should not take the dominant role.

In India many people do not have a will. Traditionally, inheritance goes to the sons, but this is not a religious mandate. Manu *dharma scripture* says all people have the same rights—whether *sons or daughters*. In this country, we write wills and usually leave our assets to our spouse and then to the children. There should be equal distribution of wealth among children. The will must specify who should take care of the spouse of the decedent. Whoever takes care of the parent will get the parent's share after his or her death. Because of the complex requirements, those having Hindu parents must clearly understand their desires and make appropriate provisions.

You must take care to assure that your parent's particular customs are provided for in their estate plan.

CHARITY: A DIFFERENT APPROACH FOR TALKING TO YOUR PARENTS

Help Your Parent Plan Charitable Gifts and Bequests

If speaking to your parents about their security, their last wishes, and their religious beliefs does not motivate them, perhaps discussing charitable giving will help. If your parents have supported a particular charitable cause, were active in their local church, or are excited about your children's private or parochial school education, helping them perpetuate their charitable wishes or memorializing their name for charitable good may give them comfort. It also can offer you tremendous financial, social, and personal benefits. Importantly, your parents don't need to be extremely wealthy to take these valuable steps. Finally, discussing charitable planning may lead to a broader estate plan that will protect them and your entire family.

Many Benefactors Want Heirs to Be Charitable

This approach can help emphasize what estate planning is really about. It is a different definition from the one most heirs use. Estate planning is not merely the transmission of wealth. And that's not what your parent may think it is about. Getting the most chips to their heirs doesn't win the estate-planning game for many parents. Your parents may not be convinced that the answer is so simple. They may be more concerned with what their heirs are going to do with the chips. What will they do with the money? How will the heirs live? Are you and other heirs going to be productive members of society? Your plans for giving back to your community may be more important to your parents than maximizing the dollars they bequeath to you. Your parents may suspect that merely getting the most dollars to the heirs will have a negative impact on them. Integrating charitable planning into your parents' estate plan may help allay their concerns and allow them to move forward in their planning.

Involvement, education, and training of heirs to be charitable are goals for many parents. For heirs to become tomorrow's donors, they must become involved in charitable and community endeavors. They must be educated in the importance of philanthropy and have experience in making charitable gifts. To the extent you show your parents that you can help them achieve these goals for most of their heirs, you may substantially encourage their further planning.

Options for Giving Charity

Whatever charitable endeavors appeal to your parents, there are many long-term or deferred charitable-gift opportunities to handle the most unusual or sophisticated charitable plans. The broad scope of charitable activities offers the flexibility to plan a charitable program that suits their personal objectives and helps you and other heirs as well. Planned giving encompasses charitable gifts that take effect in the future, such as deferred bequests under a will, current gifts structured through appreciated assets, gifts of business interests, or gifts structured through complex trusts such as charitable lead or remainder trusts.

Further, the tax laws provide considerable opportunities to structure charitable giving to meet personal, tax, estate, financial, and other needs in planning such gifts. Planning to help your parents take advantage of all of these tax benefits can result in a larger inheritance for you, more money for charity, and a benefit to all (well, except Uncle Sam).

There are many ways your parents can give money to charity:

- They can write a check out today. But the money is gone, and little remains to teach heirs about philanthropy.
- They can make a bequest in their will. This can be an effective way to make a gift and make a statement to their heirs, but again, heirs have little involvement.
- They can set up a donor advised fund either while they are alive or, in their will, following their death.

Donor Advised Fund

The donor advised fund approach, can accomplish almost any charitable objective of your parent or other benefactor, while involving you and other heirs. This can be good for everyone. Your parents benefit because the funds they designate for charity will go to charity; perhaps even more importantly, their heirs' involvement in the periodic charitable gifts from the donor advised fund will pass on the legacy of charitable giving. You will benefit if you have a hand in distributing the charitable gifts each year, especially if you have been given some discretion in choosing charities.

With this technique, instead of a specified charity receiving the payments each year, the heir determines the amount of money that charities must get (possibly subject to some minimum distribution requirements), as well as which charities should benefit. This is a wonderful way for parents to pass on the value of philanthropy and teach heirs what they can do with charitable giving. Year after year, you and the other heirs can use the ongoing payment to help set up meaningful programs and facilitate your involvement.

This approach enables you and other heirs to allocate significant funds to charity every year. These decisions can enable you to become actively involved on different boards and committees that open up tremendous social and business opportunities for you and the other heirs. Thus, a donor advised fund not only allows your parents to pass on the values of charitable giving, but also can give you and other heirs an avenue to excel from a professional or a social perspective.

Celebrity Case Study: The mother of a famous television family, all of whom shall remain anonymous, unbeknownst to most people, had an unmarried 45-year-old daughter. The tax benefits of the donor advised fund technique alone justified using it. But the mother got all excited about something besides tax benefits, exclaiming: "It's a son-in-law, it's a son-in-law!" What she was saying was that her daughter, who would be giving $50,000 a year to charity, would get herself on some prominent charitable boards where she might meet a potential mate.

Case Study: The son of a wealthy local businessman recently became a doctor. The father established a donor advised fund at a local charity. Each year, the son can allocate $10,000 to any charity he chooses. He donated half of the first year's funds to a local hospital where he has privileges, and the other half to the physicians' division of a local charity. Both donations help causes important to him and have enabled the son to become active on a committee of the hospital and the board of the local charity. These will enhance his ability to make contacts for referrals for his new medical practice and will give him an important new perspective on issues in his community that relate to his professional practice. His father obtained important tax deductions as well as the satisfaction of accomplishing two important goals: helping his son's new career and helping the community.

Exploring the options of a donor advised fund with your parents may accomplish much good, demonstrate your sincerity and maturity in dealing with inheritance issues, and accelerate the planning for your parents' estate.

Charitable Lead Trust

One of the most effective ways to structure larger charitable giving is through a charitable lead trust (CLT). This technique begins with your parent hiring a lawyer to prepare a special contract that states how and when charities will get money (the trust agreement). Once the document is completed and signed, your parents contribute money into the account set up for the trust. Then, each year, one or more charities receive a periodic payment, usually annually, for the number of years the trust is to exist. The charitable lead trust can even be combined with a donor advised fund so you and other heirs can direct which charities should receive contributions each year. After the trust ends, you and the other heirs receive the trust assets (which may have appreciated considerably). Thus, the CLT can be a real "win-win." Your parents give substantial charity; you and the other heirs can gain all the intangible benefits of a donor advised fund; and when the charitable gifts end, you and the other heirs receive the money. The CLT approach can enhance what you ultimately receive by significantly reducing estate tax for your parents. This is a sophisticated technique, and establishing the trust requires professional advice. But the benefits can substantially outweigh the costs to all.

LESSONS TO LEARN

Opening the dialogue with your parents is often the hardest step to take when attempting to help organize their estate. The line between being perceived as a greedy, ungrateful heir or a helpful, concerned child is thin and you must tread lightly. If you cannot communicate effectively, important issues regarding religious beliefs and personal desires may be ignored. This can only lead to unhappiness for your loved ones and eventually a sense of guilt that you were unable to fulfill their last requests. Without an open dialogue, many significant concerns will not receive the attention they require.

Discussing religious, charitable, and other personal preferences also will help immeasurably in creating a bond of trust between you and your parents. Lacking such trust, it is nearly impossible to involve yourself in your parents' estate planning, and you will severely inhibit your ability to protect your inheritance.

3 SECOND (AND LATER) SPOUSES CAN DESTROY YOUR INHERITANCE

THE PROBLEM

Where Are Beaver and Ward?

The good old days of the Brady Bunch were pretty simple. The show never addressed estate planning, real financial issues, and the other complexities that the hybrid family commonly faces today. In the Cleaver family, life was even more idyllic. There was no problem that Beaver or Wally could create that Ward, the all-knowing dad, couldn't solve before the end of the half-hour episode. That was the world your parents inherited but not the one that is being left for you and your children. In the era of reality TV, it is more likely that all six children will have disastrous romantic relationships, leave home as soon as they graduate from high school, and move back in as soon as they graduate from college, along with ill-assorted partners and grandchildren. Their parents will finally disinherit them out of pure disgust, leaving everything to Alice and Sam the butcher. If your parents have remarried and children of more than one marriage are involved, you need to look out for a few common pitfalls when attempting to protect your inheritance.

But first, your parents need to understand that the Cleaver family is about as relevant as a dinosaur.

Celebrity Case Studies: Jane Welch wants half of Jack Welch's (of GE fame) $900 million. When Nicole Kidman and Tom Cruise divorced, $150 million was at stake. When NASCAR superstar Jeff Gordon divorced Brooke Gordon in 2002, she sought half of his $50 million.

The Typical Estate Plan Won't Work the Second (or Third) Time Around

The typical estate plan for an average family of husband, wife, and two children is to leave everything outright (i.e., without any trusts or other restrictions) to the surviving spouse (unless tax planning creates a need for trusts—which it doesn't for most). This is the typical four- or five-page will put together by most Americans who have wills. It is not much by way of planning for a traditional family, and for second and later families, it is usually a disaster in the making.

Say Ward dies first. On June's death, she bequeaths all of the family assets to the joint and only children of the marriage, Wally and Beaver. Now everyone on the show is happy, and Thanksgiving dinners will continue happily along.

To add some American social reality, say that after Ward's funeral, June remarries. Her new husband is a lawyer in another town who doesn't really care much for Wally, Beaver, apple pie, or wholesomeness. What happens if June and her new spouse also have children; how should assets be divided between the various groups of kids? How can Wally or Beaver, as the children of June's first marriage, protect their interests?

The answer is not a simple outright bequest in Ward's will to June. The far better approach to protect her, and all spouses who remarry, is for the will of the first spouse to distribute assets in trust to protect them for the benefit of the surviving spouse, and then assure that on her death they are ultimately distributed to the intended natural heirs (not the new spouse). The classic estate-planning approach of using bypass and marital (qualified terminable interest property, or QTIP) trusts can accomplish this. These techniques are discussed in this chapter and in Chapter 11. Even without a tax, the same approaches work for any estate to protect assets for the intended beneficiaries.

Hybrid Families Generate Hybrid Problems

What if the kids from Dad's first marriage are in their 30s? They have all completed college, bought houses, and started families and careers, with much financial support from Dad. Should more of the estate be distributed to the new child with Dad's second wife? If the new child is only 4 years old, common sense dictates that she will need more money to get to the point Dad's grown children are already at. So fairness would seem to suggest setting aside more money for this younger half-sibling. But how would you, as an older half-sibling from Dad's first marriage feel about such a distribution and would you endeavor to prevent it?

What if Dad died and Mom remarried? Dad had $1 million in life insurance that Mom received on his death. How will you, as a child of her first marriage, feel if Mom uses money she received because of your father's death to maintain a higher standard of living for her new husband and children from her new marriage? Will Mom care?

The classic scenario children face today is that Dad is divorcing his first wife, who is the mother of the children, and marrying a young woman who is perhaps not as old as the eldest child from his first marriage.

What happens next? New Wife may be a brilliant brunette executive who resents being stereotyped as the blond bimbo after Dad's money. When, how, and to whom should Dad leave his money?

And, what happens if Dad is disabled? Who will be in charge of Dad's money? When entering a second marriage, Dad may seek legal guidance and sign a prenuptial agreement as well as a will incorporating many of the steps outlined in this chapter to safeguard assets for intended heirs. After all the careful planning, the same parent (even with the help of the same lawyer) may then sign a typical standard power of attorney designating the new spouse as financial agent to handle all legal, tax, and financial matters in the event Dad becomes sick or incapacitated. At his first sneeze, the new spouse may set about systematically transferring all of Dad's money to her accounts, or accounts of her children, friends, or relatives, in contradiction to the express intent of the prenuptial agreement and will. Your only recourse to help your parent, or protect your family's intended inheritance, might be a lawsuit. If there is no prenuptial agreement, what recourse will you have? If the new spouse just used the money to keep up a somewhat luxurious, but not outrageous, lifestyle, what could you prove?

Property and Family Law Can Make a Complicated Situation Even More Complex

The complexities of dealing with second marriages are vast. Did your parent sign a prenuptial agreement or postnuptial agreement? Was it done properly? What laws apply in the state or country where your parent remarried?

Celebrity Case Studies: Because of community property laws in various locations, celebrities often jump through numerous legal hoops to circumvent inconvenient regulations. Kirstie Alley attempted to avoid community property laws in California by declaring Maine her primary residence when she divorced Parker Stevenson.

Because in Britain the key in any divorce proceeding is the marriage license, Mick Jagger claimed that he and Jerry Hall were never legally married in all the years they lived together and raised their family. He declared that the minister who officiated was merely a friend posing as a minister and was not licensed to perform the marriage ceremony. If true, this would negate any obligation Jagger would have toward Hall and would minimize his obligations to the children they share.

For smaller estates, different issues may have greater importance. If your father's new wife becomes ill, or is incapacitated and requires nursing care, will these costs deplete his estate and inheritance? Will your father become impoverished? Will you end up supporting him (see Chapter 10 for Medicaid planning ideas and Chapter 4 for other insurance ideas)?

To really help your parents protect their assets from a greedy second or later spouse, or from the problems poor planning can create, you need to get professional advice.

ANNA NICOLE SMITH

No discussion of second and later marriages can be complete without telling the Anna Nicole Smith story.

Celebrity Case Study: In 1994, 26-year-old Anna Nicole Smith, a former stripper, Playboy Playmate of the Year, and Guess? jeans model, married 89-year-old Texas multimillionaire J. Howard Marshall. Marshall died a year later and, in his will, bequeathed everything to the younger of his two sons, E. Pierce Marshall, leaving nothing to his widow or elder son, J. Howard Marshall III. Thus was born the battle of the century over an estate with an estimated worth of anywhere from $46 million to $1.6 billion.

Smith immediately contested the will, claiming that her deceased spouse lived to fulfill her every wish and had promised her half his estate on more than one occasion. Pierce Marshall, the sole beneficiary, begged to differ, pointing to seven trusts and six wills prepared by his father, none of them naming either Smith or Howard III as beneficiary. Howard III, disinherited over a business dispute, also sued for a portion of the estate. Anna Nicole filed for bankruptcy, and in September 2000, the bankruptcy judge awarded her $474 million of her late husband's estate. A U.S. district court overturned that ruling and, in March 2002, awarded her a total of $88.5 million of her late husband's estate in compensatory and punitive damages from Pierce. This verdict also overturned a 1999 ruling in Texas probate court awarding the entire estate to Pierce Marshall. After six years of bitter litigation, "Miss Cleavage" had a second verdict handed down in her favor that Pierce is expected to appeal. All of this costly litigation, however, might have been minimized if Pierce had made certain that his father had clearly stated his intentions to disinherit his spouse and elder son. As it is, his inheritance has been vastly dissipated through legal fees and then awards for damages that could have been avoided.

If your dad is courting a pretty gold digger or your mom is about to marry a handsome gigolo who is younger than your son, what do you do? If the circumstances are outlandish, consult a psychologist to determine how to address the situation. Ongoing consultations may give you the insight to help your parents see what they are getting into. If the circumstances are reasonable, don't let your concern destroy your relationship. Keep close, keep in touch, and try to be open-minded. If you can get your parents to talk about their wishes and planning, perhaps they would be willing to consult an attorney to clarify their wishes in their will, as well as in other planning steps. Always encourage your parent to seek the advice of an estate specialist when second marriage and other complications exist.

HYBRID FAMILIES: CASE HISTORIES THAT ILLUSTRATE THE PROBLEMS

You don't have to be famous to face the difficult problems that fractionalized or hybrid families can create for estate planning. There is perhaps no circumstance more fraught with likely battles than improper planning for hybrid families.

> **Case Study:**   Some families insist on believing the Brady Bunch myth. Logic, and even professional cautions, can't dissuade them. The Winklers were both married for the second time, after tough divorces. Each had four children, and under their wills they decided to set up trusts. Each trust was to be comanaged by the eldest child from each family: wife's oldest son and father's oldest daughter. They are trusting each family to vote fairly for both families without any mechanism to break a deadlock or argument. This idealistic Brady Bunch might soon end up looking more like the Hatfields and McCoys. Only time will tell.

The better approach with hybrid families is to name independent and objective executors (to manage the will) and trustees (to manage trusts set up under the will or before death as separate documents). This might include longtime friends, professionals who have advised the family for many years, institutions, or some combination.

> **Case Study:**   Arthur Smith's wife died. He had rocky relationships with his children for decades. Then, when he was 81, he met Beatrice. Beatrice wasn't quite the Anna Nicole Smith type, she was 79. Beatrice was a true companion and confidante for Arthur. They became best friends and, about five years after meeting, began to live together. They both wrote wills. Arthur's estate had grown substantially with the stock market and, because he had always lived a modest lifestyle, his holdings had

increased to more than $5 million. He left half of his estate to Beatrice, his companion, and half to his son, but nothing to his daughter. The next year, on the advice of an attorney, Arthur and Beatrice married (if Beatrice wasn't married to Arthur estate taxes would take a lot of what he left her). Arthur's estate continued to grow to more than $7 million, and soon after marriage, he made gifts of more than $1 million in assets to Beatrice. He also changed many of his other accounts to joint ownership (this gave Beatrice access to the accounts and on Arthur's death would assure that those accounts would immediately become hers). A few years later, Arthur, with the relationship with his children becoming more strained, revised his will leaving everything to his now wife, Beatrice. About one year later, Arthur died. Arthur's children immediately sued their father's estate, trying to prevent Beatrice from gaining access to his assets. They claimed that Beatrice unduly influenced Arthur (at age 89 she was after his money), the lawyer failed to do her job correctly, and pretty much anything else they could think of. As the legal battle raged on, Beatrice, at 90, fell ill and passed away. Her last years were spent watching her companion die, and then seeing both of their families fight bitterly over their inheritance.

Arthur's will might have been a bit clearer, but Arthur's wishes were not a surprise and were consistent with years of changes. The real problems were the anger and greed of his children. Had Arthur's children been a bit more understanding of their father's loneliness, his desire for some warmth and family unity, instead of constantly bickering over mistakes in the past, his children would have inherited substantially more, and he would have been far more sensitive to their wishes.

THE NEED TO SIGN A PRENUPTIAL AGREEMENT BEFORE REMARRIAGE

If your mom is going to remarry, encourage her to consult a family lawyer about a prenuptial agreement to limit her new spouse's rights to her assets. About 20 percent of people with more than $5 million in assets have a prenuptial agreement. That means 80 percent don't! The prenuptial agreement could assure her of some minimum amount of support if the new marriage doesn't work out. The agreement can list in detail the assets your mother has before remarriage and assure that her new spouse has no claims on them. If she has already remarried without the benefit of a prenuptial agreement, your mother can still achieve some protection by entering into a postnuptial or antenuptial agreement. Exercise considerable caution in such situations. You don't want to offend and upset your parents. Try to help them understand the potentially adverse financial consequences if they don't protect themselves.

A LIVING-TOGETHER AGREEMENT FOR A PARENT WHO HAS A SIGNIFICANT OTHER BUT WON'T MARRY

If your dad, after the death of, or divorce from, your mom, should take up living with a new companion, without contemplating marriage, a prenuptial or postnuptial agreement won't apply. But that doesn't mean that he cannot take steps to protect himself. Your dad could consider entering into a living together contract with his new roommate or partner to minimize the likelihood of legal and financial entanglements if the relationship terminates. Such an agreement can also prevent the new partner from pilfering your future inheritance without Dad's consent.

Your dad should get a contractual arrangement governing the legal, economic, and perhaps other aspects of his new relationship. "A living-together agreement is important for partners who live together without the formality of a marriage since they do not have many of the legal protections married couples have. These include common law rights of dower and courtesy, the statutory right of election against an estate, the estate and gift tax marital deduction, and forms of joint ownership (tenancy by the entirety). The law is generally less clear as to how the rights between nonmarried partners will be applied," cautions Charles Abut, Esq., based in Fort Lee, New Jersey.

The living-together agreement attempts to establish the parties' economic, legal, and other ties during and after dissolution of their relationship. There is little assurance how many courts will treat these contracts. In some states, the concept of palimony is recognized in the law. Palimony can require that an unmarried cohabitant be paid financial support from an unmarried partner, if the existence of an agreement to provide that support can be established.

WHAT IF DAD'S NEW WIFE WANTS MORE MONEY IN HER NAME?

Beware: Tax Laws Encourage Large Gifts

Gifts made to a spouse, who is a United States citizen, in any amount, are not subject to gift tax. This means that there are generally no tax restrictions on your dad giving his new wife any portion of his estate.

Another less common transfer that also qualifies for the marital deduction (i.e., no tax) is to give the spouse a life estate with a general power of appointment. This means the spouse would have the right to the income or use of the assets for her life. The spouse will also have the right to designate who should receive the property following her death. Since this will likely be her children or family, not you and your family, this isn't an ideal option.

There is a better option than either of the preceding ones. Your dad can gift assets to a trust for his new wife, instead of directly to her. If this special marital trust (e.g., a QTIP trust) for a spouse, is properly formed during your dad's life (inter vivos), there will not be an adverse tax cost to the transfer. The best result, however, is that your dad can control who the ultimate beneficiaries will be. Typically, the funds can be given to a trust for the new wife, who will receive income (or an annuity payment) for her life. On her death, the assets can be distributed back to your dad's heirs.

Planning Tip: While this inter vivos QTIP approach can be great for many, there is a potential leak in the plan. And the leak will take more than a little Dutch boy's finger to plug. If your dad's lawyer doesn't draft the trust carefully, and if the trustee is indifferent or favors your dad's new mate, the powers given to distribute principal of the trust could effectively put all the assets in the hands of your dad's new wife. Principal distribution could be restricted to funds needed to maintain her standard of living after giving consideration to her other resources, or could be even less.

HAVE DAD LEAVE THE SECOND WIFE A LIFE ESTATE

There are often seemingly simple solutions to complex problems in estate planning. Simplicity is great; it is easier to understand and it costs less to write the will. The real issue is does it work? A common second marriage situation concerns the marital home. Mom and Dad raised the kids in the old Victorian. Dad died, and years later Mom remarried and lived together with New Husband for 10 years in the family home. Mom was getting on in years and wanted to protect New Husband's right to live in the home, but she wanted to also be sure that on his death the old Victorian would pass to her children, who had a strong attachment to and fond memories of the house.

A possible option would be a life estate. A life estate means that New Husband could live in the home for his lifetime, but on his death it would pass back to Mom's children. Life estates are used not only to allow a spouse to continue living in a home after death, but also to give children residential rights.

Celebrity Case Study: In Newport, Rhode Island, one of the largest tourist attractions is The Breakers, the former home of Cornelius Vanderbilt II. The Breakers is a four-story, 70-room summer "cottage" where the Vanderbilts would vacation, together with the rest of the Four Hundred. The cost of running such a large estate, however, became prohibitive. Additionally, the Vanderbilt family wanted to continue their tradition of supporting the preservation of art and historic homes in the area. As insurance that a change of fortune would not mean the deterioration of the family home, and to help raise funds to preserve other historic homes in the area, in 1972, the Vanderbilt family sold the home to the Preservation Society of Newport County. The home was opened to tourists with the provision that the Vanderbilt heirs, currently Gloria Vanderbilt, be allowed to live on the estate. When the family is in residence, some of the rooms are closed to public tours.

A life estate sounds great and seems simple. Regrettably, it's not—even if your place is a bit more modest than the Vanderbilt cottage. Although it may be common and inexpensive to implement, it's not always the best option when you want to maximize your inheritance. Too many ambiguities and issues are left unsettled when implementing a standard life estate. Take a look at the following simple clause for a will giving New Husband a life estate:

Sample Clause: I give, devise, and bequeath to New Husband the house located at 123 Main Street, Anytown, United States to have and to hold the same for and during New Husband's lifetime, without the necessity of paying rent or furnishing bond or other security therefore, but subject to New Husband paying all normal costs of maintenance and repair in respect thereof. On the death of New Husband, or upon such life estate beneficiary's earlier renunciation or disclaimer of the interest in said property, or on my death if such life estate beneficiary does not survive me, I give, devise, and bequeath said real property to my children.

The preceding clause is typical, but far short of what is necessary to prevent family problems. Consider the following common issues that the clause doesn't address:

• Does the life estate include any furniture, furnishings, and household effects? Do you as Mom's child have the right to remove items from the home as you see fit? This may be particularly significant if you have a personal attachment to items in the home or if you want to sell valuable antiques or artwork for reasons as mundane as that you need the money to pay bills.

• What about any insurance policies on the house? Would you, as Mom's child and executor, have the right to cash them in, leaving New Husband with the responsibility of purchasing new coverage?

• What if Mom sold the house or deeded it to you before her death? What happens to New Husband? Will he sue you for the right to live in the house as promised under the will?

• Must you pay all real property and similar taxes, assessments, and/or carrying charges on the house or is the burden to be carried by New Husband? How are these to be defined? Do you have the money to carry that burden?

• Who pays estate or inheritance taxes on the value of the house that may be taxable? Do you or does New Husband?

• Does New Husband pay fire and extended coverage insurance premiums for the full insurable value of the house? Who determines the value to insure? Who determines the type of coverage? What is to stop New Husband from getting the cheapest coverage available? Keep in mind that if there is a fire or other significant damage, your asset is being destroyed.

- The sample clause requires New Husband to pay "all normal costs of maintenance and repair" of the home. How are "normal" and "maintenance and repair" defined? Is a new roof normal or a repair? If it is a capital improvement (i.e., not a mere repair), must you as an eventual heir pay? Who will ensure that New Husband pays for necessary maintenance and repairs? If New Husband is 55, how can you limit the amount of payments you need to make for a property you may not receive for 30 years? If New Husband is in his 80s, he may not be willing to make repairs that would cost money he intends to bequeath to his own children: How do you get him to pay? Definition of each term is key to avoiding disputes.

- What if the life estate beneficiary is disabled and cannot live in the house? Should the house sit empty? The sample clause is too simplistic. It could provide that, if in the opinion of two licensed physicians, it is "unlikely" that New Husband could foresee returning to live in the home, it should be sold. What happens, then, if you as a child who was raised in that house, don't want to sell it?

A life estate is a great technique when it works, but be sure to review all possible scenarios and problems with your parent and attorney.

USING TRUSTS TO PROTECT YOUR INHERITANCE

Dad died, or Mom and Dad divorced. Mom is involved with a new beau, who lives in his VW Bug when not with her. Beau's tie-dyed t-shirts and peace symbol necklace, and general lifestyle concern you, but Mom decides to marry him anyhow. You suggest a prenuptial agreement. Mom says no—this is true love. She is, however, receptive to meeting with an attorney about an estate plan. The classic planning step is to recommend that Mom bequeath her assets to a trust. She can use the trust to benefit her beau and also assure that the assets eventually reach you and other intended heirs.

There is a common problem. If the new beau is decades younger than your mom, you might not inherit until you are in your 70s or later. Solutions exist. Your mom could leave a portion of her estate to you and other children or heirs on her death, not waiting for her new young spouse to die. Another common approach that can minimize all of these problems is for Mom to buy a large life insurance policy (or perhaps have a trust set up to own the policy). This can assure that on her death both her natural heirs (often children from a prior marriage) and new young spouse, are provided for economically. Another common problem is the spousal right of election. Mom's new beau is entitled under state law to some of her assets. The trust may not suffice.

SETTING UP A FAMILY TRUST

When planning for a second or later marriage that will result in the hybrid family situations discussed in this chapter, a common approach is to set up a trust for the new spouse in the will. Your parent can create a contractual relationship called a trust either with a separate legal document or under the will, in which case the trust will only become effective following death. The key concept of a trust is that it can separate legal ownership from beneficial ownership. The legal owner is a trustee, who can be an independent person named to be in charge of investing trust assets and distributing trust money. The beneficial owners are the persons intended to benefit from the trust assets. These can include the new spouse as well as natural heirs. The primary benefit of a trust in a second or later marriage is to separate control and benefit. Your mom can designate the longtime family accountant who has proven himself trustworthy and who is independent of family politics, especially as they concern Mom's new husband. This independent trustee can be given some flexibility to distribute assets and income between the natural heirs and the new spouse. This can be an effective way to help all loved ones, with the benefit of hindsight (i.e., the trustee can use the trust money appropriately in as yet unknown future circumstances).

There are two common types of trusts. The first, called a bypass, applicable exclusion, or credit shelter trust, can hold assets up to the amount that your parent can bequeath free of estate tax. This was $1 million in 2002 and is scheduled to increase in future years (unless Congress changes the rules yet again). This type of trust can include anyone as a beneficiary—new spouse, children from prior marriage, and others. If your parents' estate exceeds this exclusion amount, the remainder of the estate should be left to a trust that qualifies for the estate tax marital deduction. This will enable your mother to benefit her new spouse, while deferring any estate taxes, and still assure that you and the other natural heirs will eventually inherit.

Planning Tip: If your parents have remarried, these types of trust should be included in their wills, or you are unlikely to see any money other than what the will leaves you directly on the parent's death. Anything given outright to the new spouse is only going to make its way to your pocket by chance. If your parent's will is less than 10 pages, there is a good chance that the trusts are not included or don't have enough legal meat to make them workable.

QUALIFYING FOR UNLIMITED MARITAL DEDUCTION

When Mom wants to defer estate taxes and to leave assets that benefit and protect her new spouse, her estate plan should take advantage of her ability to leave unlimited assets to a spouse in trust. An unlimited marital deduction is available for qualifying bequests under your parent's will to a spousal trust. The following requirements must be met:

- The property that is intended to qualify for the marital deduction must pass from your parent to the surviving spouse. The property must be transferred under a will (or under your state's laws of intestacy if one died without a will), as a result of joint ownership between your parent and her spouse or by a beneficiary designation (e.g., in an IRA).

- The rights and property transferred to your parent's spouse cannot be a right that will terminate or fail as the result of the passing of time, the occurrence of an event or contingency (until she remarries), or the failure of an event or contingency to occur. A life estate (my spouse shall have our home for her life) or a bequest for a term of years (my spouse shall have my yacht for 15 years) are terminable interests and do not qualify for the marital deduction.

The most common exception to this rule denying a marital deduction for property interests that may terminate, however, is the exception called a "qualified terminable interest property" (QTIP) trust. This is the most popular marital trust. If the following requirements are met, your parent's estate will qualify for the estate tax marital deduction on bequeathing assets to a QTIP trust for the surviving spouse. In addition to the marital deduction, your parent will maintain control over the use and ultimate disposition of the property:

- No person can have the power to appoint the trust assets to any person other than the surviving spouse prior to the surviving spouse's death.
- Income from the trust must be paid to the surviving spouse at least annually.
- The executor of your parent's will must elect to qualify the trust for the marital deduction.
- The property must pass from your parent's estate to the surviving spouse's trust.
- On the death of the surviving spouse, the entire value of the QTIP property is included in the surviving spouse's gross estate. This fact can present some thorny tax problems on the death of the new spouse or, if the new spouse has an estate that isn't taxable, some huge benefits.

Example: Dad marries new spouse. Dad has a $2 million estate and the maximum amount Dad can give away without estate tax is $1 million. Dad uses the classic second marriage approach previously outlined and leaves $1 million in a Bypass Trust under his will to benefit his new spouse and all of his children from his prior marriage. The balance of his estate, the remaining $1 million, is distributed to a marital or QTIP trust for his new wife. His new wife has no assets. If she dies a few years later, the $1 million exclusion her estate has available is unused by her assets and may protect the entire QTIP trust from taxation. Thus, the estate potentially will save $500,000 in taxes as a result of the QTIP trust.

The preceding example illustrates an important point. Planning is not always a zero-sum game. You don't have to lose if the new spouse wins, and vice versa. Everyone, with careful planning, can benefit. This concept can be a key selling point to get your parent, your parent's new spouse, and your siblings to plan together.

PROS AND CONS OF A MARITAL TRUST

When in doubt, use the trust. Why? While a trust creates a bit more complexity and cost, it assures your parent's control over the assets. It can prevent a greedy new spouse from pilfering the inheritance intended for you and other family members. It can protect the new spouse from having natural heirs infringe on her lifestyle. The trust can work both ways and protect everyone.

A trust can also provide important tax benefits. Your parent's executor can determine what portion of the trust should qualify for the marital deduction. This can enable the executor to use hindsight to preserve some of your parent's estate tax exclusion, which ultimately will reduce taxes for the heirs. The executor can also make decisions to maximize the generation skipping transfer (GST) tax benefit using hindsight. This is the tax that would otherwise apply to multigenerational asset transfers (e.g., to grandchildren or later descendants).

As a child of the marriage, it should be an imperative in your mind that your surviving parent or a beloved stepparent be provided for on the death of her spouse. The cost of caring for an independent elder parent is high, and you may have to assume the burden for that care if your parent does not have adequate funds. Even if you have several siblings, you have no guarantee that they will share the burden of caring for your parent or stepparent; you could end up being the sole support. Keep that in mind when helping your parents plan their estate. It is one thing to inherit more; it is another thing to do it at the expense of your surviving parent.

WILL DAD'S NEW WIFE EXERCISE A RIGHT OF ELECTION?

What Is a Spousal Right of Election?

A spousal right of election, particularly as a result of the increases in second and later marriages and the growing divorce rate, can be important in determining the ultimate distribution of any decedent's assets.

The laws of almost every state recognize that the surviving spouse should be entitled to some minimum portion of the deceased spouse's estate, or alternatively that the surviving spouse should be entitled to enough assets to live on. The rationale of state legislatures is that it is in the public's interest to protect surviving spouses. Whereas many states assure the surviving spouse at least one-third of the estate, subject to various conditions, limitations, and other requirements, not all do.

The spousal right of election laws of a particular state generally apply to any married person who dies domiciled in that state. Determining the state of domicile is essential since laws differ from state to state. Domicile is generally defined as a place of permanent residence to which the person ultimately intends to return. The determination of domicile is based on the specific facts in each case.

Not Every Spouse Can Get This Benefit

Not every surviving spouse is entitled to the protection of this rule. A surviving spouse may be denied the right of election where the couple was living separate and apart in different homes, or where the couple had ceased to cohabit as husband and wife under circumstances that would give rise to a cause of action for divorce (or annulment) from the decedent, prior to death. Mere separation does not defeat the right of election.

Even if your parent's new spouse can take advantage of a spousal right of election, it is not always obvious what it will amount to. In some states, any transfer under which the decedent retained the possession or enjoyment of, or right to income from, the property at the time of death would subject the assets involved to a spousal right of election.

Planning Tip: In a few states if your parent transfers all of her assets to a revocable living trust, it could limit her new spouse's right of election. If you are advising your parent as to what kind of trust to set up hire a lawyer to investigate your state's position on elective share rights and revocable living trusts.

The Typical Entitlement of a Surviving Spouse

A typical state spousal right of election law guarantees the surviving spouse a one-third share of the estate. Not only does the percentage vary from state to state, but the definitions of what is included in the estate differ considerably. Prior gifts may be included in the calculation, there may be subtractions for assets owned by or given to the surviving spouse, and so on. If a trust such as a marital or QTIP trust (not a revocable living trust) is set up for the surviving spouse under the deceased spouse's will, it may only be partially counted.

A common right-of-election issue is, to what extent will property to be held in trust for the benefit of the surviving spouse be counted toward meeting her elective share (the amount the surviving spouse is entitled to)? In many states, property in trust is only counted at 50 percent of value. In some states, a life estate (the surviving spouse is given the right to use property, such as a house, but doesn't own it, as discussed earlier) and interests held in a trust do not qualify as satisfying the surviving spouse's right of election at all.

Example: Husband dies in 2002 leaving a $2 million estate. Of this amount, $500,000 represents joint assets that pass to the deceased husband's child from a prior marriage. The probate estate consists of $1.5 million of securities. The will leaves $800,000 in a QTIP trust for his surviving spouse. The remaining $700,000 assets are distributed to a Bypass Trust, protected from estate tax by the applicable exclusion amount. The surviving spouse and the husband's children from a prior marriage are all beneficiaries of the Bypass Trust. Under state law, the Bypass Trust is included in the calculation of the estate but may not count as an asset paid to the surviving spouse. Under some state statutes, assets in a QTIP trust will count at a rate of 50 percent in meeting the spousal right of election. If insurance is included in the estate for calculating the spousal right of election under state law, then the surviving spouse has a right of election against a $2 million estate. A one-third elective share is $666,666. The only bequest that counts toward satisfying the spousal right of election is the QTIP trust of $800,000. This only counts at a 50 percent rate, or as if the surviving spouse received $400,000. Thus, the surviving spouse would be entitled to an additional $266,666 [$666,666 – $400,000] if she elects against the estate. If your parent has remarried, you must understand these rules to protect your inheritance.

To prevent an end run around the spousal right-of-election laws, many state laws permit the surviving spouse to obtain a percentage of assets given away just before death. In some states, this includes any transfer made within two years of death of the decedent to the extent that the aggregate transfer to any one donee in either of the years exceeds $3,000. However, if the surviving spouse gave a written consent to the transfer, or joined in the transfer, the property transferred may not be reached.

Be Certain That the Surviving Spouse Waived the Right of Election

When your parent's will is to provide the surviving spouse less than the amount of the statutory election, it is common and proper to request that the surviving spouse formally sign a legal document giving up the right (waiving her right of election). This is done specifically to prevent the spouse of a second or later marriage from using the election to upset the dispositions provided for under your parent's will. To be effective, the waiver of the right of election must meet specified requirements under state law. The rules vary from state to state, but may include the following:

- The waiver must be in the form of a written contract or agreement signed by the spouse waiving the right.
- The waiver will only be effective if there is full disclosure. It would be unfair to ask a spouse to effectively waive rights under state law without knowing the assets involved. How can you agree to forgo what you don't know?
- The waiver must be both clear and certain. A waiver in a prenuptial agreement or divorce property settlement agreement can often be effective.

If you serve as an executor for your parent's estate, and the new spouse exerts her right of election, confirm whether a waiver was ever signed. If your parent plans to remarry, caution him to consult a matrimony attorney about including a waiver in his prenuptial agreement.

LESSONS TO LEARN

This chapter has summarized special situations and problems that arise with second and later marriages. If your parent or other benefactor remarries, and any of these difficulties arise, or even appear to be an issue, be certain to obtain professional legal advice. Also, keep in mind that state law differs considerably from state to state. Be careful how you address these sensitive matters (prenuptial, waiver of spousal right of election, trusts, etc.) to avoid upsetting or even alienating your parent.

In the words of one wealthy individual who remarked, when advised to have a prenuptial agreement before his third marriage,

"It's not necessary. After this one, it's either the cemetery or the monastery."

What can be done? Plenty—if your parent is willing. Most importantly, every step to protect your parent from a new spouse will also protect your inheritance. In many situations, the goals can be consistent; planning is not a zero-sum game. Parents who plan creatively can reduce their tax liability, protect their savings, and minimize family feuds. Try to gently guide your parent to recognize all of the ways your family, or the families of your parent's new spouse can cause havoc. Encourage your parent to seek professional legal advice to craft a plan that minimizes the likelihood of any of these problems having a significant adverse impact.

FOR YOUR NOTEBOOK

SAMPLE WAIVER OF RIGHT OF ELECTION

I, Jane Doe, spouse of John Doe, for one dollar and other good and valuable consideration receipt of which is hereby acknowledged, now waive and release "all rights in the property or estate" of John Doe ("my spouse") in accordance with [list appropriate state law reference], specifically the right to elect against the Last Will and Testament of my spouse executed on September 2, 2005. I further waive and release any right to elect as against any testamentary substitute or intestate share to which I would otherwise be entitled under the provisions of [list appropriate state law reference].

I further acknowledge that I am fully informed of the value of the assets owned by my spouse, including but not limited to the assets listed on the balance sheet and related financial information attached hereto as an exhibit, which I now waive and release and am fully informed of the nature of my rights in those assets.

I further represent that I have been represented by counsel in the execution of this document and I am signing this document freely and voluntarily.

Dated:_____

_____

Jane Doe

Subscribed and sworn to before me

this 12th day of June 2003

_____

Notary Public
My Commission expires:_____

4 DO YOUR PARENTS HAVE THE RIGHT INSURANCE COVERAGE?

Insurance means more than life insurance. Carefully planned insurance is essential to protect your parents' assets. A house without fire and casualty insurance may be a total loss in the event of such a calamity. A theft can be devastating to the financial worth of a parent who has never insured valuable art, coins, or other collectibles, or has insurance that is based on an assessment made 30 years ago. Elderly parents who have no nursing home or long-term care insurance may deplete their assets to the point that their children must help support them. This chapter discusses basic insurance that can protect your parents and their assets.

LIFE INSURANCE

Key Life Insurance Facts

Life insurance may be a major portion of your inheritance. Who owns the policies? Who are the beneficiaries? Do you have the authority to change the beneficiaries under your parents' durable power of attorney? Should a trust own the policies to minimize estate taxes on your parents' deaths? What will estate taxes do to insurance and what suggestions can you offer your parents to minimize taxation?

Why Your Parents May Need Life Insurance

A vital step in protecting your inheritance is ensuring that your parents have the appropriate life insurance coverage. Coverage will vary as to amount and type depending on the prospective needs of your parents' estate (e.g., payment of estate taxes, liquidity because of real estate holdings) and the objectives of your parents.

Your parents' requirements for life insurance may encompass a range of needs:

- Living expenses for the surviving spouse.

- Payment of your parents' outstanding medical bills. High costs from a last or other major illness can bankrupt a family and destroy an inheritance. If your father, for example, faces a long costly illness, what resources will be left for your mother?

- Mortgage payments or repayment of a home mortgage in the event of death.

- Funds to cover college and graduate school tuition for children, grandchildren, or other heirs.

- Payment of estate taxes. Second to die or survivors insurance is an excellent vehicle, in the appropriate circumstances to fund the payment of estate tax. The bypass trust and the unlimited marital deduction eliminate any tax on the first death, so that the tax is only due on the death of the second spouse.

- Payment of funeral costs.

- Insulation of assets from creditors. The cash value of an insurance policy held in an irrevocable trust, where there was no fraudulent transfer in making gifts to the trust to pay premiums, should have a measure of protection from malpractice claimants and other creditors.

- Dovetailing with gift and other planning. Where a wealthy individual is engaged in an aggressive gift program, insurance (term, or even decreasing term) can be coordinated with the gift plan. For example, if a five-year Grantor Retained Annuity Trust (GRAT) is used, a five-year term policy can be purchased to address the risk of the grantor dying prior to termination of the GRAT. This is a special trust used to gift large values to children with little or no gift tax. However, you must outlive the term of the trust for this benefit. Where a gift program of $20,000 per year to children, children's spouses, and grandchildren has been set up to remove $260,000 per year from the estate, a decreasing term insurance coverage plan could fund the cost of the estate tax if the taxpayer should die before completing the intended annual gifts.

- "Prepayment" of inheritance tax so other assets can be retained and spent. Many older people become uncomfortable making large gifts to reduce their estate out of concern for having adequate resources to provide for needs in later life, particularly an illness. Often the insurance premiums to fund the estimated tax look far more palatable than the substantial reduction of the estate to eliminate the tax.

If your review suggests that your parents have inadequate life insurance, you have two choices: You can either purchase the insurance on your parents' lives yourself, or you can convince your parents that they need to purchase additional life insurance to meet their needs and goals.

To purchase insurance on another person's life, you must have a sufficient legal right to do so (called an insurable interest). Although it is relatively easy to satisfy the requirement for a parent, the more distant your relationship to your benefactor, the less likely that you can meet this rule, absent a business or other relationship to justify your purchasing life insurance.

How Much Life Insurance Do Your Parents Need?

The first step in determining how much life insurance you should purchase on your parents' lives, or that they should purchase, is to identify each reasonable need for insurance, as discussed earlier. Your parents and their advisers should then estimate the amount of insurance necessary to meet those needs.

When purchasing insurance on an older parent, you seldom can apply any general rule of thumb, such as purchasing a life insurance policy with a face value of five times the person's annual income (or any other rule of thumb). Instead of using such "guesstimates," do the math for each need, and subtract the other noninsurance resources that will be available to meet it.

If your parents need insurance to pay for the needs of the surviving parent, you should estimate a budget for those costs. If insurance is targeted for covering estate taxes, then the cost of taxes should be estimated. You should factor in all their planning steps to reduce taxes, as well as the increase in the applicable exclusion amount (the amount that can be bequested free of estate taxes (see Chapter 11). If insurance is to be used to cover a mortgage or some other specific cost, then you should estimate that cost.

After roughly calculating all these expenses or needs, your parents and their advisers should also calculate the assets your parents presently hold and their likely increase (e.g., appreciation of investments) or decrease (e.g., use for living expenses). These include cash, savings, real estate holdings, securities, and any retirement plans that your parents own. Other sources of income or cash flow such as Social Security and pensions should also be factored in.

The net needs for insurance coverage will often differ from the amount actually purchased depending on your parents' assessment of their risks or needs and the cost of obtaining insurance.

Before Buying Life Insurance, Consider the Options

Before you purchase insurance on your parents' lives, or they purchase insurance for themselves, review all options. As your parents age, the cost will become greater, and physically qualifying for life insurance will become more difficult.

Before purchasing new life insurance, evaluate all of their existing life insurance coverage and any of these options:

- Will health or long-term care insurance protect assets for the surviving spouse?

- Can estate-planning techniques (Bypass Trusts, annual gift program, leveraging techniques) reduce or eliminate the need for insurance to pay estate taxes? What about state inheritance tax?

- Can existing insurance policies be used to meet the need involved?

- Can options on the existing insurance policies be used to minimize the need for, or cost of, additional life insurance coverage? For example, from the cash value that has accumulated in their life policy, depending on market rates and loan rates in the policy, your parents may be able to take out a loan at a lower rate of interest than the rates charged by banks. Some older policies have accumulated so much cash value that it may be more economical to simply cash in the policy or exchange it for a new policy that better meets current needs. Your parents' term insurance may have a convertibility option that enables changing it into a permanent insurance policy without a medical exam. Depending on your parents' ages, a guaranteed insurability option may remain that will allow them to purchase additional insurance at a set price.

What Type of Insurance Should Your Parents Purchase?

There are many kinds of life insurance. Once you have determined the needs and amounts, you can factor these decisions into the analysis of what policies to purchase. Permanent, whole life, universal life, and variable life insurance combine investment characteristics with a life insurance benefit. One of the main reasons for the popularity of whole life is that no rising yearly premiums go along with it. The yearly premiums will usually stay the same from the first year that your parents buy whole life insurance. These policies may be purchased instead of term insurance where there is a long-term time perspective or a desire to build cash value inside the policy to protect that value from claimants or creditors. If your parents' estate consists primarily of nonliquid real estate assets that your parents intend to hold, it may be prudent to always carry some life insurance. This will assure cash availability to meet carrying costs (property taxes, mortgage payments, etc.) and to pay estate tax (if any) without having to sell any property.

Term life insurance is the least expensive life insurance because it provides only a death benefit, not any savings component (term insurance has no cash value). Furthermore, the purchaser is only buying the death benefit for a fixed amount of time, usually anywhere from 1 to 20 years, depending on the age of the insured, although longer periods may be available. Term insurance is often not available past a particular age and thus may not be a viable option for your parents. Many term insurance policies will not be renewable after the age of 65 or 70, and if the policy is renewable at those ages, it is often incredibly expensive. Therefore, if your parents have term insurance with a conversion feature, they should convert to another policy such as a whole life policy before the feature lapses.

Variable life insurance is another type of permanent insurance; it has several variations. Straight variable life has fixed premiums, but the death benefit goes up and down based on investment performance. If the investments in your parents' insurance policy rise by more than the amount stipulated in the policy, the death benefit (face value) will increase. If, however, the value of their investments falls, the face value will fall to no less than the original guaranteed amount. Variable universal life has fixed premiums, and the investment earnings in the policy affect only your parents' cash value, not their death benefit.

Second to die insurance is tailor-made for couples wishing to provide for children or other heirs and take care of their estate tax. Second to die insurance is an insurance policy that only pays when the second of two people (your parents or other benefactors) dies. In effect, the insurance company is insuring two lives, but only paying once—on the death of the last of your parents to die. The insurance is cheaper to purchase than conventional insurance because the insurance company has reduced its risk. Two people are less likely to suffer an unexpected and premature death than one person. This actuarial or statistical savings reduces premium costs.

The estate tax laws provide for an unlimited marital deduction, as explained more fully in Chapter 11. Any assets that your father leaves to your mother (or vice versa) or in a special marital trust (QTIP trust) are not subject to tax on your father's death (the first spouse to die), no matter how large his estate. Thus, on the death of the first of your parents, the estate can avoid tax entirely by simply leaving everything to the surviving parent. Your surviving parent's death triggers the second to die insurance benefit making cash available to fund the estate's payment of estate taxes and expenses, and to provide bequests for heirs. Assuming your parents' combined estate exceeds the applicable exclusion amount (or double that amount if a bypass trust is used), a tax will be due on the second death. A state level estate or inheritance tax may be due on even a smaller amount. Since this is precisely when the second to die insurance pays off, the timing is coordinated. This approach is especially useful for generating cash to pay estate tax if your parents' estate includes art, real estate assets, or closely held business assets that can be difficult to liquidate.

Who Should Own Your Parents' Life Insurance Policies?

Once you have determined your parents' needs for life insurance, as well as the amount and type of coverage, a final key decision remains: Who should own their life insurance policy? There are a host of options, all of which have a significant effect on your parents and on you and other heirs.

Your Parents.   The simplest approach is to have your parents, the insureds, own the policy. If your father is insured, your mother could be named beneficiary and either of them could own the policy (there is no tax impact if both are U.S. citizens because of the unlimited estate tax marital deduction). If your father owns the policy, the policy will be included in his estate on his death. However, by virtue of the unlimited marital deduction, the policy proceeds can escape taxation if payable to your mother (or his surviving spouse if he has remarried someone other than your mother). The proceeds that remain in the surviving spouse's (your mother's) estate, however, may be subject to estate tax on her death, unless payable to a charity as the secondary beneficiary.

You and Other Heirs.   In some cases, insurance agents structure the ownership of an insurance policy with the children or other heirs of the insured as owner. This approach can remove the insurance proceeds from your parent's, the insured's, estate, without the cost and complexity of a trust to own the policy. This approach, however, presents potential problems:

- All of the children/heirs may not use the proceeds as desired. They may not make the proceeds available via immediate loan (or to purchase assets from the insured's estate), thereby strapping the estate for cash to pay taxes or expenses. Even if you carry out your parent's wishes, will your siblings?
- If you or other heirs get divorced, the cash value of the insurance could be deemed an asset in the marital estate.
- If you or other heirs are sued, the insurance cash value could be an asset attached by creditors.

You might mitigate the first concern through frank discussion with your parents about their particular desires for using insurance proceeds. You can assure them that you want to see to it that their intentions for the distribution of their estate eventuate. If your parents' concern, or your concern as an heir, is to protect their insurance assets from malpractice claims, bankruptcy, or divorce proceedings affecting the heirs, an insurance trust (see later in this chapter) would be preferable to having yourself and other heirs named individually as owners and as beneficiaries.

Family Partnership.   A family partnership can be used to own life insurance. The insured could be the general or managing partner.

Example: Father is a 1 percent managing partner of a family general partnership. Father gifts 99 percent of the general partnership interests to his children. The partnership buys a $1,000,000 insurance policy on Father. On Father's death, the children receive 99 percent of the insurance proceeds in proportion to the percentage interests in the partnership previously given to them by gift. The executor for Father's estate would take the position on the estate tax return that only 1 percent of the insurance proceeds are included in Father's estate.

A partnership could be used to own insurance and protect your inheritance from the taxman and other claimants. Instead of your parents using a trust, a family limited partnership (FLP) can be the owner of the policy and take advantage of the fact that an FLP can be modified any time pursuant to the terms of the partnership agreement. An irrevocable life insurance trust (ILIT), on the other hand, cannot be modified in most situations.

Insurance Trust.   The preferable approach in most, but not all, circumstances is to have an irrevocable (can't be changed) life insurance trust, an ILIT, own your parents' life insurance.

Planning Tip: Your parents might actually benefit from having as many as three ILITs: one for your father to hold insurance on his life for the benefit of your mother, one for your mother to hold insurance on her life for the benefit of your father, and a third trust to hold second to die or survivorship on both of their joint lives.

An insurance trust is especially useful in preserving its economic benefit for the surviving spouse (say your mother, if the insurance is on your father, and vice versa) to avoid inclusion of the funds in the surviving spouse's estate. Although almost any trust can receive insurance proceeds, a life insurance trust is generally formed to own life insurance policies on your parents' lives.

Example: In aggregate, your parents' estate is worth $4 million. Assume that their estate taxes and expenses are estimated at $800,000 [$4 million less two $1 million applicable exclusion amounts and less expenses]. They jointly purchase a second to die life insurance policy in the amount of $800,000 to cover these costs. The policy, however, is included in your parents' estate (actually, it will only be taxed in the estate of the last parent to die) since he or she will own the policy at death. Thus, your parents' estate has been increased to $4.8 million, and their taxes and expenses have increased to $1.2 million [$800,000 initial expenses plus additional estate taxes of 50 percent of the $800,000 of additional taxable insurance]. Thus, one-half of the insurance proceeds could be lost to additional estate tax costs. As an alternative, your parents could set up an irrevocable life insurance trust to purchase the policy. Since the trust owns the policy, the proceeds will not be included in your parents' estate. Their estate remains valued at $4 million and their taxes and costs remain at $800,000. But, in addition, the trustee of their insurance trust (perhaps you) now has a pool of $800,000 to purchase nonliquid assets from their estate, thereby providing their estate with cash to meet its tax and expense obligations. The value of the assets in the trust can then be used to provide for the needs of your parents' loved ones. The advantages over having beneficiaries own the polices include more control, protection from creditors of the beneficiaries, and protection from becoming a marital asset if a beneficiary divorces.

A simple example can illustrate the fundamental estate tax planning point of a life insurance trust for new insurance purchased by your parents. (If, instead, they transfer existing insurance policies to the trust, they will have to survive three years after the transfer before the insurance can be removed from the estate.)

Example: Assume that Mom's estate is worth $3 million without insurance, and she purchases a $1 million insurance policy to provide liquidity to meet her projected estate taxes. With the policy added to Mom's estate, her estate will be worth $4 million, and the tax cost on the $1 million insurance proceeds on her death could exceed $500,000 (depending on the tax rate and applicable exclusion in the year of her death). Effectively, Mom has paid for a $1 million insurance policy, but her estate and heirs will see half that amount as a result of the additional estate tax costs triggered by including the policy proceeds in her estate. To avoid this result, it is vital to plan for the proper ownership of the policy.

Now if Mom, with the help of her attorney, transfers the $1 million insurance policy to an irrevocable life insurance trust, and meets all the necessary requirements, she will have removed the proceeds of the insurance policy from her estate. Instead, on her death, the insurance trust will have the entire $1 million in proceeds, unreduced by estate tax costs, available to buy assets from her estate. This will provide the liquidity that Mom's estate needs to meet a large portion of the estate tax due.

Properly established, an irrevocable life insurance trust can enable the estates of both your parents to avoid tax on insurance proceeds— potentially a huge savings. They will obtain a measure of protection from creditors and divorce, depending on state law. Liquidity for estate needs can be provided where the trustee is authorized to purchase assets from the estate. For those concerned about publicity, the insurance proceeds in the trust are not included in your parents' probate estates. So if there is no legal challenge to the trust, the insurance proceeds, other assets, and the terms of their disposition should not be made available for public knowledge.

When properly planned, the insurance proceeds not only can avoid taxation in either of your parents' estates, but can remain in trust for your lifetime to protect the proceeds further. Trusts can be completed flexibly enough to protect your surviving parent while still safeguarding the assets. The surviving parent can receive some or all of the annual income from the insurance trust, distributions of the principal in the trust, and even a right to demand up to $5,000, or 5 percent of the trust principal, in any year. These rights can be made available to the surviving parent, while still assuring that the insurance proceeds are not taxed in her estate.

Consider with your parents the following five factors in assessing the advisability of a trust:

1. *Size of the estate.* The larger your parents' estate, the more likely the insurance should be held by a trust to avoid taxes. If their estate is unlikely to exceed the amount that can be given away estate tax free, then a trust is unnecessary; but it is still advisable because of the tax benefits to heirs, protection from divorce and claimants, and other benefits. If the insurance is to benefit grandchildren or later descendants, a generation skipping trust (GST) is necessary to qualify for certain long-term intergenerational tax benefits.

2. *Likelihood of a challenge by creditors or malpractice claimants.* If the policy will have a significant cash value, the parent who is insured would be best off to consider a trust to protect that cash value. If the challenge is likely to affect the beneficiaries (surviving spouse and then other heirs), a trust is advisable even for a term policy to protect the death benefit.

3. *Comfort in losing most rights and flexibility (if not all rights and flexibility) to amend the trust.* Some parents are simply averse to the constraints of a trust, no matter what the consequences or the benefits lost.

4. *Amount of insurance involved.* For a $100,000 policy, it is rarely worthwhile to use a trust because of the cost and administrative burdens. For a $1 million or greater policy, it may always

be advisable to use a trust. In-between amounts require greater analysis.

5. *Insured's objectives.* What are your parents' goals? Insurance trusts can address varying needs and desires.

Case Study: Parents have two children. Their son is well off and is married with children. Their 42-year-old daughter has never married; though she is self-supporting, they worry about her. The parents are concerned that if they bequeath more assets to their daughter, their son will feel insulted. Instead, they establish an insurance trust to hold an insurance policy for their daughter's benefit. The trust will protect the funds from any adverse relationship she might find herself in. Further, the son may not have to be informed about the insurance, and since the will bequeaths the estate equally to son and daughter, they believe this approach will avoid insulting the son.

Note: If you buy second to die (also called survivors) insurance to pay estate tax, you need an insurance trust. But you do not have to be rich to need an insurance trust. An older couple has a special needs child, and a very modest estate. They need substantial insurance to protect against the death of the father as breadwinner. That insurance could trigger an estate tax and make the government, not the child, the biggest beneficiary. An insurance trust is the answer. Futhermore, the insurance trust should include special needs provisions to prevent the insurance proceeds from disqualifying the special child from government benefit programs.

ACCELERATED DEATH BENEFITS AND VIATICAL INSURANCE AGREEMENTS FOR TERMINALLY ILL PATIENTS

An insured who is terminally ill may have a greater need for funds than the surviving heirs and beneficiaries (the traditional persons to receive insurance proceeds). To fund medical costs and other needs of the terminally ill, your parents' policies may qualify for a special right to receive an advanced payment of a considerable portion of the death benefit. This is called a viatical settlement or accelerated death benefit, and the amounts can be substantially greater than a payout of just the cash value in the policy.

Accelerated death benefits can be received in cash value policies, term policies, and even in some group policies. As part of the accelerated death benefit, a terminally ill parent can receive up to 90 percent of the face value of the policy at the time of his illness, instead of his beneficiaries receiving the full amount of the policy at the time of death. However, some insurance companies will only pay the accelerated death benefit if the ill parent is expected to die within the next 12 months. Furthermore, some companies will only pay the accelerated death benefit if the policyholder signed up for accelerated benefits when purchasing the policy. Some companies charge an additional fee to sign up for accelerated benefit options at the time of purchasing a policy; others charge a fee only if the option is used.

If your parents are ineligible to receive any accelerated death benefits from their insurance company, you might want to contact a viatical settlement company to determine whether they offer a better alternative for your parents. This type of company will buy the insurance policy from the policyholder for a percentage of the face value of the policy. This percentage could range from about 50 percent to 80 percent of the face value of the policy. The percentage that a viatical company will pay for your parent's policy will depend on several factors. Viatical companies will look more favorably on policies that are at least two years old, face values that are relatively large, and policies that are with well-known insurance companies. Viatical companies will also look at the life expectancy of the policyholder, your ill parent. The later the death expectancy, the less the viatical company will pay for the policy. If your parent's policy is a group policy, the viatical company may ask your parent to first convert the policy to an individual one, or else it may require some type of assurance that the policy will not be canceled after their purchase.

Under a viatical arrangement, an investor pays an actuarially determined amount to the terminally ill parent in exchange for an assignment of the death benefit under the policy.

Payments received from a viatical settlement generally will not be taxable income to your parent if they meet the tax law requirements.

Planning Note: If your parent is seriously ill, it may be advantageous for all to tap an insurance policy with a viatical or accelerated death benefit arrangement instead of liquidating a stock portfolio or selling other assets to pay for expenses. When helping an ailing parent evaluate options, this technique may warrant consideration.

DISABILITY INSURANCE

Disability insurance is designed to insure against the loss of wages. If your parents are no longer working, or are only working on a limited basis, disability insurance may be unnecessary. If your parents still have such insurance, they may be able to cancel it to save the premiums, or reevaluate waiting periods (how long the insured must wait after an injury before payments begin) to minimize premiums.

LONG-TERM-CARE INSURANCE

Long-term-care insurance might be critical to safeguarding your parents' financial worth, and your inheritance. A long-term stay in a nursing home could be devastating for your parents. With the costs of nursing home care reaching $70,000 to $100,000+ per year, such payments can quickly wipe out most estates.

Nursing home or long-term-care insurance can cover a significant portion of these costs. This type of insurance can supplement the other resources your parents have to pay for in-home care, or nursing homes. This may give your parents the peace of mind of knowing that they will have adequate assets to meet their health care needs while simultaneously keeping assets in their estate.

This type of insurance is generally purchased in coordination with an overall estate plan developed by an elder law attorney. The concept of this planning is to remove assets from your parents estate so that they can qualify for Medicaid without Medicaid reaching the assets that your parents have given away (see Chapter 10).

PROPERTY AND CASUALTY INSURANCE

The largest and best planned estate could become useless to your parents and all their heirs if there is inadequate insurance protection. When is the last time your parents had all of their property and casualty insurance reviewed and evaluated? If it has been more than several years, a review is in order. In many cases, you will find your parents cannot remember the last time, if ever, that they reviewed their property insurance. Changes in assets, risks, values, and laws can make a periodic review essential. A lapse in an important coverage could leave your parents' estate particularly vulnerable. Since each estate is different, and the laws and requirements vary so widely, the best approach is to sensitize your parents to the problems and encourage them to get a review.

There are several issues and types of property coverage that need to be reviewed.

Homeowners' Insurance

Be certain that your parents have adequate coverage in place. Has the value of the home been reviewed lately to be certain that the coverage amounts are reasonable? Home prices have burgeoned in many areas of the country in recent years. If your parents' homeowners' policy has not had automatic adjustments, they might be underinsured. Have your parents made any improvements that should be listed in the policy (e.g., added a room for a caregiver, added an apartment over the garage, built a deck)? The consequences of being underinsured can be severe. At minimum, a loss might not be fully covered. In a worst case scenario, the insurance company may be able to deny coverage if the insured value of the property drops too low.

Most homeowner's insurance policies tie coverage for ancillary structures (e.g., a garage) and personal property (e.g., furniture) to a percentage of the home value, unless the policy has special additions (riders). If the home was not insured for fair value and your parents have a burglary, the amount they can recover for damaged or stolen belongings might be substantially less than their actual loss.

Umbrella or Personal Excess Liability Coverage

Many people are unaware of excess liability protection. These policies can cover your parents if their homeowners and automobile policies prove inadequate. Homeowners and automobile policies have limits on the amount of liability coverage that they provide. These limits often range between $300,000 and $500,000. If someone is injured (perhaps because your parents' motor skills or eyesight are beginning to fail), a judgment might be rendered against them in excess of the protection provided under their homeowners or automobile coverage. Their assets would then be used to pay the claim. Excess liability coverage could thus be vital to protecting their assets and your inheritance.

Riders and Floaters

If your parents own any fine art or expensive jewelry, it is likely that their general homeowners' insurance coverage is inadequate. You should encourage your parents to have these valuables appraised and to obtain supplemental insurance coverage.

LESSONS TO LEARN

Adequate insurance is essential to protect your parents' assets. If they have not had recent reviews of all the types of insurance coverage that they should have, perhaps your pointing out some of the risks they face, and offering to help with the process, might encourage them to gain the protection they need. This protection might give your parents greater peace of mind to pursue a gift program for their heirs (see Chapter 11) and will certainly safeguard their assets to assure that they have adequate resources.

5 ARE YOUR PARENTS' ASSETS MANAGED AND INVESTED APPROPRIATELY?

A recent *Wall Street Journal* headline says it all: "Market Victim: Your Inheritance." The subheading for the article appearing August 6, 2002, was just as unsettling: "Stock Turmoil Disrupts Huge Wealth Transfer to Baby Boomers; Rethinking Estate Plans." Your parents' or other benefactors' investing style affects their security and yours. The same article estimates that the stock market decline from 2000–2002 shaved $30 billion a year off boomer inheritances. Despite the tremendous fluctuations in security markets in recent years, some people still concentrate all their assets in high-tech or other risky market segments and ignore the commonly understood benefits of diversifying to minimize risk. We live in times of financial uncertainty where world markets are regularly falling below five-year lows. Enron defrauded its investors, collapsed, and took with it the incomes and pensions of thousands of employees and investors. AOL Time Warner, WorldCom, and even Martha Stewart are not immune to financial shenanigans. Investors in today's markets are either selling scared and taking major losses simply to get out quickly or investing in the tried and true, many of which have been unmasked as shady business enterprises. By the time you're reading this book new world situations, different market conditions, and other developments will have occurred. The only investing certainty is uncertainty.

Are there alternatives for maximizing return to your parents while protecting them and still preserving your inheritance? This chapter presents information on this important issue and can help you learn how to encourage your parents to get better investment advice.

CONSOLIDATION: THE KEY TO FINANCIAL SECURITY

In helping most parents maximize their investment return and gain financial peace of mind, the first step is to organize and simplify their investment holdings. If your parents are like many older investors, their portfolio probably includes miscellaneous and scattered certificates of deposit (CDs), small bank accounts, a few government bonds, and the remnants of odd hot stock tips. Simplifying the mess should be your first priority in organizing the investment process and giving your parents the protection they need and want.

Consolidation Can Help Your Parents Meet Key Goals

Everyone wants control over their financial life. Consolidation is the key. This simple, no-cost step can help your parents achieve important financial goals: control over their finances and safety through better investment planning. Consolidation can benefit your parents by protecting them in the event of disability, advanced age, or other emergencies, and by generally achieving better investment returns with lower risk. For you, as the heir, consolidation minimizes probate expenses and delays, and may increase your likely inheritance as a result of better investment planning, and lowering the risk of misplaced assets.

"Consolidation" does not sound exotic but it works. Throughout their lifetime, the vast majority of people tend to accumulate a proliferation of bank accounts, brokerage accounts, mutual funds, and stocks and bonds held in individual names and kept in a safe-deposit box. If your parents become disabled, it can become extremely burdensome for anyone to identify and track dividend and interest payments, to marshal assets to assure proper cash flow, and so forth. In the event of a parent's death, attorney fees magnify probate costs dramatically. Time delays are exacerbated and costs increased as executors and lawyers attempt to identify and gain control over these assets, and finally from an investment perspective, it is nearly impossible to properly determine asset allocations when investment assets are held in many different forms and accounts.

It will be tremendously beneficial if your parents consolidate all their stocks, bonds, and other brokerage account assets into a single (or a few, depending on the size of their portfolio) account with one brokerage firm, trust company, money manager, or financial planner. By holding all their assets in a single account (one for each spouse is often necessary to assure assets to fund a Bypass Trust, as explained in Chapter 11), your parents conceivably could receive a single monthly statement reflecting almost all of their assets, except for a house, pension, or insurance. Be careful, however, IRA, pension, trust, and business assets cannot be consolidated with personal or other assets.

How to Protect Investments as Your Parents Age

Have your parents arrange for a duplicate copy of each monthly statement to be sent to a trusted person (e.g., their accountant, estate planner, sibling, or you). Explain to them that in the event of illness or age, it may become more difficult for them to manage their assets. This will enable you, or other trusted person, to watch the accounts and assure that no mistakes are made and nobody is taking advantage of them (see the later discussion of flimflam investment scams). Often these extra reports are generated free of charge and, even if someone other than you receives them, their mere existence in the hands of a responsible and trustworthy individual will assist the family tremendously when your parents have died and all their assets need to be located.

Another benefit is that by consolidating their liquid assets into a few accounts your parents will generally obtain a higher level of service from their financial professional, and it will truly make the broker, financial planner, or money manager part of their estate-planning team.

Maximize Investment Returns

Once all of your parents' assets are in a single account or firm, it becomes feasible to determine the percentages of the assets in each asset category. This makes it much easier to ascertain that investment allocations are consistent with your parents' risk profile and investment concerns, as explained later in this chapter. The bottom line—better returns from a better organized investment account and less headaches.

Minimize Probate Problems

When your parents have most of their securities in a single account or firm, in the event of their death, all their executor has to do is call one financial professional and arrange to make any transfers necessary from that account to the heirs or trusts or whatever is called for by the will or revocable living trust. For reporting on estate tax returns or state inheritance tax returns, the use of a single account or firm can save substantial time and expense because the firm will often provide, at no cost, date of death values (or if you are using the alternate valuation date, valuation of the securities six months from date of death). Certainly, this will be much cheaper than paying your accountant and lawyer to coordinate the information.

Planning Tip: For more ideas on how to minimize the costs, delays, and problems of probate for your parents' estates, see: Shenkman, *Complete Probate Guide* (John Wiley & Sons, Inc.) and Shenkman, *Complete Living Trust Program* (John Wiley & Sons, Inc.).

Watch the Pitfalls

Although consolidation should be the cornerstone of every personal plan, you must carefully assess the risk of default and so forth in the firm that you are using. Early withdrawal penalties on certificates of deposit and the tax costs of liquidating a mutual fund are other important considerations. Be certain that accounts are retitled where possible and not liquidated since liquidation will trigger a tax cost. There might be a problem transferring certain funds if the financial firm selected for consolidating assets does not carry those funds. In such a case, your parents will be forced to sell funds and reinvest with a comparable fund in the new firm. Obviously, you must take into account the tax, investment, and other considerations of this action.

IS YOUR PARENTS' MONEY BEING MANAGED?

Investment decisions need to be made. Too often investors have relied on hot tips, broker's advice, or chance for their investment decisions. Proper investment decisions are far from potluck and part-time guessing games. Investments should be planned by investment professionals, who can take advantage of the wealth of investment theory and data available. Individuals with well-diversified portfolios, who had used asset allocation models in their investment decisions, were hurt far less than other investors during recent stock market declines. Proper investment decisions require an analysis of financial needs, time frames, and budgets. Who is helping your parents make these decisions? Proper investment and budget planning will assure that your parents' wealth will, to the extent feasible, last them throughout their lifetime. If your parents fail to engage in careful investment and budget planning, they may run out of assets and income for their daily needs. If your parents have hired a professional to assist in managing their money, they should have signed an investment policy statement that clearly identifies their investment goals and objectives. If they have not done so, they should evaluate whether they are investing with the right professional.

"A good advisor will look at subsequent generations to make sure that there is potential for a legacy," suggests Gary Goldberg, founder of Gary Goldberg Financial Services, based in Suffern, New York. "What you are doing is coordinating an investment policy with an estate plan," he notes.

ENCOURAGE YOUR PARENTS TO PREPARE A BUDGET

Proper planning should begin with an estimated budget and determination of cash needs. No investment plan can be developed without a budget that identifies your parents' financial requirements. Your parents may resent your involvement in this highly personal issue. If your parents have an accountant or financial planner that they have worked with for years, you might express your concerns to the professional. He may be able to encourage your parents to make formalized investment and expenditure plans. Most accountants and financial planners have software to easily calculate "what if" hypotheticals. A few doses of mathematical reality may provide all the motivation that is necessary for your parents to reevaluate their finances.

If that option fails, consider whether your parents can address the subject directly with you. Many people accustomed to living on the interest from their savings are scrambling because of the tremendous decline in interest rates. The low rates existing at the time this book was written are insufficient for many senior citizens to continue this practice. If your parents—like tens of millions of others—have been negatively affected, they may be uneasy and fearful about their finances, and perhaps they will be receptive to the following suggestions:

- *Determine current expenditures.* This can be based on an analysis of your parents' checkbooks and tax returns.
- *Analyze their expenses to determine which expenses are likely to change, and then make appropriate modifications and estimates.*

For example, if your parents' medical and health costs are likely to increase, but the cost of ski trips can be eliminated, then current expenses should be adjusted.

- *Analyze all sources of cash available to your parents.* This may include Social Security, pension payments, IRA distributions, and earnings on investments.

With the preceding data, you can review various "what-if" hypothetical scenarios (sensitivity analysis) to see how changes in interest rates, life expectancy, and other factors might affect your parents resources. In most cases, planning to assure that your parents will have adequate financial resources to last them their life expectancy is foolish and risky. Life expectancy may be the age your parents are expected to live, but many people live well beyond their expectancy (and many less).

If your parents' wealth is great enough so that considerable assets will remain after gauging their life expectancy, then they will have excess funds that can effectively be invested for their heirs. This is also important because the time horizon and investment goals for such excess funds may differ greatly from the goals for the funds your parents will live on. Most elderly find comfort in knowing that they have a fairly certain monthly cash flow. They might prefer investing a portion of their wealth in fixed-income investments generating a regular distribution that provides the cash flow they need, putting only the excess in a more diversified portfolio.

Celebrity Case Study: Benjamin Guggenheim, never known for his business acumen, inherited tens of millions of dollars from his father. At the time of his death aboard the *Titanic,* where he was traveling with his mistress, he had eroded the family fortune to fewer than three million dollars. In the age before income tax, his three children went from being the heirs to millions to inheriting approximately $450,000 apiece. Had his father placed any checks to prevent his son from squandering the estate on his notoriously dissolute habits, or had the son had the discipline to budget and invest properly, the Guggenheim millions might have survived long after the *Titanic* sank.

LONGER LIFE SPANS MEAN INVESTMENT AND SPENDING HAVE TO CONSIDER THE REAL TIME FRAME

The average woman will live 22 years in retirement. In 1950, the figure was only 14 years. That is eight more years to risk running out of money and to exhaust any inheritance. The only way to assure your parents adequate resources for their retirement years is to put in place an optimal investment strategy. And the real issue is that the preceding figures are averages. An average means many people will live a lot longer in retirement than 22 years. So unlike a popular book about dying broke, your advice to your parents should be to focus on saving and spending so that their money will last to say 95 percent (or higher) of the life expectancy of people their age. In other words, do not help your parents plan investments to last for the average period that someone of their age will likely survive. Help them plan their investments so that their funds will last until say more than 95 percent of the people their current age will have died. This will assure that if they outlive the averages, they will not be sitting on a street corner with a tin cup looking for handouts.

STOCK MARKET MELTDOWN: INHERITANCE MELTDOWN

So the stock market crashed. No one wants to gamble and take risks. Just buy CDs so you can live on the income. That is what many retired folk thought, and perhaps still think. Sure the stock market declined, but that is not to say the stock market should be abandoned. History has shown that in the long term, the stock market always rises. Diversification of your parents' investment portfolio among stocks, bonds, and other assets, not abandonment of the stock market, is the surest way to protect your parents' cash flow. When the long-term effects of inflation are considered, diversification, not just CDs, is the only way to protect your parents' wealth. Many older investors simply do not realize how long they might actually live and what the ravages of inflation can do to their income over such a time period.

How do you assess your parents' portfolio and help them understand what they need to do to benefit themselves, and eventually you?

Many elderly people focus on income to the exclusion of growth. They will spend a 2 percent dividend and feel comfortable while their principal languishes and is eroded by inflation. What is an appropriate investment strategy for your parents? What can you do to help them?

ASSET ALLOCATION—KEY TO PRESERVING AND ENHANCING THE ESTATE

Asset allocation is an essential component to any thorough financial and estate plan. It can address many important estate-planning goals:

1. Minimizing the risk exposure of investment, thus giving greater security to the estate.
2. Improving total return on estate assets, thus maximizing income and capital gains and asset values over the long term.
3. Providing direction and guidance to fiduciaries where the documents (will, trust, etc.) indicate the grantor/decedent's risk tolerance and investment philosophy.

What, then, is asset allocation? It is the process of identifying the asset classes in which a particular investor will invest, and then allocating the investor's capital to those asset classes through an analysis of rates of return and risk tolerance. The basis of this is modern portfolio theory. Your parents, as the investors, must provide their personal guidance to the financial planner or money manager by answering this question: "How much risk are you willing to endure to achieve the return you desire?"

Modern portfolio theory, in very general terms, assumes that the investment markets are efficient. Therefore, deciding which asset categories should receive allocations of investor capital is more critical than picking specific assets (e.g., stocks) within any particular category. Selecting asset categories with a negative correlation (i.e., when one rises, the other tends to fall) can minimize risk while achieving the desired level of return. For those investors who had a significant portion of their assets in real estate or bonds when the stock market crashed in 2000–2002, the bonds and real estate tended to increase in value relative to the stocks that declined. This lessened the overall decline for those investors.

The relationship of asset categories can be indicated by their correlation. A correlation of +1.0 indicates assets whose values move in perfect tandem. A correlation of –1.0 indicates assets whose values move in opposite directions. The technical term to describe the relationship between asset categories is their *covariance*. Covariance is a measure of the likelihood of the assets to move in the same direction and the momentum of their likely movements.

Studies have demonstrated that more than 90 percent of the risk of a portfolio can be explained by the allocation of assets. Where a portfolio is diversified among asset categories, approximately 90 percent of the risk can be viewed as market risk (which cannot be eliminated), whereas only 10 percent or less of the risk of that portfolio will be specific risk of a particular stock.

Through an analysis of the covariance of particular assets and the expected return of those assets, a portfolio can be constructed that theoretically minimizes the risk faced by the investor attempting to achieve any particular level of return. By optimizing this relationship, in theory, an investor could earn greater returns than on his present portfolio while reducing risk.

Finally, in identifying and investing in asset categories, the categories should reflect the diverse global economy and not merely United States equity markets.

Modern portfolio theory holds that the "potato chip method" simply is not the most efficient method of selection. This approach is the one most of us use when eating potato chips. We reach into the bag of chips and look for the biggest chip. With investments,

Figure 5.1 Determine Your Parents' Asset Allocation

Asset Category	Asset Description	Share/Bond/ and so on	Cost Basis	Fair Market Value	Percent of Total Portfolio	Target Asset Allocation Percent for Category	Adjustment Required	Comment
Growth equity								
Growth and income								
International equity								
Corporate bonds								
Municipal bonds								

(continued)

Figure 5.1 *Continued*

Asset Category	Asset Description	Share/Bond/ and so on	Cost Basis	Fair Market Value	Percent of Total Portfolio	Target Asset Allocation Percent for Category	Adjustment Required	Comment
Government bonds								
Precious metals								
Real estate								
High-yield funds								

the more mundane but statistically proven superior method of allocating assets and committing to long-range strategies is preferable to market timing and individual security picking.

What does this mean to you? If your parents have invested their assets in a haphazard manner, referring them to a financial planner or money manager is appropriate. Having someone in a fiduciary capacity who can assist your parents in investing assets while considering modern portfolio theory concepts is vital to a well-organized investment portfolio (Figure 5.1).

COMMUNICATING INVESTMENT GOALS TO A FIDUCIARY

Your parents can communicate their investment goals to a fiduciary in several ways. An investment agreement with a financial professional could indicate investment goals by having your parents initial the appropriate boxes on a worksheet. The Investment Analysis Worksheet in this chapter illustrates a simple version of such a form. A preferable approach would be to have your parents complete an investment policy statement under the direction of a professional investment manager who could help them determine their risk tolerance, budget needs, investment goals, and so on (see Figure 5.2).

DIVERSIFICATION IS VITAL TO PROTECT YOUR PARENTS' INVESTMENTS

It is quite common for the older generation to invest in government bonds and "safe stocks" with the expectation that these investments will provide them with an income for their retirement. In the normal course of events, that will be the case. When the plan fails, however, disaster can ensue.

The 1990s were marked by changes in government regulation of utility companies. By the end of the 1990s, regulation appeared to be a thing of the past and utility companies saw a tremendous

Figure 5.2 Determine Your Parents' Investment Goals

Simplistic Investment Goal Work Sheet

Risk Tolerance:

[   ] Conservative; [   ] Moderate; [X] Aggressive.

Investment Objectives:

[   ] Income; [X] Growth; [   ] Total Return.

Ranking of Priorities: Assign a number 1, 2, 3, or 4 with 1 indicating your highest priority and 4 your lowest:

[   ] Preservation of capital.
[   ] Income.
[   ] Income and growth.
[   ] Growth.

Your Investment Horizon is [check one]:

[   ] 1–3 years.
[   ] 3–5 years.
[   ] 5–7 years.
[   ] 7–10 years.
[   ] more than 10 years.

increase in profits, or so it seemed. Profits were being inflated left and right, and this false economic boom spurred stock prices higher and higher. One of the worst offenders of cooking the books was Enron, a utility firm based out of Texas. At its peak, Enron's stock was trading at over $90 a share; but a mere three months later, its value was so low that it was removed from trading on the exchange. During its perceived prosperity, however, employees and other investors spent billions of dollars on Enron stock. When it fell, they lost much or all of their funds and pensions. Even the president's mother-in-law lost thousands of dollars when the accounting irregularities were uncovered.

How could that have happened—people losing their entire income in one stroke? The problem lay in many places, but the most critical factor was that employees of the company put all their eggs in one basket by investing all their funds in their own company. When company executives steamrolled the basket, the employees were left without any breakfast. Too many children saw their parents lose their entire inheritance through lack of planning and diversification. Luckily for George W., his mother-in-law had diversified her portfolio. Have your parents diversified?

Diversification can take many forms, from types of assets (real estate, art and other intellectual property, stocks, bonds, etc.) to differences within asset categories (technology stocks versus utility stocks or automotive stocks). There will always be fluctuations in values of the various investments. The goal is to attempt to invest in assets that will meet your needs, or in this case your parents' needs, and whose values will not all drop at once.

ARE YOUR PARENTS INVESTING FOR INCOME OR TOTAL RETURN?

There has been a lot of talk about investment philosophy; the phrase "total return" has been bandied about with particular frequency. What is total return and how does it affect your parents' investment planning? To understand this concept, so you can help your parents invest in the best way possible, you need to start with some definitions and buzz words (courtesy of Gary Greenbaum, president of Greenbaum and Orecchio, Inc., a wealth management firm in Old Tappan, New Jersey).

Gross Return is the "total return" you read about. Gross Return consists of two numbers—the annual income (interest, dividends), which is also called the *yield,* plus the change in price, also called *capital gains.* This is not adjusted for taxes, inflation, or any other factors.

You cannot spend total return. You have to make three adjustments to arrive at a net figure. The first subtraction is the sales commissions you pay. The *costs* of the transaction would include the load on purchasing a mutual fund. The second subtraction is the annual *operating expenses* of the investment, say the 12b1 fees. The third factor to reduce gross return is the *cost of advice*. This would be a fee for an investment manager.

The result is the net return. Quality investment advisers report "*net return.*" But, you still cannot spend net return. Three more adjustments are necessary. The first is *inflation*. This adjustment must be done to maintain purchasing power. The second adjustment is for *current taxes paid*. This is ordinary income tax on interest and dividends (subject to any tax law changes taxing dividends more favorable), plus taxes on realized capital gains. And the third component, which most people overlook, is the tax on *deferred taxes payable* that ultimately has to be paid. This is the tax that will be paid in the future on pension withdrawals. For your parents, the "future" of those taxes may be now.

When you subtract these three figures from net return, you get a figure called "*real return.*" The real return is the sustainable withdrawal rate that maintains the real purchasing power of your parents' pool of money. If their withdrawal rate exceeds the real return, then they are spending purchasing power and reducing the pot. Too much reduction will dissipate your parents' financial security, and your inheritance.

How does the time horizon affect this? For a charity, the time horizon is usually infinite. For your parents, it might be 95 percent of their life expectancy for some assets, and perhaps your life expectancy for excess assets they expect to bequeath to you.

What is the connection between time horizon and investment strategy? The longer the time horizon is, the closer your actual withdrawal rate has to be to your real rate of return: "Otherwise you go broke," warns Greenbaum. "People who say 'let's use an 8 percent return,' just don't know what they're talking about." The final years of the 1990s stock market do not represent the whole history of investing. Nor does the market decline that began in 2000. Assuming a 6+ percent actual distribution out of your parents' financial pot will, based on historical data, wipe them out if their life expectancy is long enough.

Example: Parents have a $500,000 nest egg. To cover living expenses above what Social Security pays them, they make payments to themselves of $3,500 per month from their investment account. This equates to almost an 8.5 percent payout [($3,500 × 12)/$500,000]. Unless these parents are quite elderly, this level of payout will likely deplete their nest egg to the point where they will run out of money.

If one of your parents has died, say your mother, trusts may have been formed on her death under her will to benefit your father, and perhaps other family members. How to invest these trust monies will depend on the terms of the trust and other factors. For several common trusts, some investment considerations are as follows:

- *Qualified Terminable Interest Property (QTIP):* This is the marital trust used in many wills. The QTIP must still conform with applicable tax law requirements to distribute, at least annually, to the spouse/beneficiary, your dad. For these trusts, it is somewhat more difficult to invest for total return although capital appreciation must still receive consideration, especially if the life expectancy of the surviving spouse is relatively long. "Remember," says Greenbaum, "all marital trusts are not created equal. Some trusts are intended to only pay out the minimum income necessary to comply with the tax requirements, others are intended to be relatively open to principal invasions, and there is a wide spectrum in between."

- *Bypass or Applicable Exclusion Trust:* This trust is designed to remove assets from the surviving spouse's estate while providing the surviving spouse with access to distributions from those assets. When coordinating a typical "A-B" estate plan, the QTIP Trust should contain the assets geared more conservatively for income, while the Applicable Exclusion Trust should contain assets designed primarily for growth. The purpose of this coordination, especially if it appears that the surviving spouse has a reasonably long life expectancy, is that the assets of the QTIP trust will be included in the taxable surviving spouse's estate while those of the Bypass Trust will not be. Thus, funds such as growth-oriented mutual funds, or index funds, to the extent they are part of the overall portfolio, might best be contained in the Bypass Trust. The income-oriented investments—corporate bonds or funds, tax-exempt bonds, and the like—might better be held in the QTIP Trust. Thus for investment purposes, it may sometimes be appropriate to view the entire family wealth as an overall investment pot that is subdivided for maximal estate and income tax benefits by following the guidelines noted earlier. However, if the surviving parent's estate will not be subject to estate tax, a different analysis is warranted.

FLIMFLAM INVESTMENT SCAMS THAT PREY ON THE ELDERLY

Wanna Buy the Brooklyn Bridge?

We all know about investment scams. Telemarketers call every day trying to sell your elderly parents something. Everyone gets those letters in the mail that say you have already won a million dollars . . . if you buy a lot of stuff from us. Many investment scams, however, are aimed at the elderly in particular. Making your parents aware of such scams is an important step in protecting their financial security and possibly your future inheritance.

There are as many Web sites devoted to warning the public about possible scams as there are those devoted to fleecing the public:

- www.sec.gov/investor/pubs/affinity.htm
- www.seniors.gov/articles/0401/investment-scams.html
- www.pueblo.gsa.gov/cic_text/computers/Internet_fraud /cyberfr.htm
- www.commerce.state.mn.us/pages/ConsumerTips /ConTipScams.htm

---

Tip: Even the Securities and Exchange Commission (SEC) provides information on scams that target the elderly and how to avoid them. There is a consensus between the government agencies and watch groups that there are many types of investment scams that cost the public billions of dollars every year.

State securities regulators' list of top scams includes an array of risky investments or sales practice abuses that your parents might encounter. The list includes unscrupulous brokers, conflicts of interest in analyst research, charitable gift annuities, and oil and natural gas scams. Independent insurance agents, brokers, and other purported "planners" selling risky or fraudulent securities to earn high commissions are a big problem. In one scam, sold almost entirely by independent insurance agents, investors in at least 14 states lost close to $30 million. An Arizona insurance agent was sentenced to 10 years in prison for selling $1.8 million in worthless stock and bogus promissory notes to investors. Another Arizona insurance agent was sentenced to five years in prison for scamming 32 elderly investors out of nearly $2 million by first soliciting them to purchase living trusts. Record-low interest rates and a bear market on Wall Street have created a bull market in fraud as investors, who might include your parents, seek higher returns. Con artists often pitch their scams as safe alternatives that promise high returns. You should caution your parents that this is an impossible combination.

The Recent Widow/Widower Scam

The best way to scam a consumer is to get him when he is distraught and in emotional turmoil. Many investment scams are aimed at the elderly because their age and often declining clarity make them easier targets. One easily identified category of elderly is targeted all the time. Your vigilance can keep your parent out of this trap. Scam artists read the obituaries and call surviving spouses, under the guise of offering assistance, and then scam them. If one of your parents has recently died, there is no reason in most situations to make any significant financial decisions for at least several months (but you should accompany your parent to an estate planner's office for a meeting to be sure). If anyone other than a hired professional asks your parent as a recent widow or widower to take care of any legal, tax, or financial matter, the answer should be no.

Planning Tip: For many recent widows or widowers, it is hard to say no, especially when the person asking is a family member or professional adviser. For more than 15 years, I have successfully used a simple technique. I tell all recent widows and widowers to have anyone trying to sell them insurance or an investment product to call me as their attorney. To encourage clients to use this approach, I assure them that I will never charge for fielding such a call. The motivation is simple: If someone selling investments is willing to call the widow or widower's attorney about the sale, he or she is likely to be legitimate. In more than 15 years, I have not had a single call, yet many clients have told me of frequently recommending that people call me!

Another common, and often unreported, scam of recent widows and widowers is the misuse of insurance. When your mother calls the insurance company to collect on a policy on your dad's life, some insurance companies send an agent to your mother's house to complete the paperwork. Occasionally, a sales pitch for a new policy accompanies the completion of such paperwork: Use the proceeds from the old policy to buy a new policy. Although there are occasions where such a plan might be advisable, there are many where it is not. Further, in such a vulnerable state, your mother should not generally be making such a decision without guidance from you, other family, or more importantly an independent professional.

Unlicensed Individuals Selling Securities

One of the biggest problems in investing these days is knowing whom to trust. Unlicensed individuals selling securities abound, and too often they are pretending to sell vital instruments like life insurance. Imagine what would happen if your father invested in a life insurance policy to provide for your mother and, after he died, she found out it was all a scam. Verifying that a person is licensed to sell takes only a phone call to your state securities regulator.

Their number can be found under "government" in the white pages or online at www.nasaa.org.

Affinity Group Fraud

One of the most problematic and hardest-to-spot scams is what is known as an affinity group scam. It is so prevalent that the SEC has devoted an entire Web page to warning investors and giving hints for spotting this scam. Affinity group fraud occurs when a scam artist targets a group of people using their religion, political views, or other group affiliation to build trust, and then steal their life savings. The most prevalent scams involve charity programs at churches and other religious meeting grounds and foreign exchange scams involving immigrants and foreigners. People feel that because someone is like them, because it sounds like a worthy cause, and possibly because their child's Sunday school teacher is behind it, the investment must be sound and the charity must be real. Although it may be a cliché, investors should remember that you should never judge a book by its cover. If it looks too good to be true, it probably is.

Pay Phone and ATM Sales

In recent years, at least 25 states and the District of Columbia have initiated legal proceedings against companies and individuals who were selling coin-operated telephones to ordinary citizens. With grand tales of returns on investment upward of 15 percent, they managed to bilk millions of dollars out of thousands of private citizens. Independent life insurance agents have often perpetrated similar scams using ATM machines in the place of pay phones.

Promissory Notes

A promissory note is a simple loan document commonly used in millions of legitimate transactions. And that is precisely why many con artists have used it in scam techniques. It is important to note that not all promissory notes, a kind of short-term debt instrument, are evil. Banks and large corporations regularly issue promissory notes, and the savvy investor researches them before investing his hard-earned funds. If your parents research the instruments properly, perhaps with your assistance, they will be able to spot the scam easily. Small and unreliable or nonexistent companies frequently abuse this investment instrument, offering large returns in a short amount of time. Independent life insurance brokers often sell these investments. All businesses are listed at the Better Business Bureau of the city or state in which they reside, and a few minutes and a few dollars in phone bills can save an investor thousands of dollars. You should be able to obtain a Dun & Bradstreet report for anyone who issues a promissory note. If not, warn your parents not to invest in it. If the interest rate is much higher than interest rates obtainable elsewhere, it is usually for a reason. Higher rates mean higher risks (which may not be appropriate or comfortable for many older people). Extremely high rates of interest may indicate the ultimate risk, a scam. The best approach for many, however, is to have a professional financial planner or money manager select investments in accord with a specific plan.

Internet Fraud

So you just helped your dad set up his new computer so he can get online to chat and relieve some of his loneliness. You are well aware of the problems the Internet has, or so you think, which is why your children have features limiting their access to certain Web sites. But have you thought of helping protect your parents from investment scams targeted at the elderly online?

The Internet is a vast and anonymous space. Its breadth and anonymity, however, are what make it dangerous to the average investor. Financial advice can be found in every chat room and on billions of Web pages and the surfer must always be aware that it could be a five-year-old shelling out the advice. The danger does not arise, however, from toddlers offering stock tips. The real danger of the Internet is that it makes every scam global. It takes only the click of a mouse button for scams in China to reach U.S. e-soil. Scammers use the Internet to "pump and dump" thinly traded stocks, publicize pyramid schemes, and sell offshore banking schemes. The resources of the Internet are infinite and anyone can use them—sometimes, regrettably, for unethical purposes.

Caution your parents. Ask them to review with you any online purchases. Perhaps they should limit their purchases to selected major well-known sites to avoid giving out credit card and other personal data to unknown Web sites.

Ponzi/Pyramid Schemes

This scam, possibly the most well-known of them all, was the benchmark of the savings and loan scandals of the 1980s. These scams consistently promise high yields to investors, while only those at the top of the pyramid ever see a dime. One or two swindlers begin an investment pool. They continuously seek new investors and use their money to pay off the old investors. This goes on until there is not enough new money coming in to pay off old investors and the pyramid collapses.

The most famous Ponzi scheme ever attempted was instigated in the early 1990s by Charles Ponzi himself. An Italian immigrant, he stole $10 million from investors by promising them returns of 40 percent from arbitrage profits on International Postal Reply Coupons. To paraphrase every Scooby Doo cartoon, he would have gotten away with it, too, if it had not been for those "pesky" securities fraud investigators. As it is, millions of dollars were lost to investors, and a new term appeared in dictionaries.

"Callable" CDs

Callable CDs are certificates of deposit that generally will not mature for 10 to 20 years unless the bank "calls" them. Redeeming a CD too early often results in losses totaling over one quarter of the original investment. While these investments are legal, salespeople do not always disclose all the risks and restrictions to the buyers at the time of sale. Always ask what the terms of the investment will be before purchasing. Investing in any asset can be compared with buying a racehorse. When buying a thoroughbred, if you want even a slim hope of winning, you need to know the history of the investment, the trainer behind the investment, the horse's limitations, and how fast you can reasonably expect it to run. The same holds true with any investment. Find out when it originated and how it has performed from then to now; research who is behind the investment; learn the terms and limitations of the instrument; and research how much return you can reasonably expect to see.

Viatical Settlements

Viatical settlements were originally used as a way for gravely ill individuals to pay their bills. While some of these settlements are legitimate, and in the appropriate circumstances present a valuable planning opportunity (see Chapter 4), they can be risky and occasionally they are just plain fraudulent. Simply put, in exchange for a percentage of an individual's life insurance policy on his death, the individual receives a sum of cash while still alive. Because of the uncertainty inherent in longevity, these investments are always highly speculative and you should think twice before investing in someone else's death. The policies being sold often belong to healthy individuals, and you may never see a return on your investment.

Prime Bank Schemes

This scam is aimed particularly at those people who feel they are savvy investors. Individuals promise investors over 100 percent return on their investment through access to the investment portfolios of the largest banks in the world. Often these scams target conspiracy theorists by telling them they will learn the investment secrets of some of the world's wealthiest families and Arab royalty.

Billions of dollars have been scammed out of unsuspecting investors in these prime bank scams.

Investment Seminars

On every subway car in any major city and in every mailbox on the Internet, you can find information about seminars promising to teach you how to make a lot of money in a very brief time. Every day, infomercials and standard ads on radio and TV scream to the public a hundred new ways to make money at little or no risk. A good rule of thumb is that it is impossible to get rich quickly. Anyone who tells you that he has a formula for acquiring almost instant wealth is lying. The only people who make money from these seminars are the ones who run them, through admission fees and the sale of books and cassettes. *Caveat emptor,* let the buyer beware. Particularly when investing your own money in someone else's plans.

A Final Word on Scams

The preceding list of scams is no way complete; it merely highlights some of the most common and damaging schemes. The only way to truly protect your parents, and your inheritance, is to teach them, if they don't already know, the proper way to research an investment. Charities need to be registered to maintain a tax-exempt status, and investment brokers need to be licensed. That kind of information is available through state agencies, at local libraries, or online. Businesses asking you to invest in their companies should be willing to give you time and some information to use in researching them before pressuring you to invest. Most importantly, warn your parents that if some one offers them a deal to jump at "now or never," the correct choice is always "never."

Planning Tip: For additional tips on protecting your parents, AARP and HALT are two organizations that have significant publications, Web sites, and other helpful information (see www.halt.org and www.research.aarp.org).

LESSONS TO LEARN

Diversification and consolidation are the two key terms to know when helping your parents protect their assets, improve their investment returns, and minimize probate costs. Diversification will help ensure that a single market downturn does not wipe out an entire asset portfolio or that inattention to investment principles does not deflate the portfolio. Consolidation will assist you in locating and helping to manage your parents' assets, and will allow expert financial advisers to assist in asset planning and growth. When done properly, diversification and consolidation will promote growth in your future inheritance, pinpoint the location of assets to reduce delays in receiving your inheritance, and allow you to plan your parents' investment strategy to mitigate estate taxes that could significantly reduce your inheritance. But investment planning must go further to protect your parents' security, and ultimately your inheritance. Investments and expenditures must be analyzed and coordinated to assure that your parents do not outlive their money. Rational investment strategies need to be applied, and scams must be avoided.

6 HOW DO YOUR PARENTS OWN THEIR ASSETS: JUDGING A BOOK BY ITS COVER

WHAT IS "TITLE" AND WHY IS IT IMPORTANT?

"Title to an asset" is the legal jargon for how it is owned. This seemingly simple concept is actually complex and is vital to understanding where your parents' assets will go on death. The simple addition of "joint tenants" on the name of a bank statement or stock certificate can dramatically change who will receive an account following a parent's death.

Case Study: Uncle Sidney had two nieces. One of his nieces, Jane, had a drug abuse problem. On the advice of a general practice attorney (not an estate specialist), Sidney signed a standard power of attorney form (document that names an agent to take legal action on behalf of the person signing it) naming his other niece, Frances, as agent. Frances visited Uncle Sidney every few months to look in on him. She tended, or so Uncle Sidney thought, to some occasional legal work he needed. Uncle Sidney moved into a beautiful retirement community and met a wonderful woman, Toni, who became a friend, then companion. Frances did not get along at all with Toni, and constantly warned Sidney about becoming involved with her. On the other hand, Toni's son, a compassionate and caring son, was friendly and warm to Sidney, and encouraged both Toni and Sidney to meet with an estate attorney to be certain that their personal affairs were in order.

Sidney wanted to leave 40 percent of his estate to a trust to protect his niece Jane, 40 percent to his beloved niece Frances, and 20 percent to his

---

111

new companion, Toni. His old will had simply split his assets 50/50 between Frances and Jane. Sidney's primary concern was to have Jane's money protected because of her drug problem. As part of that process, the estate attorney assembled a balance sheet of Sidney and Toni's assets. Some strange things started to surface. The titles of many of the individual stocks that comprised much of Sidney's estate had been changed to read: "Sidney and Frances, as joint tenants with the right of survivorship." Frances had changed the title to almost all of Sidney's assets so that when Uncle Sidney died, she, and not her sister, would inherit. If on his death the stocks had just listed Uncle Sidney's name, his first will would have divided the stocks between Jane and Frances, and the new will among Jane, Frances, and Toni. The new titles, however, made the will irrelevant. On Sidney's death, the stock would have passed automatically to Frances by operation of law (i.e., without probate).

Sidney did not realize what was going on because he continued to see all interest and dividend payments automatically deposited to his accounts. When Frances was confronted with her acts, she denied any wrongdoing and insisted that she changed the assets at Uncle Sidney's instructions. It took a legal proceeding to force her to re-title the assets back to Uncle Sidney's name alone. Frances would have cheated her own needy sister Jane out of a financial safety net. As the case proceeded, Frances did everything possible to upset Uncle Sidney in the apparent hope that the strain would kill him before the trial date. Frances hired an attorney known for nasty and vicious litigation tactics. When Uncle Sidney was deposed by the attorney, he questioned Uncle Sidney, then ailing and age 88, about his sexual relationship with Toni! The questions and conduct were so vile that Sidney's attorney almost came to physical blows with Frances's shark! After a long and costly legal battle, a settlement was reached with Frances to avoid trial. Sidney revised his will, obviously leaving Frances nothing. Sadly, he died not more than a year later.

A simple unsuspected change in a few words on a stock certificate that almost went unnoticed would have eliminated any inheritance Sidney intended for Jane or Toni. The abuse of a power of attorney, one of the most basic and frequently used legal documents (forms are available at any office supply store and take about five minutes to complete), was all that was required. Is someone tampering with your parents' assets? You must understand what legal title means, and what key estate-planning documents can do, to protect your parents and your inheritance.

What do different types of ownership mean? This chapter addresses how to find them and how to determine whether they need to be corrected. The title and structure of asset ownership is a critical, and often misunderstood or overlooked, component of estate planning. The most obvious implication is that the title to assets affects who will inherit them. Title, however, can mean much more.

The ownership structure of assets can affect the ability of your parents to make gifts of their assets (e.g., to help a particular heir or to reduce estate taxes), the likelihood of creditors (including nursing homes) reaching the assets, and the rights of a surviving spouse to exercise a right of election against those assets (see Chapter 3). Title to assets can affect the ultimate beneficiary, asset protection benefits, tax-planning implications, asset management issues, and so on. This seemingly mundane factor can affect virtually every key aspect of your parents' financial and estate planning.

Title is also far more complex than simply choosing between joint tenants, tenants in common, and tenants by the entirety. Title includes whether your parents should own assets in their names, in a revocable living trust, or in a family limited partnership. Many of the common titles in which individuals hold assets are reviewed in this chapter.

DETERMINING HOW YOUR PARENTS OWN ASSETS, AND WHAT THAT FORM OF OWNERSHIP MEANS

Your parents need to understand how their assets are owned and what the title means. Few nonlawyers ever fully appreciate the impact of this legal issue. Your parents, like Uncle Sidney, might be surprised at what they learn. This task is almost always far more difficult than it sounds because most people simply do not know the actual legal ownership of many of their assets.

If your parents are not positive about the title to a particular asset, help them review all relevant legal documents:

- For real estate, the top portion of the first page of the deed will state to whom ownership was transferred. That will be the present owner.

- For stocks and bonds, look at the actual certificates if your parents are holding them in their safe-deposit box (almost always a mistake).

- For brokerage accounts, check the statements; but to determine the exact ownership of the assets, it is more important to review a copy of the papers filed to open the account. This is because statements often truncate the title to an account, sometimes inaccurately.

- Personal assets such as jewelry, art, and antiques are sometimes harder to identify. Your parents may have simply purchased them and no records are available, so the presumption might be that they both own them. If the property is valuable, it should be listed on your parents' homeowners insurance policy as a "scheduled" or "floater" item, notes Howard Honigfeld, of KRA Insurance in Springfield, New Jersey. This listing might be required to protect the property in the case of a theft or fire.

Planning Tip:　If personal assets (i.e., not a stock certificate that has a name on it indicating ownership) are held in a safe-deposit box, the legal presumption is that the owner of the box owns the assets.

Case Study:　Roslyn has a fabulous and valuable antique silver collection. On the advice of her brother-in-law, an accountant, she opened several large safe-deposit boxes in the name of her antique business, a corporation. When she goes to Florida for the winter, she keeps her valuable collection in these safe-deposit boxes. She owns the company, so what could the problem be? The company is a C corporation for income tax purposes. If the corporation owns the safe-deposit boxes, the legal presumption is that it owns Roslyn's collection as well. There could potentially be a huge income tax cost to Roslyn's heirs to obtain ownership of the silver collection after her death.

GATHER KEY DATA THAT YOUR PARENTS' ADVISERS WILL NEED

Once your parents ascertain the titles to their assets, you need to help them obtain other information to verify that the titles are the determining factor. This information will enable your parents' estate planner and financial adviser to recommend the best ownership or title for those assets:

- If your parent is in a second or later marriage, a prenuptial agreement or other legal arrangement may govern ownership. For example, a typical clause in a prenuptial agreement might require further investigation to determine who owns a particular asset if the marriage terminates. If your mother's new spouse leaves, who will get the Waterford?

Sample Clause: In the event of a suit for the termination of the marriage, property acquired during the marriage if not attributable to separate funds, inheritances, or gifts shall be divided equally.

If mom divorces the new spouse, she might have to prove whether the Waterford crystal was purchased with marital funds or her separate assets, or was an inheritance from her sister Patti Sue.

- Determine your parents' (the owner's) tax basis (investment) in the property. This will depend, in part, on how the property was acquired: gift (carryover basis, which is the tax basis of the donor), inheritance (step-up basis at date of death or the alternate valuation date—the fair value when the testator died), or purchase (acquisition cost). This is important because under current estate tax rules (which are to change in 2010, well maybe!), on your parents' death, assets that have appreciated will be given a new tax basis equal to their present value.

Example: Mom purchased shares in EndRun, an oil company, 20 years ago for pennies. Each share is now worth thousands. If Mom sold her EndRun shares before her death, she would incur a huge capital gains tax. However, if she holds the stock until her death (since she is confident the price will continue to rise), the tax basis will increase from pennies to thousands of dollars when you inherit it. Thus, you will not face any capital gains tax if you sell the day after Mom bequeaths the EndRun stock to you.

This increase in tax basis, and hence the elimination of capital gains, is an important factor to consider in planning how assets should be owned.

Planning Tip: If your dad is very ill and your parents each have a $1 million stock portfolio, it might benefit the family to put the appreciated stock into Dad's name, and the not-so-appreciated stock into Mom's name. If Dad dies first, the stocks will all receive an increase (step-up) in their income tax basis and capital gains taxes may disappear. The IRS is hip to this, too, so if the transfer is within one year of Dad's death, the tax laws will prevent the step-up. If it is more than a year, the family wins.

- Are there any co-owners? If so, determine the contribution of each co-owner and when the contributions were made. The timing could be critical to properly allocating the contributions and appreciation to determine tax benefits. Also, timing is critical where a divorcing husband and wife acquired property while married and while living in a community property state. For example, you, your father, and his new wife are all listed on the deed for a vacation home. For tax purposes, how much you each own might depend on how much of the purchase price you each contributed.

- Determine legal consequences of ownership interest. This could include a review of applicable local law as well as the application or contract documents for the bank, brokerage firm, or other legal entity involved with establishment of the asset. Legal help is always advisable.

- Have your parent's accountant and estate planner analyze your parent's overall personal, tax, investment, and liquidity situation to determine the optimal, or at least a preferable, method of ownership. If either spouse is not a United States citizen, they should consider a limited gift tax marital deduction for noncitizen spouses, as well as the requirements for a bequest to a noncitizen spouse not to be taxed. A special trust called a "QDOT" must be used. These rules are complex and if either parent is not a citizen, encourage them to seek the assistance of an estate-planning specialist.

- Consider the costs and difficulties of restructuring the ownership interest. Where real estate is involved, transfer and recording fees may be incurred and environmental review may be necessary to approve the transfer. Changing title may require the consent of all tenants under leases, and mortgagees on any loans to the owners, a new title policy, and so on may be called for. Is it really worth it? Not always.

- Consider how your parents' wills treat particular assets. If your mother's will leaves her vacation home to you, but the property is retitled to joint ownership with her new husband, you will lose out. Your parents' wills affect assets in many other complex and subtle ways. How will the tax allocation clause, simultaneous death provision, and other items be affected by a change in the title to key assets? For example, an attempt to retitle a house to permit the transfer of an asset to a Bypass Trust on the first spouse's death (see Chapter 10) will be defeated if the will has an improper simultaneous death clause. That is, a clause automatically transferring residential real property to the surviving spouse. Also consider the consequences to the tax allocation clause.

Example: Your dad's will leaves you his favorite painting, which he knew you always admired. His attorney never thought much about the technical intricacies of the estate plan since your dad hired the attorney based on the cost of doing a will, not on expertise (many parents think cheap is better—they won't be here when the problems occur—you will!). Your dad's estate is large enough that a federal estate tax is due. The clause in his will says every beneficiary must pay a share of the tax based on the assets received. You now have to come up with 50 percent of the value of the painting in cash to pay your share of the tax. Where are you going to get it? Many heirs end up selling the specific assets their parent or other benefactor wanted them to have, not really because of Uncle Sam's evil death tax, but because of Dad's incompetent lawyer!

HOW THE TITLE TO ASSETS AFFECTS ESTATE TAX PLANNING IN A TRADITIONAL FAMILY UNIT

Basic financial information is critical to estate planning. At least once every several years, or following any significant financial event, you should advise your parents to analyze their assets with a professional estate planner to be certain that their estate plan takes advantage of all tax-planning opportunities available. If your parents are married, they may wish to take advantage of the $1 million (in 2002, but increasing in 2004 and later years) available to each of them. They will have to divide ownership of assets between them so that the estate of the first parent to die can fund a Bypass Trust (the name reflects that the assets bypass the surviving parent's taxable estate).

The surviving parent is generally provided for by this trust, but the trust assets will not be pulled into the surviving parent's

taxable estate. This technique is one of the most commonly used es-
tate-tax planning strategies. Joint ownership of all assets could defeat this type of planning since the assets will pass to the joint
owner (e.g., niece Frances, as described earlier) instead of through
the will to this tax and asset protection trust.

JOINTLY HELD PROPERTY

Common-Law Definition

Joint tenancy is a possessory interest in a property where all co-
tenants own a whole or unified interest in the entire property. Each
joint tenant has the right, subject to the rights only of the other
joint tenants, to possess the entire property interest.

Joint Title as a Will Substitute

Jointly held property is often advocated as a will substitute. While
a will is not necessary to transfer ownership of jointly held property,
this approach is never a substitute for a will because your parents
can never be sure they have dealt with every asset. Joint ownership
impedes proper tax planning in a larger estate because estate planners cannot control the disposition of the assets held in joint title
unless they first eliminate the joint ownership of the property involved. Assets owned jointly will pass to the surviving joint owner
and not to trusts under the deceased joint owner's will, which could
protect those assets. Jointly held property may be an imperfect will
substitute for yet another reason. If your parents, as the two joint
tenants, die simultaneously, the Uniform Simultaneous Death Act
presumes that the property should be distributed as if it were tenants in common, namely one-half to the heirs of each joint owner.
This may not be the intent of your parents, especially if it is a second or later marriage. Also, this rule is not binding on the Internal
Revenue Service, which therefore could argue to include some portion or all of the property in the estate of each joint tenant. This

could result in more than 100 percent of the value of the jointly held property being taxed. Now that's a winner!

Joint Property—What Language to Use

Where you own property jointly ("Sandy Smith and Jeff Jones, as joint tenants with right of survivorship"), the asset will automatically become owned by the second joint tenant on the death of the first. Even where the account is simply listed as "Sandy Smith and Susan Smith," a presumption exists that the tenancy is a joint tenancy with right of survivorship. The preferable approach is to play it safe, and if joint ownership with right of survivorship is desired, the account title should so specify. This is especially important where one of the purposes of establishing the joint ownership is to protect the property from the creditors of one of the joint owners.

Distinguishing Joint Tenancy from Other Forms of Ownership

Joint tenancy should be distinguished from tenancy in common, where each person owns an undivided interest in the property. Although both types of ownership allow your parents and a second person to own equal interests in property, the legal consequences are substantially different. On the death of a joint tenant, the survivor obtains ownership of the entire property. On the death of a tenant in common, the deceased parent's will governs where ownership of his interest in the property will go.

Where property is owned jointly by a husband and wife, it can become a special form of joint ownership called tenancy by the entirety. Joint ownership can be distinguished from tenants by the entirety, where asset protection planning is an important goal. Tenants by the entirety cannot convey or encumber their interest in the property. A mere joint tenant, however, can encumber his interest in the joint tenancy property. The key asset protection aspect of this form of ownership is that having a joint tenant makes the property less valuable, and hence less desirable, to a creditor or claimant.

Income Tax Trap of Joint Ownership

If the property transferred to joint ownership has a mortgage or other liability in excess of the donor's tax basis, the transfer could be characterized as a part-sale (to the extent that the liability exceeds basis) and part-gift (for the balance) to the extent of the interest given up.

Example: If your parent transfers a $10,000 asset to you where the basis of $1,000 is exceeded by a mortgage of $4,000, a gain should be realized by your parent of $1,500 [½ × ($4,000 − $1,000)]. The rules, however, do not apply in the case of savings bonds and joint bank accounts.

Estate and Gift Tax Consequences of Joint Ownership

Where an account is taken in title of joint tenants with rights of survivorship, the account title itself constitutes a beneficiary designation. Where an account is established "John Doe, payable on death to Niece Dana," or "John Doe, ITF (in trust for) Niece Dana," the beneficiary designation is similarly accomplished by the mere titling of the account. From an estate-planning perspective, this arrangement determines the beneficiary and avoids probate. However, several issues must be considered.

Will the parent or other benefactor's dispositive scheme really be accomplished? In many cases, the answer is no. It is a mistaken belief that if a parent designates, for example, half his accounts in joint name for each of his two children that each child will receive one-half of the estate. This distribution scheme is far more likely to eventuate through having all assets held in the decedent's name alone and distributable to the two heirs under the will. The problems often overlooked are that different accounts may grow at different rates (e.g., one account was invested in dot-com stock and the other in CDs). Furthermore, funds may be accessed in one account to meet the decedent's expenses.

Does the parent have control over his assets? The tax consequences of joint property must be considered. The rule for assets held in joint name is that the entire amount is included in the estate of the first to die unless the survivor can prove his or her contributions. Where the joint owners are spouses, a special presumption applies, namely that the assets are presumed owned 50 percent by each spouse. For an aunt, uncle, or other benefactor, the results could be unfavorable and this rule needs to be planned for.

Example: You purchased a summer home with your Uncle Ned. You each put up $100,000 and own one half. Title is listed on the deed as "Nancy Niece and Uncle Ned, as joint tenants." The IRS will presume, unless you can prove otherwise, that the entire property is taxable in Uncle Ned's estate.

Joint ownership can also create some notable tax problems that you should be aware of before you title any significant assets (other than a small joint checking account) in joint name. As stated earlier, the general tax rule is that, on the death of a joint tenant, the entire value of the joint property is included in the estate of the first joint tenant to die. If, however, the executor can prove that the surviving joint tenant contributed some portion to the property, then some portion of the value can be excluded from the estate of the first joint tenant.

The consideration furnished by the surviving joint tenant will not be counted where it was provided to the surviving joint tenant by the deceased joint tenant. If Uncle Ned gave you $100,000 to buy a vacation home with him, it will not be treated as if you contributed half of the cost of the purchase.

Additionally, where contribution is demonstrated, it is not just the amount contributed that is removed from the gross estate of the decedent (first joint tenant to die). It could be argued to also include a proportionate amount of any appreciation in the property in determining the contribution by the surviving joint tenant. Income earned on the property given to the joint asset counts toward contribution.

Case Study: John Crawford and Sam Lester purchased a beach house years ago for $55,000, as joint tenants with the right of survivorship, and on John's death, the entire $400,000 fair value of the beach house will presumptively be included in his estate. However, if John's executor can demonstrate that Sam contributed $30,000 of the original purchase price, a proportional amount of the value of the beach house will not be taxed in John's estate. If the executor is successful, then $218,182 will be excluded from John's estate [$30,000/$55,000 × $400,000].

Where the joint tenants are husband and wife, the presumption is that half of the value of the jointly held property is included in the estate of the first to die.

Creating a joint tenancy can also have important gift tax consequences. If the joint tenants each own half of the property, but only one joint tenant contributed to the purchase of the property, then the joint tenancy will create a gift equal to one-half of the value of the property from the contributing joint tenant to the noncontributing joint tenant. Joint owners will generally report equal amounts of income on their respective tax returns. However, if one joint tenant is a minor under age 14, the Kiddie Tax may apply.

What happens if the tenants decide that it would be preferable to terminate a joint tenancy? There could be tax consequences if you and the other joint tenant receive different percentages than you own. If you and a stepparent owned real estate equally, but on division of the joint tenancy, you let her take a 75 percent ownership interest, this could constitute a gift by you to her equal to 25 percent of the value of the property. A similar result could occur where the joint tenants have very different ages. If you are 25 and your benefactor/joint tenant (your grandfather), is 85, there could be a tax cost to an equal division of the property since his life expectancy is so much less than yours. This is because according to actuarial calculations, your grandfather would be entitled to much less than a 50 percent share.

Caution: It is important to review the laws of the state where your parents are domiciled (permanent residents) to ascertain whether there are any special rules affecting joint ownership. If your parents own real estate in another state, that state's laws should also be consulted. The rules differ for community property states: Arizona, California, Idaho, Nevada, New Mexico, Texas, Washington, and Wisconsin.

The tax consequences to the surviving joint tenant are also important. The surviving joint tenant should receive a step-up in tax basis of that portion of the property passing to the surviving joint tenant from the deceased joint tenant. Thus, it could be advantageous for the joint property to be included in the estate of the deceased joint tenant. This could occur if the estate tax is less than the income tax cost that the survivor would realize on sale. This situation could arise where the deceased joint tenant's estate is in a lower tax bracket, or especially where the decedent's estate is small enough that the unified credit eliminates the estate tax cost. Although basis step up (increase) on death is scheduled to be repealed in 2010, most taxpayers will still qualify to increase basis.

Types of Property That Joint Tenants Can Hold

Joint tenancy can be used for real and personal property. A common example of nonreal property held in joint title is a bank account. Care must be exercised, however, to review the terms of the underlying bank application agreement to properly ascertain exactly what type of legal title/relationship has been created.

Some property transfers may affect a joint tenancy and create an unexpected gift tax cost. If your parent has conveyed property to you by creating a joint tenancy, there may be a current gift tax cost based on the concepts discussed in this chapter. Similarly, if your parent later unilaterally makes payments on a mortgage on the jointly held property, each payment could be construed as an additional gift to you, the joint tenant.

Severing a Joint Tenancy

A joint tenancy can be terminated (severed) in four ways:

1. Partition is the dividing up and distributing of joint property for the purpose of terminating a joint tenancy, selling part or all of the property, and so on.

2. Mortgaging the property may also sever a joint tenancy. In some states, where one joint tenant grants a mortgage on the jointly held property, this severs the joint tenancy because the mortgagee will only be permitted to foreclose on the divided one-half interest of the joint tenant who granted the mortgage.

3. Leasing the property can destroy the joint tenancy in some states.

4. Conveying the property to a third party severs the joint tenancy by destroying the requisite four unities described earlier. For example if two joint tenants hold the property ("Bob and Sam as joint tenants"), Bob's transfer of his interest to Joe would result in "Joe and Sam as tenants in common" as there is no unity of time.

Where a joint tenancy is converted into tenants in common, there should be no income tax consequences.

Severing a joint tenancy, however, could have varied tax ramifications. The way that the property is severed could trigger gift tax consequences. If there was no completed gift on the transfer of the property to the joint tenancy, and on severing, the joint property reverts back to the contributor, there should be no gift tax consequences. If the property is instead transferred, even in part, to the other joint tenant, the transaction could trigger a gift tax cost to the extent the value of such portion exceeds the annual exclusion amount.

Other Types of Joint Ownership

There are many other types of joint ownership. For example, where a corporation, limited liability company (LLC), or partnership owns an asset, the principals (shareholder, members, or partners, respectively) are joint owners of the property. Time shares are another form of joint ownership, and life estates can provide a means of having more than one person own an interest in property, although those interests are not effective at the same time.

COMMUNITY PROPERTY CONSIDERATION

Generally all property that a husband and wife acquire during their marriage while they are domiciled in one of the community property states belongs to both of them. If one of your parents remarries and lives with the new spouse in a community property state, these rules could have a huge effect on what you may ultimately inherit. The rule in community property states is "share and share alike." They share not only in the physical property acquired but also in the income from the property and their salaries, wages, and other compensation for services. At the same time, each may have separate property. Spouses may also hold property between them in joint tenancy and generally may adjust their community and separate property between themselves (i.e., use a transmutation agreement).

Celebrity Case Study: Community property issues may become a bar to a quick and easy divorce for Jennifer Lopez. Lopez, an actress and multi-platinum musician who commands a salary of millions of dollars per movie, filed for divorce in 2002 after only a few months of marriage. Lopez was married and domiciled in California, a community property state. Unless she had her husband sign a prenuptial agreement, on the dissolution of their marriage her husband could be entitled to millions of dollars of her hard-earned cash.

Celebrity Case Study: In 1988, slugger Barry Bonds married Sun, a Swedish immigrant, in Las Vegas. Subsequently, they moved to California, a community property state. Although Bonds had Sun sign a prenuptial agreement stating that assets he acquired during the marriage were not to be considered community property, Sun did not have a lawyer present at the time. Their 1999 California divorce was marked by Sun's challenge to the agreement, at the conclusion of which the court found it to be valid. On appeal, however, the Appellate Division found that since Bonds had changed the ownership on three of his properties to a joint ownership, Sun was entitled to half the value of those three homes. As a result of the scandal, legislation was passed in California requiring that both parties have a lawyer present at the signing of a prenuptial agreement for it to be considered valid, a law common to most states.

Prior to marriage, couples can state in a prenuptial agreement that they will not be bound by the community property laws of their state of domicile. Generally, community property assets retain that character even after the parties have moved to a noncommunity property state, unless the parties are able to adjust their rights between themselves. This may be important with respect to your parents' actions concerning the assets held by them.

Real estate will generally retain the form of ownership assigned to it. Real estate in a community property state acquired by either spouse while married may be treated as community property without regard to the domicile or residence of the spouses. The law of the location (situs) of the real estate determines whether the income therefrom is community property.

There are various methods for determining whether property is categorized as separate or community. Property acquired before marriage retains the form of ownership it had when acquired—separate, joint, or other. Property that one of the parties acquires during the marriage by gift or inheritance, such as gifts received by a spouse from his or her parent, retains the character in which it was acquired. Common sense, as well as the law, dictates that property purchased with community property is community property, and property purchased with separate property is separate property. Additionally, property purchased with commingled community and separate property, so that the two cannot be separated, is community property. This means dad's new wife, not you, inherits.

Community property is included in the estate of the first to die only to the extent of the decedent's interest, generally half of its value. Only that half will be subject to probate. Transfers of community property between spouses qualify for the marital deduction.

If a couple lived in a community property state before marriage and were married in a noncommunity state, community property laws should not be applicable since the couple was not husband and wife at the time of living in a community property state. If your parent (or other benefactor) plans to remarry, this could be a critical point for you to be sure they understand to protect your inheritance.

It is harder in some states than in others to have a prenuptial agreement upheld if it precludes property from attaining community status. Texas, for example, adopted the English common law and the Spanish civil law of the community system of property rights of the spouses. If your parent (benefactor) plans to remarry, encourage him to sign a prenuptial agreement, and to consult an attorney about how different state laws will affect him, it is important to protect your inheritance.

A spouse's separate property consists of:

- Property owned by the spouse before marriage.
- Property acquired by the spouse during marriage by gift, devise, or descent.
- The recovery for personal injury sustained by the spouse during marriage, except the recovery for loss of earning ability during marriage.

Community property is any assets, other than separate property, acquired by either spouse during the marriage. The presumption is that each asset is community property if property was held by either spouse during or on the dissolution of the marriage. Therefore, proper recordkeeping to prove a particular asset is separate property is important to protect your inheritance.

A spouse may record separate property in the county where they reside and where real estate is situated. A spouse has the sole management, control, and disposition of separate property. Each spouse has the sole management, control, and disposition of the community property that he or she would have owned if unmarried.

On the death of one spouse, all property belonging to the community estate of the husband and wife vests in the surviving spouse if there are no children of the deceased spouse or descendants of the children. If there are children of the deceased spouse or descendants of these children, then the surviving spouse is entitled to one-half of the community property and the other one-half of the community property vests in the children or their descendants.

Prenuptial agreements require care, especially in a community property state like California, observes Ginita Wall, an accountant in San Diego. "I had a client who kept his separate property trust separate in his name alone. He never deposited any community monies to the account, or so he thought. As it turns out, he had periodically loaned money from his trust account to the family to buy a house, take trips, and so on. When the community property had surplus cash, he repaid the money to the separate property trust. Even though he thought these transfers were simply loan repayments, the court characterized them as community property. He had to analyze years of statements and treat each repayment, and the earnings attributable to it, as community property."

Whether or not your parents reside in a community property state, if either is contemplating a second, third, fourth, or even fifth marriage, be sure you advise drawing up a prenuptial agreement. The last thing you want when you have just lost a beloved parent is to lose much of your inheritance from simple neglect of such an agreement.

Tenancy by the Entirety

Tenancy by the entirety is a special type of tenancy available only to husband and wife. This concept arose out of the common-law concept of treating husband and wife as a single person. The surviving spouse has the right to the property by operation of law on the death of the other tenancy by the entirety (the deceased spouse). You or other heirs won't receive anything.

Tenancy by the entirety can be distinguished from joint tenancy in that the methods to sever or terminate a joint tenancy do not apply to sever the tenancy by the entirety. The spouses, however, can terminate a joint tenancy by agreement or divorce. Thus, neither tenant alone can force the termination of the tenancy by the entirety or the partition (division) of the property. For this reason, this ownership structure has significant value in the context of asset protection planning where only one spouse is a target for creditors or malpractice claimants. It may, however, jeopardize your inheritance if you are trying to protect your interest in your parent's assets from a new spouse.

When making this assessment, you must consider many possible eventualities. For example, if both your dad and his new spouse were owners of business interests then both spouses might be at risk if a creditor succeeded in a lawsuit. The laws of the particular state must be consulted. Many states permit each spouse to convey or encumber such spouse's one-half interest in the property.

Tenancy by the entirety can be useful from an asset protection perspective. Transferring separate property into a "tenancy by the entirety" ownership substantially reduces the value of the property to a prospective creditor. But weigh the risk of losing your inheritance. There may be a better way to achieve all objectives—your parent could use a trust.

TENANCY IN COMMON

In a tenancy in common, two or more persons share ownership in a property at the same time but each party has a separate undivided interest in the property (as contrasted with joint tenancy where each has an equal interest in the whole). A key consequence of this difference is that a tenant in common can bequeath property anywhere he wishes, whereas the joint tenant property passes to the surviving tenant by operation of law. This is critical from an estate-planning perspective. For example, where a key asset is the house, it is typically owned as joint tenants thus defeating the ability to use a one-half interest in the house to fund a Bypass Trust under the will of the first spouse to die. (This is a trust intended to save estate taxes by holding assets up to the amount that can pass free of estate taxes in a trust to avoid taxation in the surviving spouse's estate.) Converting the ownership interest to tenants in common (by deeding the house from "John Doe and Jane Doe, his wife" or "John Doe and Jane Doe, as joint tenants with right of survivorship" to "John Doe and Jane Doe, as tenants in common") is sufficient to permit the spouses to fund the Bypass Trust.

Note: Converting a house owned as tenants by the entirety into a tenants in common arrangement will allow the parties to fund a Bypass Trust using that asset under the will of the first spouse to die. The change in title, however, may also expose the property and make it vulnerable to attack by the creditors of either spouse. Although a creditor of one tenant by the entirety can generally not attach that spouse's one-half interest in the property, a creditor of a tenant in common can attach the tenant/creditor's interest in the property. Which is more risky to your inheritance—estate taxes or a lawsuit?

Beneficiary Designations for Bank Accounts

The status of bank account titles can be troublesome to your inheritance. Many people, especially senior citizens, may establish a joint account to facilitate management of that asset (e.g., to enable a younger family member to assist by paying bills). Unaware of the use of a revocable living trust or durable power of attorney, they often opt for the method suggested by a bank clerk. In other instances, the intent of such an account is to pass assets on the death of the transferror (i.e., for the account to serve as a will substitute). Yet in other instances, the intent of establishing a joint account is to make a gift (e.g., parent wishes to give child money but may want to keep parent's name on the account to make future gifts or help the child make investments). Difficulties arise because the person establishing the account (only sometimes really being a donor) could have such a broad range of intents, and those advising that person often do not understand the legal and tax implications of the available account titles. If Mom's main account is joint with your sister you may loose out on your inheritance regardless of what Mom's will says.

For the following discussion, assume that "Parent Taxpayer" is the person establishing the account and placing funds in the account. "Junior Taxpayer" represents you, as the child of Parent Taxpayer and the hopeful heir.

"Junior Taxpayer"

Where Parent Taxpayer opens an account solely in the name of Junior Taxpayer, the funding of the account should constitute a completed gift for gift tax purposes. Junior owns and controls the account. Its your money. Slam dunk.

"Parent Taxpayer in Trust for Junior Taxpayer"

In these instances, your parent may wish the funds to be transferred to your control only on his death. Thus, your parent likely has the right to revoke, in whole or part, the account at any time simply by withdrawing funds from the account. This type of account will not constitute a completed gift until such time as funds are spent on your benefit or your parent dies, resulting in a transfer of the balance of the account to you. This account should not permit you to withdraw without your parent's approval. In almost all situations, your parent possesses the exclusive right to control or withdraw funds. If your parent, as she ages, becomes influenced by a new spouse your potential inheritance of this type of account may be undermined. But there may be a solution to save your inheritance.

Planning Tip: Although the account should not constitute a completed gift on formation, cases have arisen where the beneficiary attempted to demonstrate that the depositor intended a completed gift. This type of account is often called a *Totten Trust,* a name derived from a landmark case which held that the depositor's right to withdraw funds at any time, thereby revoking the gift, did not serve to revoke the arrangement and thereby deny the survivor (Junior Taxpayer) from receiving the balance on Parent Taxpayer's death.

"Parent Taxpayer and Junior Taxpayer, Jointly, with Right of Survivorship"

In this type of account, either joint tenant can generally withdraw all of the funds. This is perhaps the most common arrangement for a joint bank account. Your parent, however, has the right to revoke, in whole or part, the account at any time simply by withdrawing funds from the account. This type of account will not constitute a completed gift until such time as you withdraw funds, funds are spent for your benefit, or your parent dies resulting in a transfer to you of the balance of the account. Thus, this is a safer arrangement than the previous ones to protect your inheritance.

The Uniform Probate Code provides that while both joint tenants are alive the presumption is that the account balance is owned in the proportion of the contributions of each joint tenant to the account. This would result in your parent owning the entire balance of the account until death.

On death of your parent, you will succeed to the entire property interest. The deceased parent has no right to transfer the joint account by will or otherwise. Thus, this type of ownership has often been used as a will substitute. If someone influences your parents to write you out of their will, you'll still inherent any accounts or other assets you own jointly, unless they also change the account too.

"Parent Taxpayer and Junior Taxpayer"

This type of account is likely an artless attempt to establish the account referred to previously—a joint account with right of survivorship: "Parent Taxpayer and Junior Taxpayer, Jointly, with Right of Survivorship." Courts have held that the fact that the depositor/parent could control the right of withdrawal from the account did not invalidate the intended survivorship feature. But to safeguard your inheritance clearer is always better.

"Parent Taxpayer, Payable on Death to Junior Taxpayer"

This type of account, often referred to as a "POD," is not a completed gift. The account balance should be included on your parent's estate tax return which means if your parent or other benefactor has a taxable estate, you might bear some of the cost. This account will be transferred outside probate directly to you at such time. This may save time and money and make it harder for another potential heir to reach this asset.

Issues Affecting Various Types of Bank Accounts

Controversies can arise where on the death of the depositor, your parent or other benefactor, both the estate of your parent and the survivor (yourself) claim the funds.

Being a joint account (e.g., "Parent Taxpayer and Junior Taxpayer") is not always conclusive that you should inherit the balance in the account on the death of your parent. As mentioned, your parent may have set up the account merely as an administrative convenience and not with the donative intent necessary to make a gift or even an ultimate transfer on death. Overcoming the presumption of your inheritance, however, is likely to be a difficult task.

Caution: Uniform Probate Code § 6-104 requires that someone challenging the inheritance of Junior Taxpayer would have to present "clear and convincing evidence to the contrary intent." But remember what Mom always said—better safe than sorry. If you want to be sure, have your parent write a letter confirming her intent that you get the particular account or if substantial money is involved encourage your parent to put the money into an irrevocable trust for you.

Where a creditor of one but not both joint account holders seeks to reach the assets, what protection exists? If one tenant has the exclusive and complete right to withdraw funds from the account, the funds in that account are more likely to be reached by a creditor. If the two tenants own the property as joint tenants, a creditor of one joint tenant often does not have rights against the interest of the other joint tenant. If the joint tenant who owes the debt dies first, the surviving joint tenant may be able to take the entire asset free and clear of any creditor claims. If you're worried about malpractice claims, it might be better for you if your parent retain all her assets in her name until death or gift them to a trust—not use the account arrangements mentioned previously. Where the IRS exerts a lien over an account, the levy will be on the entire account even if only one of the joint owners is liable. Similar concepts have been applied to assets other than bank accounts, such as securities.

SAFE-DEPOSIT BOX

The title of a safe-deposit box does not necessarily determine the title and ownership of its contents. Instead, the title to each item in the safe-deposit box will determine the ownership of that individual item. However, jewelry, gold bullion, art, and other items that may not have a title or clear legal ownership, are deemed to be owned by the owner of the safe-deposit box.

Caution: If Mom put her safe-deposit box in your sister's name to avoid probate, your sister may inherit the crown jewels, not you! If your mom had the box in joint name with your sister, your sister may help herself to the gold bullion before you even knew it existed.

U.S. SAVINGS BONDS

U.S. Savings bonds are commonly held in joint name. The ownership will pass to the surviving joint owner by operation of law.

Where the bond is issued to "Parent payable on death to Child," the government will pay only Parent during Parent's lifetime. There is no completed gift at the time of the purchase of a bond by Parent in the joint name of "Parent and Child" because Parent can cash in the bond and reclaim all monies. However, where the bond is redeemed by Child or reissued solely in Child's name, a completed gift will occur. The value of the bond where a gift tax is due is based on the redemption value of the bonds. Redemption values are found in the Table of Redemption Values available from many banks or the U.S. Superintendent of Documents.

BENEFICIARY DESIGNATION FORMS

Among the most critical documents to address, and they must be addressed on an account-by-account and asset-by-asset basis, are beneficiary designation forms. These simple (often one page or shorter) documents may determine who inherits everything as well as what share the IRS will glean from your inheritance. A beneficiary designation form specifies legally who shall receive an account or other assets such as life insurance following the owner's death.

LESSONS TO LEARN

How your parents own their assets is important to protecting their rights and interests. It is vital in determining who will ultimately inherit those assets and has many significant consequences for those heirs. The rules are often complex and legally technical, so it is essential to have a skilled estate planner review your parents' assets. To help your parents make the best decision, they will need to understand the consequences of how each asset is owned, beneficiary designations, liability risks (weighing yours and theirs), taxes, sibling rivalry concerns, and more!

7 JEWELRY, VACATION HOMES, FAMILY APARTMENTS, AND OTHER TOUGH-TO-DIVIDE ASSETS

There are probably more estate battles over Aunt Nellie's diamond wedding band than almost any other issue. There are also few quarrels harder to deal with than fights over tangible property. This chapter helps you explore the myriad questions, issues, and problems affecting your parents' tangible property and offers suggestions for handling such bequests to safeguard your inheritance.

Planning Tips: Check to make sure that your parents have properly insured these assets, as explained in Chapter 4. See www.laweasy.com for more information, including a sample annotated will.

UNIQUE PROBLEMS RAISED BY PERSONAL PROPERTY

Often assets such as jewelry, art, and other personal property have tremendous sentimental value for your parents and many heirs, so their proper distribution is important. If your parents will let you address the topic with them, there are several ways you can help them assure that their wishes are carried out.

- What is Aunt Nellie's wedding band worth? Valuing personal assets is often a difficult task. When the value is largely sentimental, the task becomes impossible. Your parents should consider this carefully in determining how to handle personal property. Often, the best solution is for them to specifically identify which asset should be given to which heir. A personal letter or note may be helpful in this regard.

- If your parents list each item of personal property in their wills, the distribution of those items, as they have specified, will be assured. Well maybe.

Sample Clause: I give, devise, and bequeath my wedding band to my favorite nephew, Joseph Fordham.

And exactly which wedding band was Aunt Nellie referring to? The one from her first or her sixth marriage? Which one was actually bequeathed?

- Personal property is often tough to track.

Case Study: The case of the disappearing brooch. Aunt Gertrude bequeathed her diamond brooch to her niece Joanne. Her other assets were generally divided up by specific bequests as well—$50,000 to one nephew, $75,000 to another, and so on. However, when Aunt Gertrude died, no one, not even the executor, could find a diamond brooch among her belongings. There were no letters indicating that she gave it away before she died. It was not listed in any insurance policy. No claims had been filed for its loss or theft. Joanne really wanted the brooch. The more she wanted it, the more the value of the brooch seemed to soar. Aunt Gertrude's executor could not prove it was missing. How do you prove a negative? The ensuing legal battle, which ultimately was settled for $10,000 paid from the estate to Joanne, probably cost the family $25,000 in combined legal fees and fractured the family relationships beyond repair. Legal fees exceeded the value of the brooch so every heir's inheritance was diminished!

- What happens if your parents decide to give a particular item of jewelry to a different person? If their lawyer convinced them to list their jewelry distributions in their will, they must go through the formality and cost of signing a new will. Not something they will likely be pleased about, especially if they periodically update the bequests of jewelry, as many people do.

- Depending on the state your parents live in, they might be able to write up a list of personal property and simply state in their will that their personal property should be distributed as provided in that list. The problems with this approach can also be significant. Some states will not recognize this arrangement. How do you prove which list governs?

Again, if you know your parents are anxious to leave a specific asset to a particular heir, helping them achieve this goal in a cost-effective and secure manner will help win them over to your involvement in more estate-planning issues.

Planning Note: The preceding point sounds almost trite. Is it really likely that if you show Aunt Elle how to make sure that her needlepoint pictures will be given to her grandniece Susan, you will begin to build a bond that encourages Aunt Elle to involve you to a greater degree with her personal planning? Twenty years of practice says "Yep." Often small and inconsequential steps help win the trust of a parent or other benefactor, especially when you make sincere efforts on behalf of heirs other than yourself.

THE CASE OF THE MISSING EMERALD BRACELET

Although the heading sounds like a title from the kids' detective series Nate the Great or Encyclopedia Brown, poorly planned estates can create huge battles over simple matters. "Mom promised me the emerald bracelet!" Well, how can anyone know she made that promise if the will fails to say so? What if your parents make a last-minute gift to you in their lifetimes of assets specified to go to someone else in a will written 30 years earlier? Changes in dispositive schemes need to be set out in a will. Otherwise, everyone will be asking what happened to the art collection or the gold coin collection; and if you were meant to get one of them, you will be out of luck. Once your parents have given away personal property, it is pretty much gone. If your parents are dividing up art, jewelry, and

similar personal property, they will have to apply common sense
and enough care to create an approach that works for you and all
their other heirs. In many cases, heirs will simply work it out ami-
cably, but not always. And planning to avoid the "not always" situation is how to protect your inheritance.

Celebrity Case Study: Shoeless Joe Jackson is one of baseball's eter-
nal icons. He was a great ballplayer (.365 batting average). He was also
one of the players accused of throwing the 1919 World Series for a gam-
bler's bribe, which became known as the "Black Sox" scandal. Jackson
was illiterate and rarely signed his name. One of his few signatures was
on his will. When his wife Katie Jackson died, two charities, the American Cancer Society and the American Heart Association, were beneficiaries under her will. They sued trying to get Shoeless Joe Jackson's
will, claiming it was Katie's personal property and bequeathed to them
under her will. The court held that his will did not belong to Katie so
the charities under her will could not get it. Two lessons to learn to
protect your inheritance: First, avoid lawsuits by expressly planning for
every asset and issue with an attorney specializing in estate planning.
Second, be mindful that any potential heir may sue to enforce their
rights. This means anyone, even a charity.

Often parents can just leave it up to their children. Encourage
them to at least leave a note of nonlegally binding instructions, label
the back of pictures with the name of a child they suggest should
take that particular painting, or leave a video discussing how they
might wish the children to handle these matters. If you are pretty
sure that your siblings will be reasonable, have your parents write a
letter of instruction. Your parents can also provide that if you cannot get the particular asset you want, you will at least get the cash
value of your share of the estate.

   If your parents have named an independent person, friend, family member, bank, or other institution to manage their estate (executor or personal administrator), explain to them that they might
wish to give that independent person authority to make decisions.
However, only encourage your parents to take this step if you fully
trust the person or institution they have appointed. And even if you
do, still monitor their activities!

   In some cases, your parents might simply set up a mechanism for
the children to pick the things they want, within a structure that

gives all the heirs a reasonable chance to choose what they prefer. A few years back, *The Oprah Winfrey Show* featured a family that had a dot race to determine who would get what assets from their parents' estate. While both parents were still healthy, each of their four children was assigned a color and given a sheet of dots in that hue. At the shriek of a whistle, the children raced through the house placing their dots on any item they wanted to inherit that had not already been claimed.

YOUR PARENT'S WILL: DIFFERENT WAYS YOUR PARENTS CAN DIVIDE ART AND JEWELRY

There many ways your parents can distribute personal property in their wills. They need to discuss their goals with a professional estate planner to determine which approach will minimize the likelihood of later personal, tax, and legal problems.

Planning Tip: If your parents are using a revocable living trust as their primary estate document (instead of a will) the living trust can only be used to distribute personal assets if those assets were transferred to the trust while your parents were alive, or their will pours the assets into the trust. The trust isn't necessarily better than the will. The trust may avoid probate, but the keys to planning are carefully crafting the will or trust to address your parent or other benefactor's circumstances.

As Directed by the Executor

A simple approach to avoid many of the problems of distributing jewelry and other personalty is to leave it up to the discretion of the executor (person in charge of the will and the estate). If the executor is reliable and objective, this can be the easiest approach. Your parents merely communicate their desires to the executor and successor executor (in the event that the executor does not serve) and rely on the executor's integrity. What often makes this approach practical is that many changes typically occur to personal property after a precise distribution list has memorialized them in a will. Your parents can communicate general ideas and let the executor use discretion to implement them thus avoiding the problem of an outdated will.

Sample Clause: I give and bequeath such articles of my tangible personal property, wherever located, to and among such persons as the Executor may direct, including the Executor (if appropriate) and appoint by a written instrument delivered to each appointee with respect to the specific article or articles so appointed. The receipt of the appointee if adult, or if a minor of his or her parent or the person with whom he or she resides, shall be a full and sufficient discharge to the Executor from all liabilities with respect to the specific article or articles so appointed.

Even if your parents choose to rely on the executor, they can provide him with an informal, nonbinding letter and/or specific list to give some direction in making distributions. As long as this is a suggestion list and is not legally binding, it does not create any complications if property is lost, sold, or given away before death.

Sample Clause: I request, but do not require, that the Executor dispose of my tangible personal property in accordance with such wishes as I may have expressed to such Executor. I direct that any articles not effectively appointed shall be sold by the Executor, and the net proceeds of any such sale shall be added to and form a part of my residuary estate and be dealt with and disposed of accordingly.

By Lottery to Designated Persons

Sometimes it is difficult, or simply impossible, for a parent to determine how to divide personal assets. It might be hard to know what the children or other heirs will want. The values of different assets might change considerably over time. One method to deal with this uncertainty is to have a lottery. Let each heir pick an asset, and then reverse the order.

Sample Clause: I give and bequeath to such of my children [or other heirs], as shall survive me, the balance of my personal property as may be selected by each of them. In making such selections, eldest child [or other heir] shall choose first in each round. All other beneficiaries shall draw lots to determine who shall choose second and who shall choose third, and so on (in alternate rounds their positions shall reverse) in each round. Each person shall have the right to select one item per round, and this procedure shall continue until all of the property designated in this provision shall have been selected or three of the above-named persons, at the end of a round, have no interest in proceeding. Any items not selected shall be sold by my Executor and the net proceeds of sale shall be added to and form a part of my residuary estate and be dealt with and disposed of accordingly.

As Adult Children Shall Agree

In some cases, it is easiest for parents to leave the division of personal assets up to the heirs. If the heirs are adults and reasonable, a parent may like the simplicity of just letting them work it out for themselves. Any assets that cannot be agreeably divided are sold and the proceeds divided.

Sample Clause: I give and bequeath all of my tangible personal property, in such manner as my adult children shall agree within Sixty (60) days from the date of the appointment of my Executor. If my children fail to agree as to any property, then any such property not agreed to shall be sold by my Executor, and the net proceeds of such sales shall be divided, to the extent possible, in the manner to most closely equalize the value of all personal property distributed under this provision, and all cash distributed under this provision.

GIVING AWAY THE HOUSE WITHOUT A FIGHT

A family home or vacation home can create financial, legal, and tax nightmares when the parents or other benefactors die without having implemented proper planning. If at all possible, sit down with your parents and help them to carefully evaluate whether they should bequeath the house to one child and not to all of them. What if that child does not want the house or other children want it as well? In most cases, however, no child wants to live in their parents' home (usually by then they have established themselves in their own homes, possibly far away). Most often, in bequeathing a house, parents are bequeathing a problem that the child has to dispose of.

What happens if they bequeath the home to one or more children, but then sell it before they die? What if they want to put restrictions in their wills so that their heirs must keep the house? The neighborhood could deteriorate; the property may need substantially more repair than anticipated. Remind them what a tremendous burden it might be on their heirs and try to discourage them from that course of action. A nonbinding expression of their wishes that the home be kept in the family is fine.

Often parents bequeath their house to one child and money or other assets to another child. Your parents should consider all possible eventualities, including the probability of the house appreciating (depreciating) substantially after they sign their wills. The child receiving the house then would inherit a substantially greater (lesser) portion of the estate than the parents had planned. Additionally, what if that heir later cannot afford the tax burden and is forced to sell leaving no child with the family home?

An alternate approach is to let siblings choose who will buy the house—if, in fact, one or more children express interest in purchasing it. Consider the following:

Sample Language: I direct my Executor to provide both of my Children the right to purchase, at its appraised value for federal estate tax purposes, any residence, which I shall own at the time of my death and which I shall be occupying on a permanent, temporary, or seasonal basis at such time ("House"). If either Child shall be interested in purchasing any such House based on the appraised value obtained by my Executor, such Child shall be granted the opportunity to purchase such House. In consummating such purchase the Executor is directed to permit such Child to use any portion of such Child's inheritance under this Will to pay for such House. If both Children shall be interested in purchasing the same House, and if they cannot between themselves resolve which one shall purchase the House, then the following shall apply.

Should my older Child (the "First Child") wish to buy the House, and my younger Child (the "Second Child"), also wish to buy the House, then the First Child shall initiate the reciprocal buy/sell procedures of this provision by providing Notice to the Second Child that she wishes to engage in a reciprocal buy/sell transaction (the "Buy/Sell Notice"). The Buy/Sell Notice shall designate a price at which the First Child is committed to purchase the entire House, or alternatively, to permit the Second Child to buy the House.

Upon receipt of the Buy/Sell Notice, the Second Child shall have the right within Thirty (30) days to indicate by Notice to the First Child whether or not the Second Child shall agree to buy the House pursuant to the terms contained in the Buy/Sell Notice provided by the First Child. If the Second Child agrees to let the First Child buy, or does not otherwise provide Notice within such Thirty (30) day period that he rejects the opportunity to buy the House, then the First Child must purchase the House on such terms. If the Second Child shall indicate by Notice that he wishes to buy the House upon such terms, then he must purchase the House on such terms.

Any Buy/Sell Notice provided pursuant to this provision shall set forth the proposed terms of such transfer, including the purchase price for the House being sold, the terms of payment, and any other material terms. Such terms must include, however, a period of at least Ninety (90) days to close the transaction. All closings shall take place at the office of the attorney then representing my estate.

If either of my Children do not survive me, this right shall not be granted to the issue of the deceased Child.

If both Children do not survive me, or if both Children do not wish to purchase any House, then this provision shall not be applicable.

THE FAMILY VACATION HOME OR RENTAL APARTMENT

When a vacation or rental property is given away, your parents can take simple steps to minimize the costs and problems, thus maximizing the inheritance to all heirs.

Frequently, vacation or second homes are located in different states and your parents' estate may require two legal proceedings to transfer property distributed under their will (probate). The first probate will be in the state in which your parent resided (domiciled). The second probate (ancillary probate) will be in the state in which the real property is located. They can avoid this cost and hassle if they transfer the vacation home to a revocable living trust while they are alive. Alternatively, if the property is rented, they could transfer it to a family limited partnership or limited liability company to avoid ancillary probate and obtain some measure of protection from suits by tenants or others.

When such a property is rented part time and used personally other times, it can create problems. If one child uses it personally for two months, the other heirs lose rental income. If some use it more than others, there might be fights over the expenses. Your parents could address these issues in several ways. They could create a partnership to own the property while they are alive and gift some percentage ownership to each heir. As part of this gift, each heir would sign an agreement specifying how the property should be used, how heirs will pay for personal use in order to be fair to all, how they will divide expenses, and so on.

Planning Tip: See the sample "Tenants-in-Common" agreement form in the real estate section of the Web site www.laweasy.com.

If your parents are reluctant to transfer any interests in the property while they are alive, they could set up a trust in their will managed by an independent trustee who can make decisions to avoid fights between heirs. They might opt simply to direct their executor to sell the property.

LESSONS TO LEARN

Personal property and family real estate, while seemingly simple for your parents to bequeath, can raise emotional, personal, tax, legal, and a host of other practical issues. Helping your parents address the distribution of these assets can help minimize legal disputes and probate expenses, thus enabling the entire family to inherit more.

8 IDENTIFYING HIDDEN ASSETS

You cannot help your parents or other benefactors plan what you do not know about. Elderly people, out of fear of losing control or of someone taking their money, often hide assets in various and sundry places. This can include cash in a strong box, jewels in the basement, deposits in scores of bank accounts, and other random secret places. Giving your parents peace of mind and comfort through proper planning can help curb this behavior. But when a parent has begun to scatter assets, how do you know? How do you find them?

Case Study: Jim and Steve were brothers, but they had little in common other than extreme animosity toward each other. Their father, Harold, was aging and ill. Jim, the proverbial good son, took care of his father, saw to his needs, and handled his financial and legal affairs. Steve, the classic bad kid, was always in trouble as a teen. He disappeared in his 20s and was rarely heard from except when he needed money. When Harold died, his son Jim set about cleaning out his father's house. Steve did not wait more than a day or two before hiring a lawyer to sue Jim, accusing him of pilfering his father's money at the expense of Steve's inheritance. While Jim was cleaning, he noticed a loose floorboard under the bed; and when he lifted it, he discovered it led to a secret storage area containing boxes full of cash. He called his lawyer, who hired a video company and public accounting firm. Professionals videotaped the entire procedure as independent certified public accountants removed the boxes and counted the money. The cash was reported in full on Harold's estate tax return. Fearing the risks of litigation, Jim did not want to give his evil brother Steve a chance to have any claim on him.

While you might need the help of a forensic accountant to determine whether cash is missing, you can probably identify many other hidden assets. This is important not only to identify assets in the estate after your parents die. It is also necessary while your parents are alive since many older people lose track of their own assets. There is also an army of vultures who prey on elderly people, pilfering their assets. One of the best sources to identify these assets is an income tax return because most assets and accounts will generate a tax statement for the IRS that must be listed on your parents income tax return. Other data on the typical income tax return can also help you identify missing parental assets and bring them under your parents' control. How can you read, identify, and understand an income tax return to find assets?

If your parent has already died and you are trying to marshal (collect) assets for the estate, how can you use a tax return to help find assets you may have missed? How do you review the mail to identify new assets? Can a credit report help you? How? This chapter shows you how to play the sleuth that you may have to be to identify assets that if missed, will escheat to the state. This is a legal process that transfers unclaimed property ownership to the state in which your parents were living at the time of death. Onward Sherlock Holmes.

USING AN INCOME TAX RETURN TO FIND ASSETS

Obtaining a Copy of Your Parents' Income Tax Return

An income tax return is the first place to look when attempting to identify assets. The threshold issue, however, is whether your parents will give you a copy of their return, or authorize their accountant to release a copy to you. If they are hesitant, explain to them the many planning issues you can identify from the return to help them. If they remain hesitant because of privacy concerns, try one of several alternate approaches:

- If your parents have named you as agent under their durable power of attorney, you will have the authority not only to see their tax return, but possibly to receive refund checks and sign a return for them. If they cannot trust that you have their best interest at heart now when they are well, how can they trust you with even greater power if they become disabled?

- If you still have no success, encourage your parents to have a planning meeting with their accountant to review their return. If they will permit you to be present, then you can review planning at that time. If not, at least a professional will review planning issues with them including identifying assets and making sure they are safe. If you are not present, perhaps your parents will agree to take a list of ideas that you suggest (after your review of this book) for their accountant to review with them (everything from investment analysis to insurance coverage).

Sleuthing with Your Parents' Tax Return

It is well known that the only sure things in life are death and taxes. Not only are income taxes inevitable, but almost every asset your parent owns will have some income tax return consequence. A tax return can also tell you what kind of necessities your parents are missing. For example, it is possible to tell from their tax return that they may have insufficient health coverage, something you want to avoid and can help them remedy immediately, because it can be a tremendous drain on their assets and income and even yours if you have to help. A tax return can tell you what kinds of assets your parents have invested in and whether their portfolio is diversified (or at least give you leads to their funds and brokerage accounts to find out). And it can tell you if they need to change their investment strategy because of falling returns on capital. Depending on what kinds of investments your parents have made, the tax return can point you to the next step in your investigation. If your parents are shareholders in a closely held business organized as an S corporation (no tax paid at the corporate level) to plan they must determine what is the most appropriate business succession plan in their situation. Is there a shareholders' agreement? Are they aware of their rights under the agreement? Your parents may be entitled to payments that they have forgotten about.

Form 1040—The Basic Income Tax Return

Page 1—Dividend Income   Large amounts of dividend income on your parents' tax return may indicate substantial equity holdings. If so, is the portfolio appropriate for your parents considering the many points discussed in Chapter 5?

Determine whether any of the dividends that your parents are receiving are from closely held businesses. This can raise many planning issues for owners:

- *Insurance coverage may be essential to cover estate liquidity needs.* This can include covering costs to hire an executive to replace the deceased owner's work efforts and paying estate taxes. An irrevocable life insurance trust may be used to remove such proceeds from your parents taxable estate. Failing to do this planning can result in almost half the insurance proceeds being lost to taxes!

- *Buyout and operating, partnership, or shareholders' agreements.* These are essential to assure a transition to new owners and managers without fights.

- *Business succession planning.* Such planning may be warranted, even critical, to safeguarding your inheritance.

- *Adequacy of dividend distributions.* Pay attention to the accumulated earnings tax and the personal holding company taxes, which can be a tremendous burden.

- *Adequacy of records.* If the closely held business is a corporation, properly completed corporate minutes and records are integral to maintaining the corporate integrity. Most closely held corporations do not maintain adequate records. In the event of a lawsuit or IRS challenge, your inheritance could be decimated.

- *Charitable Remainder Trust (CRT).* It may be appropriate to dispose of some portion of such stock with a CRT.

- *A Grantor Retained Annuity Trust (GRAT).* A GRAT may be useful as an estate-planning tool to remove the closely held business interest. Have your estate planner contrast this with a sale to a defective grantor trust. These are sophisticated gift and estate tax minimization techniques for larger estates that can save millions in estate taxes.

Page 1—State and Local Taxes. If your parents are reporting a recovery or refund of state and local taxes, consider whether your parents are reporting as residents of the correct state. If they have more than one home, which is their domicile for tax purposes? This simple sounding decision can have huge implications to their cash flow, general planning, and your inheritance. If your parents could, with some planning, be treated as residents in a lower tax state (e.g., they are spending seven months a year in Florida instead of New York, which until recently had been their primary home), they might save substantial state income taxes immediately. This can help them meet their living expenses and perhaps preserve more for future heirs. Estate and inheritance tax issues differ considerably from state to state. The state they are treating as their permanent residence (domicile) may have a significant estate or inheritance tax on death. Therefore, if they can demonstrate that the state with the lower estate/inheritance tax is really their permanent residence, all of their heirs could benefit substantially.

Caution: Even if your parents' estate is less than the federal estate tax exclusion amount (i.e., the amount on which they will not have to pay federal estate tax), it does not mean that their estate will not pay a state inheritance or estate tax. Many states have lost millions in tax revenues as a result of the estate tax changes in the 2001 tax act, and they have changed their laws to assure that in many cases they will receive tax payments even if a federal estate tax is not due.

Schedule A—Itemized Deductions

Medical and Dental Expenses. Even though your parents do not qualify for a tax deduction, if they have listed large amounts of medical expenses, it could indicate inadequate health insurance or inadequate long-term care insurance—since only nonreimbursed amounts are deductible. It could also give notice of large recurring charges for a family member's illness, such as nursing home care for an elderly parent, which could be a serious cash drain. Medicaid planning might be appropriate (see Chapter 10).

If a parent's second spouse has recurring high medical expenses, the reason needs to be known so the estate plan can address the issue. For example, if there are significant medical expenses, a durable power of attorney and health care proxy/living will may be indicated. In other cases, a revocable living trust may be warranted to provide for even more formal management of assets pending a disability. For an older couple, Medicaid planning may be important.

State and Local Taxes.   State and local tax deductions may indicate planning opportunities to help your parents and enhance your inheritance. First, review any municipal bonds that your parents own to determine if they purchased state-appropriate bonds. Most people purchase bonds issued by their state or municipalities or agencies in their state. This is because these bonds are not subject to state income tax in the state of issuance. While there are financial arguments for purchasing out-of-state bonds (e.g., a New York or California resident might purchase a bond issued by Montana if the net of state tax return is higher), depending on your parents' income tax situation, this approach may not be beneficial. Has optimal residency been considered? If your parents are splitting a significant time between two or more states, establishing residency in one or the other of those states may minimize the state and local tax burden. If your parents have closely held business interests, there may be benefits to receiving dividend or salary income to minimize tax in a state in which they are not residents.

Real Estate Taxes.   Evaluate the real estate taxes your parents are paying. Are these taxes, for example, incurred only for one residence in New Jersey, or are they also paying taxes on a winter/vacation home in Florida, the Poconos, or New York? If your parents have real property outside their state of primary residency, then the estate plan must take this into account. Before undertaking a plan of action, you must consider the probate and gift tax laws of the other states. Real estate in another state will trigger ancillary probate proceedings (a second legal step), but the creation of a trust, partnership, or other entity to hold title to the real estate can eliminate that ancillary probate problem. What about liability exposure for those properties?

Is there adequate casualty insurance for the properties owned? Review your parents' liability and excess personal liability insurance to be certain that all properties are properly covered. If a property is rented or used for a business or other use, be certain that such use does not void their personal insurance coverage.

Personal Property Taxes.   Consider which property is taxed and whether the transfer to a revocable living trust or other arrangement may be a preferable result.

Do your parents have adequate provisions in their will and letters of instruction to deal with this property?

Is insurance adequate?

Home Mortgage and Interest Deductions Might Indicate Planning for Home Ownership Generally.   Few parents take the time to undertake the basic planning of completing a home inventory. This is essential to assure proper insurance coverage, demonstrate a loss to an insurance company should one occur, and identify personal property to be listed in the estate plan for your parents.

The ideal way to address this is to help your parents complete a detailed listing for each room in their home and attach copies of bills, receipts, photographs, and other supporting documentation. As a stopgap measure, and to supplement the paper listing, assemble a photo record (stills or video) of the entire house and store it off-site, in a safe-deposit box (or preferably a safe designed for protecting valuable papers). Once the listing is complete, you need to help your parents address a host of planning considerations. The first question to consider is whether insurance coverage is adequate. Have scheduled items (e.g., expensive jewelry or art) been properly listed? Next, discuss with your parents whether they have properly addressed the distribution of personal property in their wills. Has the tax allocation clause been modified accordingly (i.e., should beneficiaries of expensive personal property bear their share of estate taxes)? Have administrative expenses (insurance, shipping, and other costs) been provided for?

If the estate plan calls for a life estate (e.g., the right to live in a house for your life), how should the personal property (the furniture in that house) be handled? Additionally, if the estate includes business interests that are subject to special distribution provisions (e.g., to a child in the business), has business property been distinguished from personal property?

When planning your parents' estate, has business or rental property been sufficiently distinguished from nonbusiness personal assets for purposes of insurance? Also, if business is conducted in entity format, such as a limited liability company, has personal property been properly retitled in the name of the entity? Frequently, closely held businesses do not address the formalities of transferring assets to the entity. A bill of sale, assignment of contract, or a deed should be completed.

Interest Deductions Generally.   The interest portion of the tax filing may help you identify your parents' debts. It can also help identify whether your parents have been the victims of a scam artist preying on older investors. If you see interest deductions for anything other than a known home or other loan, inquire.

The tax rules for interest are hopelessly complex. Interest payments must be carefully categorized so that the rules applicable to each type of payment can be properly applied. Review interest expense items: Sometimes minor restructuring of a transaction, or having the appropriate legal documents put in place, can secure a deduction your parents may otherwise lose. Personal interest, including interest on credit cards, is not deductible for tax purposes. However, reviewing it will alert you to be sure your parents have a listing of all of their credit cards, the account numbers, and emergency telephone numbers. This is important in case your parents lose their wallets or are robbed.

Planning Tip: An easy way to get this information is to have your parents photocopy the contents of their wallets, front and back.

Home Mortgage Interest.   It is important to determine in whose name the house(s) is (are) titled. For the funding of a Bypass Trust (an applicable exclusion trust), it might be necessary to retitle the house from joint ownership (the most common) either to one spouse's name or to tenants-in-common. Then your parents must consider the liability issues with respect to the property.

Other Expenses—Safe-Deposit Box.   Safe-deposit boxes raise multiple planning issues. First, your parents must decide in whose name to put the safe-deposit box. Should it be in the name of an entity to prevent any closure or other issues on death? If it is in the name of an entity, who owns the contents? Whereas this may not be an issue for a deed or other titled property, it could have significant tax and legal consequences for cash, jewelry, and other nontitled property. Next, your parents must determine who can have access to the box. Finally, make sure a detailed inventory of the box is maintained for emergency use and to prevent other greedy heirs from walking off with valuables that were not intended for them.

Schedule B—Interest and Dividend Income

Dividing Title to Assets to Facilitate Funding of Bypass (Applicable Exclusion Amount)Trust

- Your parents should determine whether they need to restructure the ownership of some portion of their assets to better equalize their estate with that of their spouse so that they can increase the likelihood that whoever dies first will have sufficient assets to fund the applicable exclusion amount. This might be necessary to minimize or avoid federal estate tax (or state level estate tax).

- Community property warrants special consideration. Generally, community property assets retain that character even after the parties have moved to a noncommunity property state, unless the parties themselves are able to adjust their rights between themselves. This is important when considering their actions with respect to the assets held. For example, their restructuring of title to any assets presently owned individually or in joint name could affect the community property status of the asset involved. Therefore, consider the caveats and issues with an independent and specialized estate counsel before changing how any asset is owned. In particular, in the event of a future divorce, the steps either or both of your parents take now in establishing title to their assets could affect their retention of assets at such time.

- Large amounts of interest income from one institution may indicate that the principal of your parents investment is in excess of $100,000, the amount guaranteed by the FDIC. If that is the case, some changes may be appropriate.

- Interest is occasionally received on behalf of another. This should be recorded as interest received as a nominee, and then deducted on a second line. Investigate the relationship to be certain all is in order and that sufficient legal documentation exists to support a nominee arrangement. Again, be alert to someone trying to scam your parents with unusual transactions.

Dividend Income

Your parents should consider title to each of their securities and which spouse earned the income. This latter part can be important in determining the allocation of assets between spouses, which is basic in planning to maximize the Bypass Trust (applicable exclusion trust) in the estate of each. If your parents invest in dividend reinvestment plans (DRIPs), consider steps to determine the tax basis in each stock.

Is anyone monitoring the dividends and interest checks to be certain that they are all being received as required?

Schedule E—Rental Real Estate and Businesses

Income or losses from real estate rental properties, partnerships, passive activities, and S corporations are reported in Schedule E of your parents' personal income tax returns.

Rental Real Estate and Royalties. If the properties are in a state other than the state your parents live in, this factor must be considered in their estate plan, particularly to avoid ancillary probate (a second probate proceeding). Even though the information may not be listed on the return, you also need to know who holds title (ownership) to the property. This information is important to ensure that your parents maximize their estate tax applicable exclusion amounts (the amount that can be given away tax free). Title could also be important to secure discounts for lack of marketability and control.

Example: Instead of your parents each owning 50 percent of a partnership or S corporation, which owns real estate and other assets, each gifts 1 percent to each of their three children. Now each parent only owns 47 percent and a discount on the value may be available in the event of their demise. This is because less than a 50 percent ownership means you don't have control so the value of the asset is reserved for estate tax purposes (your parents' estate saves taxes) and for creditors (it helps protect your parents' assets for your inheritance).

Income or Loss from Partnerships and S Corporations. For every entity in which your parents own an interest, they need to organize certain minimum information so that their attorney and other professional advisers can protect their interests. These items include copies of the documents used to form the entity (e.g., a certificate of incorporation), a recent income tax return for the entity, a shareholders' or similar agreement, buyout agreement, employment agreement, and termination or retirement agreement. These items can be used by a business or estate-planning attorney to be sure that your parents' interests in the business entity are known and protected. People retiring from a business often fail to focus on their retirement or buyout benefits or, in many cases, continued obligations to the entity.

For each entity, your parents should address several considerations with their accountant to assure that they have done appropriate income tax and financial planning:

- Passive loss limitations.
- At-risk rules.
- Basis limitations.
- Performance of proper entity formalities.

In case of a general or limited partnership, your parents should review with their advisers whether the entity should be restructured. Many limited partnerships will benefit from being restructured as a limited liability company(LLC) if no restrictions or approvals are necessary and an individual is serving as general partner. Such a restructure can eliminate the general partner's personal liability for lawsuits against the partnership/LLC. This can prevent a claimant of the entity from reaching their personal assets and thus preserve your inheritance.

REVIEWING MAIL TO IDENTIFY ASSETS

Perusing your parents' mail can provide much information about the location of their assets. Banks are required to send monthly statements detailing account activity for each account held at their branch. Safe-deposit boxes generally require a small fee for maintenance, and that will usually show up in the bank statements.

Credit card bills can also pinpoint asset location. In this plastic world we inhabit, many major purchases are placed on a credit card. The credit card bill will furnish you with the customer service number of your parents' credit cards, and with their proper authorization, the customer service desk will send you an itemized copy of your parents' purchases. If your parents generally shop in the same establishment using a store-issued credit card, the credit office of the establishment will have on file an itemized list of all purchases made on that credit card.

Information about investments your parents have made in time shares, mutual funds, and certificates of deposit will be sent in the mail, as will property tax assessments and financial statements from companies where your parents have investments. Much of your parents' junk mail comes from companies with whom they have previously conducted business. If automotive companies or like establishments are sending mail to your parents, it is generally a good idea to ask your parents whether they have made any purchases at these commercial establishments (or investments in those companies).

Careful study of the mail that comes to your parents' house will go a long way in helping you identify their assets. Remember, however, rifling through the mail to look at return addresses is one thing; stealing your parents' mail is another. Never take your parents' mail without permission: That is one of the surest ways to destroy trust in a relationship. If your parents keep a post office box, not all important mail may come to the house, and a record of its existence may not be readily apparent. If they do not have a post office box, obtaining one may be the best way to assure control over their mail, especially if they travel a lot. Once a parent becomes disabled, especially if institutionalized, having all mail routed to a post office box can be helpful to you—allowing you to pay Mom's bills and monitor her financial situation.

CONTACT THE STATE TO FIND MISSING ASSETS

If your parents leave an account inactive long enough, the account may be forfeited (escheated) to the state. To prevent this, consolidation and monitoring of your parents' accounts is essential. If you think your parents may have already lost accounts, search online for their state's forfeited or escheated property to identify missing assets. Their state will have an Office of Unclaimed Funds, or similar department. Many older investors lose track of accounts, CDs, bonds, and so on. When you search these records, you might also write prior bank and brokerage firms your parents used. Be careful to conduct the search under all variations of your parents' names: maiden, nicknames, and so on. If your parents are alive and well, they will need to sign the letters personally. If they are alive but disabled, the agent under their durable power of attorney will have to sign. If they are deceased and you are trying to identify missing assets, the executor under their will should sign.

REVIEW PROPERTY INSURANCE POLICIES FOR LISTED OR SCHEDULED PROPERTY

If your parents heeded the advice to have valuable personal assets listed or scheduled on their homeowners' insurance, that listing will provide a valuable indication of their art or jewelry assets.

HOW FRIENDS AND FAMILY MAY HELP

If you have been living away or estranged from your parents for a lengthy time, you may not have complete knowledge regarding their likes and dislikes or where they might have invested money or purchased property. If your father has only developed an interest in fishing in the past few years, and you have been estranged during those years, you would have no reason to suspect he might have a cabin retreat or fishing boat where he goes to indulge his hobby. Friends and other family members who may go on fishing expeditions with him, however, would be in a much better position to know.

Additionally, your parents might have consulted with friends and other family members about investment opportunities that crossed their path. You may have no knowledge of those investments for reasons ranging from estrangement to your parents feeling that they should not have to consult with their children before investing their own money. Possibly, they knew you would take issue with their plan so they simply decided not to tell you. Whatever the reason, others may be in a much better position to know about these investments than you are, so do not hesitate to ask.

Your parents may also have invested with friends or other family members or told some family members the location of heirlooms while keeping that information from others (possibly for fear of their being lost or stolen). If all else fails, your friends and family may still prove to be an immense indirect help if you need to initiate an Internet or phone search in multiple states or municipalities for hidden assets. Identifying hidden assets is a time-consuming task, and the more help you can get, the faster you may obtain results.

CONTACT FORMER EMPLOYERS ABOUT CONTINUING BENEFITS

Various government agencies have on file a list of all the places in which every taxpayer has worked. Whether it is for Social Security, Medicare, or income tax purposes, that information is vital to the government and, as such, can be retrieved through the appropriate channels. A credit report will generally give a snapshot of a person's financial history from birth until the date it is generated. What this means is, if your parents cannot or will not give you a complete list of all the places they have worked, there are ways to find out this information on your own.

Once you have a list of all your parents' former places of employment, discuss each job with your parents and determine if they know whether there are continuing benefits and what they are (e.g., medical benefits, life insurance policies, matured or outstanding options). If your parents have documentation, ask to see it and verify the information with the company for which your parent worked. If your parents do not know, or are unsure of the information, the onus will generally lie with you to find the answers to these questions.

The first step is to attempt to get the information from the former employer. If the firm no longer exists, you might need to contact the company that has purchased or merged with it to see if records exist of possible continuing benefits. If your parent was a union member, the union should have on file information relating to benefits received under union contracts and whether they are expired or continuing.

LESSONS TO LEARN

The search for hidden assets takes time and effort. Your parents should have documents in their possession that can help you with that search. Tax forms, bank statements, and credit card bills can provide assistance, as can conversations with friends and other family members. In addition, former employers, unions, and professionals your parents consulted over the years, may be able to give you much needed information in your search for hidden assets.

9 DO NOT OVERLOOK THE PAPERWORK

PAPERWORK IS CRITICAL

Whatever your parents' wishes and assets may be, you must assure that they have the essential legal documents in place to protect them while they are alive and to transfer their assets when they die.

When it comes to protecting your parents and your inheritance, there is much truth in the old adage: "No job is done until the paperwork is finished."

Proper legal documentation will protect your parents' dignity as human beings (health care proxy), recognize their religious beliefs (living will), minimize estate taxes (wills, trusts, beneficiary designation forms), and verify their personal wishes (all of the preceding documents). Parental estate planning is not only about wills. Your parents need to have many ancillary documents to protect themselves and to maximize your inheritance. This chapter explains the most significant documents. Chapter 11 reviews the estate tax benefits your parents' estate (and hence you) can gain from properly using and planning with these documents.

WHAT HAPPENS IF YOUR PARENTS DO NOT HAVE ESSENTIAL LEGAL DOCUMENTS?

Your parents' lack vital protection if they do not have a durable power of attorney (a document in which an agent is authorized to make legal, tax, and financial decisions when they are disabled) and a living will/health care proxy (an agent to make medical decisions if your parents cannot). If they become mentally incapacitated without legal documentation, a court proceeding is necessary to appoint a person to be in charge of these matters (a guardian, conservator, or committee). This can be an expensive and time-consuming process. If you have had trouble discussing estate planning with your parents, these personal issues that are essential for them, and that offer primary or sole benefit to them and not to you, may be a selfless way to begin.

The most common legal document is the will, and everyone knows it is essential to have one. Yet a surprisingly large percentage of people do not have a will, and many people who do have wills rely on simplistic forms that hardly address their personal circumstances. Even knowledgeable and skilled expert attorneys have died without signing a will. The result is that their heirs suffer. No parents want to inflict such problems on their children.

Celebrity Case Study: Warren Burger was the longest sitting twentieth-century chief justice of the U.S. Supreme Court. He retired in 1986 at the age of 74. Burger, a widower, typed his will on his home computer . . . it was a single-page document. When he died in 1995, he left behind an estate valued at $1.8 million. Federal and state estate taxes totaled upward of $450,000. In his will, Justice Burger neglected to bestow on his executors the power to sell his real estate. Therefore, his co-executors, who were his son and his former assistant, a federal appellate judge, had to go to court and petition for those powers. The cost of litigation drained the estate of a considerable portion of its assets.

What should he have done? Justice Burger could have bestowed specific powers on the executors. If his children were wealthy, he could have set up generation skipping trusts to avoid some of the $1.8 million from being taxed in their estates. He could have set up other trusts to keep his assets private, and cut down on probate costs. He could have made gifts in trusts to his children and/or grandchildren that would have reduced his estate and saved on taxes.

Intestacy: If Your Parents Do Not Have a Will

If your parents die without a will (intestate), state law provides rules to determine who will be the executor and to whom and how your parents' assets will be distributed (outright, in custodial accounts for minors, or to a guardian if the beneficiary is incapacitated). The typical intestacy distribution scheme provides for a fixed dollar amount and a significant percentage of the remaining assets to the surviving spouse, with the remainder to be shared between the children. If there is no spouse or children, the assets will be distributed to more distant relatives in order of the nearness of the family relationship (consanguinity). While the rules differ from state to state, generally grandchildren, then parents, then siblings, then nieces and nephews may take in that order.

If your potential benefactor is not a parent, unless you are the closest living relative to benefit under state law, you may be completely out of luck. All the promises in the world from second cousin Sue will be for naught if she has a bevy of siblings and first cousins. The fact that you are the only living human being she has talked to in the past three decades is irrelevant. If you want to protect an inheritance you expect to receive from anyone other than a parent (and even from a parent), your first priority should be making sure the person has a will that properly, legally, clearly delineates what you are to inherit.

Intestacy can create additional costs, problems, and delays compared with probating a will. All of this will diminish any potential inheritance.

Be certain that your parents are aware how expensive and difficult intestacy can be, and how it can result in people other than their intended heirs receiving their assets. Few parents or other benefactors would wish to take that risk.

Guardianship: If Your Parents Do Not Have Powers of Attorney or Living Wills

The court can appoint a guardian if your parents are incapacitated and thus unable to manage their lives and assets. To avoid this legal action—and everyone wants to avoid it—your parents should have a durable power of attorney and a living will and ideally should fund a revocable living trust. When the court has to appoint a guardian, the court, not your parent, has the final say in choosing the appointee. Not a pleasant thought. There may be a host of reporting and oversight provisions. The guardian may be required to report to the court on what seems like a far too frequent basis, in considerable detail. If the person is disabled, the guardianship could result in significant restrictions on your parents' personal rights and independence. The consequences of the appointment not only will attack the your parents' dignity but also will affect many family members and friends.

A guardian (referred to as a *guardian ad litem*) is the individual, or individuals, designated by the court to take care of an incapacitated or incompetent person and to protect and represent the incompetent's interest. A court-appointed guardian may have little interest in your concerns.

The specter of guardianship is usually quite a motivator for any elderly or infirm parent to address estate planning. The key is to emphasize that not only is estate planning about inheritance, it is about protecting your parents while they are alive.

ESSENTIAL DOCUMENTS YOUR PARENTS SHOULD HAVE: WILLS AND MORE

Your parents need to have a number of documents to protect their interest and to ensure you receive your full inheritance on their death. While the necessity of drawing up a will is readily apparent, there are several ancillary documents you should discuss with the older members of your family as well.

Will

"Too many people get estate planning and financial advice from bank tellers who usually are not trained in these matters and can make dramatic mistakes doling out inappropriate advice," cautions Gary Goldberg, founder of Gary Goldberg Financial Services based in Suffern, New York. Whether it is from a bank teller or lawyer, bad advice can hurt your chance of inheriting what you are entitled to, and it can destroy your parents' intentions. Even the rich and famous fall prey to poor will drafting.

Celebrity Case Study: The estate of Marilyn Monroe takes in more than a million dollars a year. Her fortune is going into the bank account of a woman Marilyn did not even know. In 1962, Marilyn left the "remainder" of her estate to Lee Strasberg, her acting coach. Six years after Marilyn died, Lee married. At his death in 1982, the licensing and royalty deals from Marilyn's estate, along with Lee's estate, went to his widow—a stranger to Marilyn. Incidentally, this "remainder" estate is now many times more than the value of Marilyn's estate at the time of her death.

Be Sure Your Parents Do the Basics.   The most well-known document associated with death and inheritance is a will. The will sets out in detail a person's intent for asset distribution after death. It may also include final messages to loved ones and (nonbinding) directives as to how the deceased would like the various assets to be used.

For a will to be binding, it needs to be dated, signed, and witnessed. Additionally, it should be notarized at the time it is signed. Although notarization is not always required by law, a will that is not notarized will need to be presented along with extrinsic evidence of its validity. To ensure that the will has covered all details, it is preferable to have it written by, and signed and witnessed in the presence of, a reputable lawyer familiar with the laws in the state where your parents permanently reside. Although that does not guarantee that nothing has been missed, it mitigates the potential for large errors.

Planning Notes: Rules differ by state so be certain your parents consult with an estate-planning specialist in the state of your parents' permanent residence. If they are vacationing in California, but live in Maine, the work should be done and the documents signed in Maine unless health or other emergencies necessitate an interim will or plan in another state. Do not underestimate the critical importance of formalities. The slightest variation from state law as to the requirements of a valid will could jeopardize all planning.

How bad are the consequences of an improperly drafted will, a will that doesn't meet state law requirements, or bequests not reflected in the will? In one word, "disastrous." The estate and the heirs of one of America's most eccentric billionaires suffered the consequences.

Celebrity Case Study: Howard Hughes, who led a reclusive billionaire lifestyle, left many disputed wills. When all was reviewed, none of the wills was deemed valid and the great fortune passed to distant relatives. During his lifetime, Hughes had indicated he wanted to leave his money for medical research—but he never put that in writing. This oversight cost the estate hundreds of millions of dollars in taxes, and—who knows—that lack of funding may have caused the loss or delay of some medical cures. Hughes wishes were probably never realized!

Wills can be simply crafted leaving everything to a single beneficiary, or they can be more complex. Suggest to your parents that they include a comprehensive list of their assets and their locations, to whom they are being left, and possibly the intended tax plan for the estate in their personal record along with a photocopy of their will. The original will should be kept in a secure place. This will greatly cut down on fees and the time it takes to locate assets and settle your parents' estate after their deaths.

Planning Tip: See www.laweasy.com for more information including a sample annotated will.

Parents Should Name Trusted and Objective Fiduciaries.   One of the most important questions for your parents or other benefactor to address is naming an executor and, if applicable, trustees (generically called fiduciaries). The success of their estate plan depends on picking appropriate persons as fiduciaries. Your parents should consider the following checklist in selecting fiduciaries. They should evaluate each person on their possible fiduciary list:

- *Integrity:* No attribute is more important.
- *Common sense:* Unfortunately, this attribute is far from common. Even if your parents' fiduciary has inadequate skills, if he

has the common sense to recognize this and hire the appropriate professionals, all will bode well.

- *Ability to manage assets:* If there is an interest in a business or other difficult-to-manage asset, consider the specific skills necessary to manage those assets.

- *Ability to get along reasonably well with the beneficiaries:* If your father, for example, has a second wife, the best way to balance her needs and those of you and other heirs of your father might be to have an independent person named as fiduciary. Your father should seek someone who can be objective and who does not owe allegiance to his new wife or other heirs.

- *No conflict of interest:* Your longtime business partner may be your mom's most trusted friend and be financially astute, but if her personal objectives for the business could adversely affect your family's interests, she is not the best choice for executor.

- *Judgment to determine the needs of the beneficiaries:* The most financially astute person may not exhibit the sensitivity you want toward your parents' beneficiaries. One solution to this dilemma is to name cofiduciaries. One fiduciary can have substantial investment or estate and trust management expertise. The cofiduciary can be someone who exhibits the personal sensitivity and skills you desire. Together, they may be able to do a better job than either would alone.

What happens if your parents do not name a qualified fiduciary? A famous estate illustrates the sad tale.

Celebrity Case Study: Elvis Presley's last wish was that his fortune should be used to take care of his daughter, Lisa Marie. Within two years of his death, the estate was almost broke. Because Elvis had not arranged for effective tax planning, taxes took nearly half of his estate. Also, he named Vernon Presley, his father, as executor and trustee of the estate. Due to Vernon's botched management, the estate was valued at less than $500,000 by the time Priscilla, Lisa Marie's mother and Elvis's ex-wife, got control and saved the inheritance for their daughter.

Also, encourage your parents to review with an estate-planning specialist (not a general practice attorney) the interplay of the person named as executor with the provisions of the will, and perhaps even state law, governing the rights of executors. They should review the provisions of any trust set up and perhaps even state law governing the right of trustees. Failing to consider these details can be detrimental to your parents' wishes, and devastating to your inheritance.

Celebrity Case Study: Tom Carvel, who founded the Carvel ice cream franchise, had a $200 million estate when he died in 1990. Unlike Justice Burger, who was guilty of drafting too simple a will, Carvel created a too complicated one with seven executors. In 1998, eight years later, the estate, which was to be passed to his wife and on her death to a foundation, was still tied up in court and she had yet to see a penny of it.

What should he have done? Tom Carvel had too many executors. He should have chosen people he trusted (charges of alleged improprieties hovered around some of his executors), and not nearly as many. He should have included provisions for the resolution of conflicts among executors. He had 80 bequests in his will. He could have given bonuses instead while he was alive, because many of these were to employees. Bonuses would have been deductible to the business and would have reduced the overall estate. He could have made a gift to others during his lifetime, thus simplifying the bequests in his will.

The choice of fiduciaries is critical. A poor choice can embroil your parents' estate in litigation for years. The ensuing cost can substantially diminish an inheritance. If you are well known, even in your small town, the newspaper and media hype could be extraordinarily embarrassing to the family.

Celebrity Case Study: Doris Duke, dubbed the "richest girl in the world," became an heiress at age 12 when her father, James Buchanan Duke, founder of the American Tobacco Company, died. At that tender age, the child heard her father say on his deathbed, "Trust no one." Seemingly, that warning formed the basis for her entire life, including the poor choice she made for executor of her own estate, estimated at $1.2 billion. Duke died in 1993, at the age of 80, surrounded by hired help. At least six times before her death, she rewrote her will. The last revision named her butler, Bernard Lafferty, as primary executor of the estate. He claimed to be an alcoholic and a drug addict. The coexecutor was U.S. Trust. The two-year battle over Duke's estate that ensued included highly publicized allegations covering the gamut from murder to undue influence. By one estimate, attorneys challenging and defending the tobacco heiress's will generated more than $50 million in legal fees while nothing was going into the foundation Duke had intended to be one of the nation's largest charities. Eventually, Surrogate Judge

Eve Preminger approved a settlement removing Lafferty as coexecutor. The decision was based in part on questions over whether Duke was of sound mind when she scrawled her signature on her last will from her hospital bed in 1993, and whether her unconventional choice of primary executor was competent to assume such duties. Preminger also ousted U.S. Trust for failing to control Lafferty. U.S. Trust was later reinstated.

What should she have done? Doris Duke should have thought about what she wanted to do with her assets and made decisions when she was mentally competent. Also, making such decisions just before death increases the likelihood of a last illness or simply age affecting competency. This increases the risks of mistakes or worse. It also increases the likelihood of a lawsuit (will challenge). Thus, signing a will near death can decrease the chance that your parents' named beneficiaries will get their bequests, because their will might be contested. You should encourage your parents to think through all their decisions long in advance. Have a will written by an estate-planning specialist. Everyone will benefit, and it is more likely that your parents' wishes will be respected.

Do Not Forget the Taxman.   If you need to hum the Beatles song to your folks, go for it, just do not let them forget the taxman. And there may be many taxmen—IRS plus any state in which your parents lived or owned assets.

Celebrity Case Study: In 1965, Joe Robbie, a successful entrepreneur, cofounded the Miami Dolphins, a franchise that turned into one of the highest profile and most lucrative teams in professional football. Robbie never planned to deal with estate taxes. When he died in 1990, his storied franchise and the stadium he had built and that bore his name passed estate tax free to his wife through the estate tax marriage deduction. She died not long afterward, and a split among his nine children along with a staggering estate bill (estimated at $47 million) forced the cash-poor family to sell Robbie's legacy—both the team and the stadium—for $138 million in 1994. While the sale price, even minus the estate taxes, was impressive, the value of the Dolphins and the stadium, no longer named after Robbie, may be twice as high today. More important, however, Robbie's dreams were shattered: His family was removed from the success he worked so hard to build.

What should he have done? Robbie could have bought a survivorship life insurance policy that would have kept the stadium and team in his family. He could have encouraged his advisers to be less defensive; they blocked the path of people who might have helped him create a better estate plan. He could have used sophisticated estate tax minimization techniques such as grantor retained annuity trusts, sales to defective irrevocable trusts, charitable lead trusts, and so on, to reduce estate taxes.

Having trouble motivating your parents to estate-planning action? Few would appreciate knowing that their failure to plan and act will result in Uncle Sam becoming a prime, if not the largest, beneficiary. The estates of many famous people have succumbed to this fate.

Celebrity Case Study: When TeleCommunications, Inc. (TCI) founder Bob Magness died of cancer in 1996, he left about $55 million to his second wife [of which $35 million was in a qualified terminable interest property (QTIP) trust]. This is a marital trust that defers tax on the first spouse's death. He bequeathed approximately $25 million to charitable contributions, and the rest of his estate was to go to his two sons from a first marriage. On the surface, his estate plan sounds well planned. In reality, it proved too rudimentary. The fight that ensued contesting the distribution of his estate and accompanying estate taxes reached almost epic proportions. At his death, the stock in his company was valued at roughly $750 million, while his estate totaled $1 billion. His second wife contested the will, although she received more than the share specified in their prenuptial agreement. Additionally, few provisions were made to pay a staggering estate tax bill that, at the time, was the largest ever in the state of Colorado (the first installment on Magness's federal estate tax bill was roughly $500 million). In addition, no redemption agreements were in place to assure orderly transition of business ownership. In TCI's case, the story had a happy and profitable ending thanks to settlements and a surprising bidding war for the stock. But it almost did not turn out that way. TCI's saga is more an example of everything working out despite the poor planning and other obstacles, than of a well-planned estate facilitating this success.

What should Magness have done? There were many handwritten notes and amendments in the margins of his 20-page will. Anyone with a large estate is wise to have all relative facts ferreted out and made clear. A no-contest (In Terrorem) provision in his will might have helped (not only did his second wife challenge the will, but also his two sons challenged her claims). A stock redemption agreement might have helped when it came to selling company stock. He needed life insurance to help pay estate taxes. (Malcolm Forbes, who died with a $1 billion estate, had enormous amounts of life insurance that allowed his family to preserve his estate.) Magness could have used corporate or split-dollar plans to buy huge amounts of insurance without incurring gift tax costs. The interest on the estate tax installment payments was probably close to the premiums he might have paid on insurance. Magness could have used gifts to trusts, private annuities, and other sophisticated estate-planning techniques to move assets out of his estate.

See Chapter 11 for a discussion of how to help your parents or benefactor reduce estate taxes.

Protect Your Parents with a Properly Crafted Durable Power of Attorney

Another document necessary to a well-planned estate is a properly crafted durable power of attorney. With this document, your parent can name a person (agent) to handle tax, legal, and financial matters. The power of attorney should expressly include language (that conforms to state law requirements) that will remain valid even if your parent becomes disabled. Otherwise, it will be of little use.

Powers of attorney should not be treated lightly as routine and simplistic documents. Consider with your parents the following technique—a "special" rather than a "general" power of attorney. A special power of attorney is limited in scope. It will allow your parents' agent to handle only one particular transaction or perhaps one type of transaction. A special power might be useless for general planning if your parents become disabled because they do not know what legal and financial issues they are going to face or what problems will arise. It is not possible to know what type of limited powers should be given to an agent under a special power of attorney. This is why, for general protection and estate planning, your parents should give someone a general power that will be broadly effective if they are disabled, and will enable the agent to handle any foreseeable financial matters. If the broad privileges of a general power still concern your parents, they should use the opposite approach and have their attorney modify a general power to exclude specific powers that concern them. For example, they may be comfortable with giving their financial agent almost unlimited powers (except prohibiting him from changing beneficiaries on insurance or retirement accounts).

Ensure that your parents understand the implications of appointing an agent "separately" (either agent can act alone) or "together" (jointly—meaning both must agree on any action) in their power of attorney.

Also, it is imperative that your parents understand the scope of the power to make gifts. Many attorneys routinely give an agent the power to make gifts of one's money. Be sure this is what your parent really wants, and restrict it so that the agent cannot haphazardly distribute your future inheritance to all and sundry people while your parents are still alive. One should almost never sign a power that permits unlimited gifts unless it is necessary for Medicaid and elder law planning (see Chapter 10).

Discuss with your parents whether they really want to give their agent the right and the power to change beneficiaries of their IRA or other retirement plan. This could enable the agent appointed to change the beneficiary of any retirement plan thus dramatically altering the distribution of assets. Similarly, the right to effect insurance transactions could enable the appointed agent to change the beneficiary of any insurance policy. This could dramatically alter the distribution of your parents' estate.

Another thing for your parents to consider is a "springing" power of attorney. This is a power that becomes effective (i.e., springs into use) only when your parent becomes disabled. This prevents the agent from having any authority until your parent is actually disabled and in need of assistance. For your parents, this may be the better approach if they prefer not to grant any authority to their agent until it becomes absolutely necessary. The argument against the springing power of attorney is that, in general, one should not grant any power of attorney unless one trusts the person named. If trust is not then an issue, why risk restricting the power of attorney until your parent becomes disabled? If you are given springing power of attorney, be sure your parents specify some way to determine when disability has occurred (e.g., consensus of two medical doctors) to avoid legal wrangling over the matter. Otherwise, all kinds of questions could be raised as to whether the power of attorney has become effective (i.e., whether your parent is disabled).

Why include so many restrictions in a durable power of attorney? They may be necessary to win your parents over to the idea of planning. Your parents, as well as their heirs, are likely to be better off with a restricted power in place, than with no power in place.

If you have to agree to restrictions, such as making your powers to act contingent on your parent becoming disabled and forgoing the right to change insurance or IRA beneficiaries, accept the restrictions and move your parents' planning forward. It might be a great compromise approach to get a recalcitrant parent to sign on.

The Safest Approach: A Revocable Living Trust with an Institutional Cotrustee

A revocable living trust can be key to protecting your parents and their loved ones, such as a minor child or a spouse.

Case Study: Ira wanted to have his will done, and at the time, his wife was in poor health. The attorney recommended they prepare revocable living trusts with a bank as a successor trustee because there were no close family members to help them out if something happened to the husband. The concern was that the wife, given her physical and mental condition, would not be able to take care of herself properly. The only family members were grandchildren who lived a substantial distance from their grandparents. Second, Ira was concerned whether the grandchildren would provide adequate care for their grandmother. He was hesitant about working with an institution because, like many others, he had some predisposed idea that institutions are bad. He did not complete the plan, but about three years later, Ira called his attorney again. Circumstances had changed dramatically. He was in the hospital, terminally ill, and had a very short time to live. Ira called his attorney to the hospital and told her that he had thought about what she had said. He now realized that, to take care of his wife and help protect her, he needed to structure the type of trust with independent management that they had spoken about years earlier. Ira was relieved to know that he could arrange care for his wife, the most important person in the world to him, and that ultimately his grandchildren would benefit even more.

A power of attorney is a simple approach to enable someone to act in your parents' behalf in the event of their disability. However, a living trust can be a far more effective vehicle. A living trust can provide far more detailed provisions and contingency plans for dealing with disability than does the typical durable power of attorney. The authority of an agent under a durable power of attorney could be less certain than that of a successor trustee under a revocable living trust. The successor trustee (the trustee that takes over if the first named trustee becomes disabled) has legal ownership (title) to the assets in the trust, so the line of authority of the trustee is perhaps stronger than that of an agent under a power. Additionally, banks and other financial institutions may more readily accept the authority of a trustee than an agent, since the agent under a power of attorney may not be subject to the same requirements of maintaining books and records as would a trustee.

The two documents, a living trust and a durable power of attorney, however, are not mutually exclusive. A durable power of attorney should always be signed as part of any estate plan. There are few exceptions to that rule. When a living trust is determined to be an appropriate tool for your parents' estate and financial goals, they still should consider signing a durable power of attorney. The durable power of attorney should give their agent the right to make gifts and, most importantly, should have an express provision giving their agent the authority to transfer assets to their living trust. Rarely does anyone transfer every asset they own to their living trust when they set it up. A checking account, gifts received after the trust was formed, personal property acquired after the trust was formed, and assets that are costly or difficult to transfer (perhaps a car) are often not in the trust. If your parent becomes disabled, the only mechanism to get these assets into their trust is for their agent, acting under a durable power of attorney, to transfer these assets.

A living trust is an excellent vehicle for a single benefactor who cannot rely on immediate family to handle financial matters in the event of disability. A comparison should also be made with another option for providing for financial management of a disabled or incompetent person—have a court appoint a guardian, conservator, or committee. The definitions and functions of each differ under each state's laws.

If your parents become disabled and cannot manage their personal affairs, then their successor trustee (or successor cotrustees if they named two persons to serve) will take over management of their trust assets. If they instead named an initial cotrustee who has served from the beginning with them, that cotrustee, and the next successor cotrustee appointed in the trust document, will then together manage the trust assets on your parents' behalf. At this time, their agent, acting under the durable power of attorney may transfer any assets that your parents then own in their own name (i.e., that were not previously transferred to the trust) to their living trust. The disability provisions in the living trust will be vitally important for determining when this switch occurs and when your parents can resume control of the management of their trust assets if they recover. This is important to consider since disability can frequently be short term and not permanent. This is another soft point you can highlight to your parents to show them how planning actually will keep them in control of their assets as long as feasible.

Few living trusts contain detailed rules for determining when disability occurs and ends. This is ironic, because one of the primary benefits of a living trust is the management of assets without court intervention if one is disabled. If the trust document does not have clear tests, court involvement may become necessary. If your parent has a living trust, review those sections; if they are not clear, you or your parent should contact the attorney who prepared the document and find out why.

An important part of the disability provisions of a living trust is detailed instructions for your parents' care in the event of disability. Many trust forms do not provide for personalized detail. Do your parents want to avoid being placed in a nursing home as long as possible? Do they have preferences for the type of health care facility they should be placed in if it becomes absolutely necessary? If geographic preferences are important to them, they should specify in their living trust that in the event of disability they wish to be placed in a facility that is located in a certain part of the country (perhaps near family). If religious preferences are important, they might specify a health care facility that meets their religious dietary requirements or that is located near a church, mosque, or synagogue where they could attend services. Never assume that trustees "will know" that kind of vital information. These instructions might give fearful or uncomfortable parents some reassurance that their needs and wishes are really being addressed.

Thus, those who argue that living trusts are never necessary, advocating instead a simple durable power of attorney, miss the point.

Celebrity Case Study: Salvadore or "Sonny" Bono, with wife Cheri-lyn Sarkisian, formed a successful pop music duo "Sonny and Cher." They became cultural icons in the 1960s and eventually starred in a popular television variety show. In 1974, divorce ended their marriage and business partnership. In 1986, Bono married his third wife, Mary Whitaker Bono. Gone from the public eye, but a successful restaurant owner, Bono tried his hand at politics in 1988 and won the mayoral race in Palm Springs, California, by the widest margin ever. Bono's political career hit new heights when he was elected to Congress in 1994. Successful in his work and family life, he seemed to have it all when he died in a skiing accident in Nevada in 1998. His lack of estate planning turned his family's already tragic experience into a nightmare. Incredibly, the man who had astutely managed both an entertainment and political career apparently made little or no attempt to plan for the future disposition of his estate—he did not even have a will. For one-marriage families, the lack of a will can cause enough grief. For Bono, who married three times and had several children, this oversight has caused his survivors more than a probate headache.

What should he have done? Sonny Bono could have established a revocable living trust and a pour-over will. The trust may have kept his estate more private, if he had transferred his assets into it while he was living. Trust assets would have avoided probate. The pour-over will could have provided a safety net for assets that were not transferred into the trust. A QTIP trust and a Bypass Trust, which would have governed the disposition of the assets in the revocable trust after he died, would have distributed assets to family members most efficiently. Chastity (his daughter with Cher) could have been the remainder beneficiary of the Bypass Trust (with the unified credit in 1998 of $625,000), and the balance, no matter how large, could have gone into the QTIP trust, which would have qualified for the marital deduction. His wife could have drawn income from both trusts in her lifetime, and then passed on the trusts' assets at her death. He could have made his gifts equal to his children by buying supplemental life insurance, owned by a trust, with each child named to receive the inheritance he wished. To help pay estate taxes on his wife's death, he could have purchased a second-to-die life insurance policy owned by a trust.

LESSONS TO LEARN

Proper estate-planning documents can protect your parents' dignity, assure that their personal wishes are carried out, provide them the structure to keep the most control for as long as possible over their own affairs, and address their personal wishes (see Figure 9.1). Meeting these goals, and helping to show your parents that you have done so, might be the keys to moving them forward in the estate-planning process. This is also essential for protecting your interests.

Figure 9.1 Parents' Estate-Planning Documents

Type of Document	Date Signed	Fiduciaries Named	Location of Organization	Status	Key Points	Planning Comment
Parents' will						
Spouse's/partner's will						
Parents' power of attorney						
Spouse's/partner's power of attorney						
Parents' living will						
Spouse's/partner's living will						
Parents' revocable living trust						
Spouse's/partner's revocable living trust						
Insurance trust						
FLP/LLC						
Other						

Many devices are available to ensure proper asset distribution in an efficient manner on the death of a loved one. Joint ownership, wills, powers of attorney, trusts, and other kinds of legal status and documents will ensure that you receive what is lawfully yours when a loved one dies. Some of these instruments and documents work better than others, and whenever your parents use one of them, make sure that they have paid proper attention to the planning, details, and long-term care and tax ramifications of their estate plan. If they fail to detail their wants, needs, and expectations now, there is little likelihood their plan will eventuate as they intended.

Planning Tip: See www.laweasy.com for more information. See: Shenkman, *The Complete Living Trust Program* and Shenkman, *The Complete Book of Trusts* (both published by John Wiley & Sons, Inc.), for more information and sample forms.

---

10 MEDICAID NURSING HOME COSTS

Few things can be more devastating to a potential inheritance than a parent's lengthy stay in a nursing home before death. With costs exceeding $100,000 per year in many facilities, it does not take long to erode even a large estate. Many people are affected. Some studies have shown that nearly 45 percent of persons over the age of 65 will spend some time in a nursing home. Some estimates suggest that the average nursing home stay could be nearly three years. Be careful with statistics and averages because they can be misleading. These time periods may comprise days or weeks for strokes, heart attacks, and other acute conditions. For those afflicted with advanced Parkinson's or Alzheimer's, the duration could be years, even a decade or more. Few estates are large enough to withstand the financial impact of these longer stays. This risk, which frankly worries most senior citizens, is the motivation behind a particular subspecialty of estate planning, called "elder law" planning. Your parents must engage in elder law planning to safeguard their life's savings; it is the planning you may have to encourage them to consider if you are to have any inheritance.

What can you do about this risk? This chapter provides an overview of basic elder law planning—the art of trying to protect assets from nursing home and other medical costs.

There are generally five ways to finance nursing home costs and care: Private pay, long-term-care insurance, Medicare, Medicaid, and veteran's benefits. Maximizing the payments from long-term-care insurance and government programs, while minimizing private payments from your parents' assets, will maximize your inheritance. How does long-term-care insurance work? How can you help your parent apply and determine what type of policy to obtain? What can you do to protect your parents' assets? Although the laws differ tremendously from state to state, this chapter describes the general rules that are common to most states. These rules include an explanation of the minimum assets that your parent can retain without losing them to Medicaid (i.e., while remaining covered so their assets do not have to be used), and a description of excluded assets that can be held without being dissipated. Medicaid qualifying trusts to protect assets from being eaten up by Medicaid costs are also discussed.

If your parents are extremely wealthy, they may choose to fund payments of expenses from their own assets. If they are veterans, special benefits from the Veterans Administration may be available.

Planning Tip: See www.elderlawanswers.com and www.naela.com for more information.

WHAT IS ELDER LAW PLANNING?

Elder law planning is a field of law that is growing rapidly, along with the aging of the American populace. In essence, it is a specialty within the estate law that focuses on the needs of senior citizens. Estate-planning practitioners provide services that range from writing wills and living wills and establishing trusts to planning for death and disability with a focus on life insurance and estate taxes. Elder law specialists in the estate-planning community focus on Medicare, Medicaid, and Social Security benefits. Elder law also addresses abuse against the elderly in nursing homes and medical care facilities.

Since elder law encompasses such a wide range of interests, lawyers in this field usually have specific areas of specialization. If you need assistance with Social Security benefits, you do not want a lawyer who specializes in wills and trusts. On the other hand, you may be able to consult with a lawyer who specializes in disability claims and appeals.

The National Academy of Elder Law Planning provides a list of areas included in elder law. It includes in part:

- Preservation of assets for spouses when one enters a nursing home.
- Medicaid.
- Medicare claims and appeals.
- Social Security and disability claims and appeals.
- Supplemental as well as long-term health insurance issues.
- Disability planning.
- Conservatorship and guardianship.
- Estate planning during life and disposition of the estate on death.
- Probate.
- Elder abuse.

Many more issues should also be addressed, depending on your parents' circumstances. The fields of law that pertain to the specific needs of the elderly are too many to count, and you can always find someone who is eager to meet those needs. For example, if your parent is elderly and infirm, with the specter of a nursing home looming, a lawyer who specializes in asset preservation will be able to sit down with your parent and work out a plan to protect his assets from the nursing home and the government.

RULES DIFFER FROM STATE TO STATE

The rules of elder law, like most fields of law, differ from state to state. The state of California, through the California Partnership, has instituted a program that allows elders to protect a greater amount of personal assets. Under this new program, if a person purchases long-term-care insurance through the California Partnership, an amount equal to whatever monies they spend on that person's behalf is added to the amount of assets he can protect in his estate while still qualifying for Medicaid or Medicare. For example, if your parent purchases long-term-care insurance from the California Partnership and they pay $200 a day for four years on nursing home care for your parent, an additional $292,200 of your parent's estate will be protectable [$200 \times 365 \times 4 + 200 = 292,200$]. If you add that to the standard $2,000 allowable amount, your parent can hold $294,200 in assets and still qualify for Medicaid or Medical benefits. That figure may include a home, automobile, or other assets.

Planning Point: If you consult an elder law attorney on behalf of your parents, to learn how they can better plan, be certain to consult an attorney licensed in, and practicing in, the state where your parents reside, unless the plan is to relocate them.

MEDICAID

Medicaid is a program that is funded by the federal government and state governments, but is administered by the individual states. Medicaid can pay for nursing home care, and certain home care, for qualifying individuals. To qualify, your parent will generally have to meet several requirements:

- *U.S. citizen and resident, and a resident in the state where benefits are sought.* Be careful if your parent has recently relocated. If your parents are planning to relocate to a new state, encourage them to consult with an elder law specialist in the new state before moving.

- *At least 65 years or older or blind or disabled.*

- *Medically eligible as determined by an examination conducted by a Medicaid nurse.*

- *Limited income.* The cap varies by state, but is low in all instances. All types of income are counted in making the calculation.

- *Limited resources.* Your parents may own only a modest amount of assets, including certain specified assets that are categorized as "excluded resources," if they are to qualify. The excluded assets may include a car, home if occupied by appropriate persons (community spouse, child under age 21 or blind or disabled, sibling with an ownership interest, or a child-caregiver who meets additional requirements), limited personal belongings such as a wedding ring, and prepaid burial fund if the payments are held in an irrevocable trust.

Once your parent or benefactor qualifies, a look-back rule will be used to test prior transfers. The purpose is to assure that if your parent transferred significant assets before applying for Medicaid, some of those assets will be applied to the payment of nursing home costs. If your parent transferred assets to heirs, such as yourself, then all of those transfers within the past 36 months will be considered. If your parent transferred the assets to a trust (see later in this chapter), the look-back period is expanded to 60 months.

If your parent is living in a nursing home and Medicaid is paying for his care, the first thing to know is that there is an issue of a recovery against the estate for costs. If your parent still owns a home when he dies, the government can tax the estate for the death value of the house to pay for any outstanding bills. In some states, like Arizona, this is only done if the nursing home spouse is the last spouse to die. This can completely dissipate whatever inheritance you may have had coming to you.

How can you avoid this? Have your parents consult an elder law attorney and review the benefits of signing a deed to the house to you in their lifetime, while creating a life estate for themselves. That means they will be able to live in their own home during their lifetime and your inheritance will be protected from the government after they die.

The house is not the only asset that the government can reach to reimburse Medicaid for monies spent on your parents' behalf. Generally, when children discover exactly how much of their parents' estate is vulnerable, they encourage their parents to sign everything over to them as soon as possible so the assets will be protected and the government will pay for care. There are a few problems with this reaction. The largest, however, is that if the assets change hands for less than fair market value, they are still reachable unless the transfer occurred three years before your parent applied for assistance. Additionally, if an irrevocable trust is involved, any transfer within five years of the application may make your parent ineligible. Living trusts are particularly troublesome because all your parents' assets in the trust remain vulnerable to creditors.

If your parents transferred assets during this "look-back" period of 36 or 60 months, a calculation must then be made to determine how long they will remain ineligible for Medicaid. During that penalty period, your parents' resources—your inheritance—will be used to cover costs.

Planning Tip: What if your parent is incapacitated mentally and cannot make the transfers necessary to protect assets? If your parent had taken the precaution earlier of signing a durable power of attorney that permitted gift transfers, the agent under the power might be able to make the Medicaid planning transfers. Absent that, you will have to consult an elder law attorney in your state to determine if a guardianship proceeding can be used to authorize the transfers.

MEDICAID TRUST

If your parent transfers all of his assets to you and other heirs, there might be a gift tax cost. The assets, once transferred, will be subject to the risk of your being sued or divorced. Thus, some parents may prefer to transfer assets to a trust to provide some protection for those assets.

LONG-TERM-CARE INSURANCE COORDINATION WITH ELDER LAW PLANNING

When planning for their golden years, your parents should consider investing in both long-term-care insurance and catastrophic illness insurance. Long-term-care insurance benefits cover a long stay in a nursing home or an extended period of home care. Catastrophic illness insurance covers the costs of hospital care that are greater than a person's medical insurance coverage. For example, if your elderly parent were in a severe accident, Medicare would cover a stay in the hospital per incidence of illness plus a lifetime reserve. Catastrophic illness insurance would kick in following the 150-day period. Long-term-care insurance will not cover hospital care, but if the accident was debilitating, it will pay for nursing home costs or home care during the period of time purchased by your parent.

What happens if your parents do not have insurance or the insurance runs out? They will be stuck paying the bills out of pocket unless their resources are below the standard set by Medicaid. These thresholds are generally low. What assets can your parents retain if they are dependent on Medicaid to foot their bill? As explained earlier, not much.

LESSONS TO LEARN

When planning for long-term care with your parents, seek a lawyer who specializes in elder law planning. It requires familiarity with Medicaid guidelines, assets-protection planning, and an understanding of different kinds of long-term-care insurance. Finding a lawyer who knows the particulars of the law of the state in which your parents live is a vital component of ensuring they have effective and competent counsel. This is the best way to prevent the nursing home from walking away with your inheritance or forcing your parents to spend it all to qualify for government assistance.

11 ESTATE, GIFT, AND OTHER TAXES THAT CAN DECIMATE YOUR INHERITANCE

Together, income and estate taxes can easily deplete 70 percent or more of your inheritance unless you take action to protect it. This chapter describes gift, estate, and generation skipping transfer taxes, as well as income with respect to a decedent (IRD), and explains how they can decimate an heir's potential inheritance. Some basic steps to protect your inheritance (e.g., a gift program) are also presented.

It is important to encourage your parents to pursue estate tax planning to safeguard their wealth. What can you tell them that will help them minimize, if not eliminate, the estate tax? Although the government has proposed a repeal of the estate tax, it continues to lurk, and future legislative changes might occur. Even if the tax is repealed, it could be reenacted.

Do your parents have wills that include the appropriate language to help save taxes? Are your parents' assets structured (titled) to realize tax savings? This chapter points out the basics of transfer taxation and offers a few simple legal ways to reduce taxes.

Although this chapter focuses on gift, estate, and generation-skipping transfer taxes, income tax planning is critical to safeguarding your parents and maximizing your inheritance. Setting up a trust in a carefully selected state can minimize or eliminate state income taxes. Stretching out the payments on your parents' IRA (a stretch IRA) can defer income taxes for decades or longer, tremendously enhancing family wealth.

GIFT AND ESTATE TAXES

The transfer tax system consists of three separate, but related, taxes:

1. Gift tax, which is assessed on gratuitous transfers of assets while the donor is alive. Even if the estate tax is repealed, the gift tax is an independent tax that will remain indefinitely. If your parents pursue Medicaid planning, as discussed in Chapter 10, the gift tax may be an important consideration.
2. Estate tax, which is assessed on transfers of assets following a person's death (e.g., assets bequeathed under a parent's or benefactor's will or revocable living trust).
3. Generation skipping transfer (GST) tax, which is assessed on transfers made during a person's life or following the person's death to people two generations younger, such as grandchildren, grandnieces, and grandnephews (or trusts for the benefit of such people). This tax applies only to the wealthiest taxpayers, so the discussion in this chapter is brief. However, because the GST tax is important in planning the ideal way for you to receive your inheritance, it is addressed again in Chapter 15.

These three transfer taxes are all based on the transfer of your parents' assets. While the tax rates are extremely high, there are many exclusions, deductions, and other planning benefits. Encouraging and helping your parents to take advantage of these transfers may be the key to preserving your inheritance and giving your parents the satisfaction that Uncle Sam will not be the primary heir to their lifetime of work.

The three federal transfer taxes—gift, estate, and GST—can be distinguished from the inheritance tax assessed in many states. An inheritance tax is assessed, not on the owner's transfer of assets, but on the recipient of the property. In all cases, the result is the same. You get less.

Caution: The 2001 Tax Act phases out the credit that the federal government had paid states to share estate tax revenues. As a result, states must either increase inheritance taxes or find other taxes to make up for the lost revenues. Thus, your parents' estate may not be subject to a federal estate tax, but could still incur a hefty state level death tax.

GIFT TAX

Transfers That Trigger the Gift Tax

The gift tax is charged on the person's right to gratuitously distribute assets while alive. Although in everyday usage the term *gift* implies a donative intent, tax law does not require showing that the donor had the intent to do this. All that is required to trigger the gift tax is your parents' transfer of assets to another for less than full payment of value (consideration).

A Gift Must Be Complete to Be Taxable

No gift is made and considered taxable until it is completed. For a gift to be complete, the donor (your parent) must transfer beneficial interest in the assets to the donee (you or any other recipient) and must give up sufficient control over the asset so that the gift cannot be rescinded. In other words, the gift must be beyond recall.

The delivery of the gift property should also be completed. To complete a gift to a trust for your benefit, your parents not only must take all of the steps necessary to transfer the asset to the trust, but must establish appropriate terms for the trust as well. For example, if your parent has substantial control over the trust, the gift may not be complete. This concept is used intentionally in some trust planning to avoid income and gift taxes. Additionally, if your parent is a trustee, or has reserved significant powers, such as the right to terminate the trust, the gift may not be complete.

For tax purposes, is it better to complete the gift or not complete it? As far as safeguarding your inheritance is concerned, a completed gift to you ensures that your parents cannot bequeath those assets elsewhere, because they legally become your property. For tax planning, the answer is not necessarily as clear. It depends on your parents' circumstances and everyone's goals.

Note: Incomplete gifts have been used as an intentional planning technique when setting up many different types of trust. Very wealthy parents can set up an intentionally defective grantor trust (IDIT) to which they can sell assets without triggering capital gains tax costs. Transfers to a foreign situs asset protection trust can be structured so that parents concerned about lawsuits retain sufficient powers to avoid a completed gift. Otherwise in addition to a gift tax, they may face a substantial excise tax applicable to transfers of assets overseas. For less wealthy parents, some elder law trusts preserve rights to minimize income or gift taxes. Gifts, however, must be legitimate transfers. Some parents, as the following famous case study illustrates, go too far!

Celebrity Case Study: In the summer of 2002, the Regis family, who ran one of the largest cable companies in the United States, Adelphia, found themselves under investigation by the Securities and Exchange Commission (SEC). In July 2002, John Regis, the CEO of Adelphia, and two of his sons were taken into custody for using company assets as their personal piggy bank. Among other things, they allegedly appropriated company funds to buy homes, build a personal golf course on the family estate, and pay for personal vacations.

Tax Benefits That Can Help Your Parents Avoid Gift Tax

Four tax benefits can help your parents minimize or entirely avoid the gift tax. The most common is that any person, including your parent, can give away up to $11,000 a year (the amount is indexed for inflation), to any person, without incurring a gift tax. This is called the annual gift tax exclusion. Your parents can each make this gift to as many people as they want during each calendar year. Because donors often complete this gift every year to the same person, the recipient can accumulate substantial gifts over several years. For a large estate, the $11,000 limit may sound piddling, but it can be substantial when used to the maximum extent feasible.

Example: Tony and Helen Taxpayer have three children. Each child is married and has two children. Tony and Helen set up trusts for each of their six grandchildren. Tony can gift $11,000 to each of the six trusts each year. Helen can gift $11,000 to each of the six trusts each year. Thus, the Taxpayers can gift $132,000 per year to trusts for their grandchildren. In two years, they can gift $264,000. Since the $11,000 gifts can be made in each calendar year, the Taxpayers could make gifts of $132,000 on December 31 and $132,000 on January 1. Thus, in a short period they could give more than a quarter million dollars to trusts for their grandchildren.

If your parents make gifts to trusts for children, grandchildren, or other heirs, rather than outright to the intended donee, the gifts must meet special requirements to qualify for the gift tax annual exclusion. If your parents are using trusts, then they should consult an estate tax specialist to assure that they are meeting these requirements. Trusts often are used to ensure that the funds will be used for an intended purpose. The trust agreement can include restrictions on expenditures and, if carefully crafted, even some lifestyle control. These controls can assure grandparents that their grandson Hotrod-Howard, has to use the money for college and not a new hog.

Planning Tip: If your parents are recalcitrant about making gifts, explaining the controls they can assert through carefully drafted trust documents might pave the way for largesse, by giving them the assurance that their money will be used for purposes they deem appropriate.

In addition to the $11,000 per year, per person, your parents can pay unlimited amounts to a qualifying educational institution without incurring any gift tax. A qualifying educational institution is one that normally maintains a regular faculty and curriculum and normally has a regularly enrolled body of students. Your parents can also make unlimited payments for medical care if the funds are paid directly to the person or organization providing the medical services. Tuition and medical payments must be made directly to the providers.

What about children, grandchildren, or other heirs who are not yet in college? Most parents view education as an admirable goal of any gift program. An ideal way to accomplish this for future college expenses is to make gifts to college savings plans. If your parents make gifts to these Code Section 529 college savings plans, a special exception to the $11,000 per year rule permits them to accelerate five years of gifts into one year. Your parents together can thus give anyone's Section 529 plan $110,000 in one year without adverse gift tax consequences. If they have six grandchildren and make this gift to all six in one year, your parents can complete a tax-free gift of more than $1 million in a single day. Money inside a Section 529 college savings plan grows tax deferred and can be withdrawn for college use without any income tax consequences. The 529 plans are an estate and financial planning powerhouse.

If your parents make a taxable gift in excess of the exclusions available, there is one last, but substantial, tax break available to offset any gift tax that would otherwise be due. This break is called your parent's lifetime exclusion, and it is the cornerstone of gift and trust planning for most taxpayers. The amount is fixed at $1 million per year. It is not increased when the estate tax exclusion is increased (see following Caution). Thus, each of your parents can give away $1 million before any gift tax is assessed. This is vitally important if your parents want to engage in the elder law planning discussed in Chapter 10.

Caution: In 2004, the estate tax exclusion is scheduled to increase to $1.5 million and eventually to $3.5 million in 2009. The gift tax exclusion, however, will remain at $1 million. When the estate tax is repealed in 2010, the gift tax exclusion will still continue, at the same $1 million level.

Example: In the year 2005, your mother gives away $900,000. She can still give away $100,000 ($1 million – $900,000) without incurring a gift tax. If she dies before making any more gifts, her estate will be entitled to a $600,000 exclusion [$1,500,000 exclusion available in year 2005— $900,000 previously used]. The gift and estate tax exclusions remain unified, only the limit on lifetime gifts is lower.

Your parents can each give away up to $1 million above the $11,000 annual exclusion amounts without incurring a gift tax.

> **Example:** Your father Paul, a widower, has made no gifts before the current tax year. Paul gifts $11,000 to each of his three children on January 10. No gift tax is due and none of Paul's applicable exclusion is used. This is because Paul's gifts are each offset by the $11,000 annual exclusion available on gifts to each recipient. On June 1 of the same year, Paul gifts each of his three children an additional $400,000. The annual exclusion has been used up on the January gifts. Therefore, he has made $1,200,000 (3 gifts × $400,000 per gift) of the transfers, which can be offset, in part, by his $1 million exclusion (2002 or 2003). Paul owes gift tax on the remaining $200,000. In the next year, Paul pays $64,036 for tuition and medical expenses of his children and grandchildren direct to the educational institutions and medical care providers. No portion of this uses his annual exclusion because these gifts qualify for the special exception described earlier for medical and tuition payments. Paul dies three years later, when the exclusion has increased to $1.5 million, having made no additional gifts. Paul's estate can use his remaining exclusion of $500,000 [$1.5 million – $1 million] to offset the tax on assets passing under Paul's revocable living trust.

The preceding example also illustrates the close relationship of the gift and estate tax although the exclusion amounts will eventually differ. When helping your parents, you cannot plan for one and ignore the other. When planning with trusts, your parents also need to review the gift tax rules, the nature of their trusts, and the consequences to their overall plan.

The gift tax is a vital consideration when planning most types of trusts. Although the tax can be costly, it can be reduced dramatically with careful planning and judicious use of the exceptions and other special rules. Even after the 2001 Tax Act, you must pursue this type of planning. It would be foolish for your parents to waste their exclusion when they cannot know with any certainty the future of the gift and estate tax, the size of their estate, and other factors that might affect them and their loved ones.

ESTATE TAX

Understanding the Estate Tax Is Essential for Proper Planning

The estate tax is a transfer charge that is assessed on property your parents own at the time of death. The actual tax, however, is much broader and more complicated than it seems at first glance. Why is it so important to plan for this complex tax? Estate tax rates can reach as high as approximately one-half (higher when state taxes are added), and even though they are to be reduced to 47 percent, planning will remain important for them. Many states have capped their exclusions at levels lower than the federal levels so that state tax might be due even if federal tax is not.

These high rates are even costlier if the generation skipping transfer (GST) tax, which can be assessed on gifts and bequests to grandchildren (and other heirs considered to be two generations younger than your parents), is added into the mix. Minimizing this tax burden is essential if your parents want to pass on the maximum amount of assets to their heirs; the key to accomplishing this is the proper use of trusts.

For most taxpayers, a Bypass Trust (to fully use the exclusion available to both spouses), a marital trust (QTIP or QDOT), and perhaps an irrevocable life insurance trust can eliminate most or all estate taxes. Proper use of these instruments can also protect assets from second and later marriages, keep creditors at bay, provide professional management, and more. If your parent does not have a spouse, a qualified personal residence trust (QPRT), grantor retained annuity trust (GRAT), or a common law grantor retained interest trust (GRIT), other fancier trust techniques may eliminate the estate tax burden. These all require consultation with an estate tax specialist.

Example: Your father is considering using a GRAT to gift interests in a rental property to his children. The GRAT will discount substantially the value of the gift for gift tax purposes. If your father does not survive the term of the trust, however, the entire value of the rental property will be pulled back into his taxable estate. As an alternative, your father's estate planner suggests transferring the rental property to a family limited partnership and making gifts to his children. Gifts made in this manner would be removed from your father's estate no matter how long he survives.

To intelligently discuss these options with your parents and/or their estate planner, you need to understand how the estate tax works.

Scaring Your Parents into Estate-Planning Action

A great way to motivate parents who are reluctant to plan is to show them an estimate of the estate tax on their estate if they do not plan. If your parents' estate is taxable, they will usually find the numbers sufficiently upsetting to be motivated to plan. Few people want their hard-earned assets to disappear into the abyss of the federal budget. In making the calculation, you must identify all property that is included in the gross estate for federal estate tax purposes. This includes a lot more than most people, including your parents, may realize.

Many taxpayers substantially underestimate the size of their taxable estate and as a result fail to take the steps necessary to avoid estate taxes. Your parents may simply not feel as wealthy as the IRS and the estate tax laws view them. Your parents' house may have appreciated substantially, but it is not a spendable asset as long as they live in it. Life insurance that they own can be included in their estate, but while they are alive, they are unlikely to view the death benefit as valuable. Pension assets often do not seem valuable because usually they are not a spendable asset until retirement. Thus, your parents could have a substantial estate for federal tax purposes without feeling wealthy.

The tax law defines property interests for inclusion in an estate very broadly. In some cases, property that your father gave away during his life can be required to be included in his gross estate. If he transferred property but retained the right to the income, or even the right to designate who will obtain the income, these assets will be taxed as part of your father's gross estate. If your father gave you title to his house, perhaps as part of the elder law planning discussed in Chapter 10, but he retained the right to live there for the rest of his life, the entire value of the property is included in his taxable estate. This result will occur even if the approach effectively insulates the house from Medicaid.

Your parents might also confuse their taxable estate with their probate estate. *Taxable estate* means assets that will be subject to estate tax on your parents' deaths. *Probate estate* refers to assets that must pass through the probate process on a person's death. Thus, if your mother sets up a revocable living trust and transfers all of her assets to the trust, her probate estate may be nonexistent. Her taxable estate, however, may be substantial because it will include all assets in her trust. Insurance, IRAs, pension assets, and jointly owned property may all pass to her heirs without becoming part of her probate estate. However, each can be part of her taxable estate. When your parents' estate planner estimates the tax cost, be sure that he has been advised of all of their assets.

Joint property presents another costly trap for many parents, as they may mistakenly believe that joint ownership removes assets from their estate. Joint assets are not included in your parents' probate estate since on the death of the first joint tenant they automatically pass to the surviving joint tenant. However, the value of these assets is included in your parents' taxable estate.

Certain transactions that occurred within three years of death are pulled back into your parents' estate for tax purposes. These include:

- Gift tax paid on gifts made within three years of your parent's death (the value of the gifts is not pulled back in unless one of the other special provisions pull it back in). So if your father made a large taxable transfer to his children, like the $200,000 taxable gift by Paul in the earlier example, the amount of gift tax he paid is added to his estate.

- Life insurance policies that your parent transferred to a trust within three years before death.

The preceding are just a few of the many estate tax traps for the unwary parent. Getting your parents to sit down with an estate tax specialist to highlight the magnitude of the potential estate tax cost problems might be the only way for them to realize the cost of inaction.

How to Take Advantage of Special Estate Tax Valuation Rules

Once the assets to be included in your parents' taxable estate are identified, they must be valued. The fair market value of the assets at the date of death is the amount generally to be included in your parents' gross estate for calculating estate tax. However, special valuation rules can greatly reduce the estate tax. These special rules might enable your parents to reduce taxes without giving away more assets than they planned, just by carefully planning which assets they are going to give.

Real estate is generally valued at its highest and best use. For example, say your mother owned land she used as a tree farm, which could be developed as a subdivision. If no special rules apply, the land would have to be valued as if it were to be sold to a developer. This result can create hardships. It could place an excessive burden on the family farm to require application of the general rule, maybe even forcing you, your mother's heir, to sell the farm to pay the tax. Thus, the tax laws permit the executor to elect to value the land based on its current use, up to a maximum decrease in the value of the gross estate of $750,000. What does this mean? If your mom is willing to give away assets today, perhaps she should choose assets other than the farm or other real estate that will qualify for this special benefit.

If your parents own interests in a family limited partnership or other closely held business, but own less than 50 percent at death, their interests might qualify for a discount for tax valuation purposes. The theory is that a less than 50 percent interest in a business is a noncontrolling position that should generally be valued at less than a pro rata percentage of the whole.

Example: Dad owns 60 percent of Widget Manufacturers, Inc., an S corporation operating a family business. Instead of making cash gifts of $11,000 to each heir to reduce his estate, Dad might make gifts of $11,000 net value of stock in the business. These gifts will themselves be discounted so that Dad might actually be able to gift the equivalent economic value of $15,000 of stock, with an $11,000 tax value (because the $15,000 of stock, as a noncontrolling interest in the company, is valued at less than its face value). If Dad is able to give away enough of the stock so that on his death he owns 48 percent of the company, that 48 percent may be reduced by a third or more of its value for estate tax purposes since it is a noncontrolling interest. The savings can be huge. On a $2 million company it could be $500,000.

The moral of the valuation story is that if your parents carefully plan their gifts, without giving more away, just giving it away more wisely, they can save a fortune in estate taxes.

Deductions, Expenses, and Credits

When estimating your parents' estate tax, remember that every estate is allowed deductions for funeral expenses, debts, administrative costs, legal and accounting fees, and casualty or theft losses. Certain claims against your parents' estate can be deducted, as can qualifying charitable contributions. Credits that may also be applied to reduce applicable estate taxes include a credit for prior transfers and for death taxes paid to your parents' state. The big number that every plan focuses on is the "applicable exclusion." It is the amount that your parents can transfer without any estate tax cost. Just be sure that they consider the comments earlier in this chapter before assuming that their estate is not taxable. The chart that follows shows gift and estate tax rates after the 2001 Tax Act.

Gift and Estate Tax Exclusions and Tax Rates

Year	Top Gift and Estate Tax Rate (%)	Estate Exclusion Amount ($ Million)
2002	50	1
2003	49	1
2004	48	1.5[a]
2005	47	1.5[a]
2006	46	2[a]
2007	45	2[a]
2008	45	2[a]
2009	45	3.5[a]
2010	Repealed[b]	N/A[a]
2011	55	1

[a] The gift tax exclusion is limited to $1 million, but the estate and gift tax exclusions remain unified so that using the gift tax exclusion will reduce dollar for dollar the estate tax exclusion remaining available.
[b] Gift tax rate is pegged to the maximum individual tax rate of 35% when the estate tax is repealed (if repeal happens).

Who Pays the Estate Tax Can Be as Important as
How Much Tax Is Paid

Few taxpayers or heirs, and unfortunately few attorneys drafting wills, focus on the critical issue of who pays the tax. The estate tax, even after the 2001 Tax Act, will remain substantial for many millions of taxpayers' estates. You must address a key issue: Who will pay the federal and state estate and inheritance taxes? Which trusts or other beneficiaries under the will should bear the tax burden? Many wills include a special provision addressing this issue, called the "tax allocation clause." Since this subject is complex, the following discussion illustrates one issue to demonstrate the importance of addressing tax allocation matters with your parents and their estate planner. Improperly handled, this provision can cause huge fights among siblings or other heirs.

Example: Dad married wife number four. One of the most common estate tax planning benefits is the unlimited marital deduction. This deduction is available on gifts and bequests to a spouse who is a United States citizen. Qualifying marital gifts or bequests can be made outright (i.e., directly to the spouse) or in a QTIP trust. When a QTIP trust is used, the assets in the trust qualify for an unlimited estate tax marital deduction on the death of the first spouse. On the later death of the second spouse (i.e., the spouse who was the beneficiary of the marital trust), these QTIP trust assets are generally taxable in the estate of the surviving spouse, Dad's fourth wife. Unless the will of wife number four explicitly provides to the contrary (which usually it will not, at least not intentionally), the executor of her estate will recover any estate tax payable with respect to the QTIP assets from the QTIP trust itself, or the beneficiaries of the trust (you and your siblings). This should be the result if wife number four's will does not address this matter. This will also be the result if wife number four's will directs that the QTIP assets bear their own tax. If wife four has a large estate, you could have a bigger tax and inherit less!

Example: Your father dies and is survived by his fourth wife. Your father's estate has allocated $1 million (2002) to a Bypass Trust with the $3 million balance to a QTIP (marital) trust, as income to his second wife for her life. On her death, it will pass to the children of his first marriage (you and your siblings). On the death of your father's fourth wife, her estate consists of $1 million, plus the QTIP assets, which remain worth $3 million. Assume the estate tax is assessed at a flat 50 percent rate. If the tax is $2 million, $500,000 will be paid out of her assets passing to her

children, and $1,500,000 will be paid out of the QTIP passing to you and
your siblings.

What if in the preceding example, your father's will, which
formed the QTIP (marital) trust, and his fourth wife's will were
both drafted to include a tax allocation clause providing that all
taxes should expressly be paid from the QTIP trust (and state law
allows it)? Then you and your siblings would receive the entire QTIP
trust, diminished by estate taxes of $2 million, or a net of $1 million—the same amount that wife number four's children received!
If that is, indeed, what your father and his fourth wife are planning,
make sure your father really understands the consequences.

LESSONS TO LEARN

The ramifications of gift and estate taxes are many and varied.
When attempting to assist your parents in crafting an estate plan,
you can contribute little if you do not understand the basic rules of
these federal tax schemes. Researching these rules and finding a
competent estate-planning attorney with a firm grasp of these issues are key components to ensuring that the government does not
shanghai your inheritance.

Although the 2001 Tax Act effectively protects a larger chunk of
your inheritance, lifetime gifts can still significantly reduce any possible tax. Additionally, the proposed 2010 repeal of the estate tax
may never eventuate. The knowledge of alternative valuation methods for your parents' assets and the particulars of gift tax exclusions can be invaluable to maximizing your inheritance. The
concepts outlined in this chapter can assist you and your parents
when you finally sit down with an estate planner to outline your
needs and wants. This is particularly true if your parents use trusts
to implement their estate plan.

12 IS YOUR MOM'S LAWYER BILLING EXCESSIVE FEES AND EXPENSES?

Legal, accounting, and other professional fees can eat up a large part of an estate. Fees ranging from 1 percent to 10 percent and higher are often justified, appropriate, and helpful to beneficiaries of complex estates. Costs multiply when the estate includes business interests, involves litigation, needs sophisticated tax planning, or requires additional special court procedures (e.g., getting a photocopy of the will admitted by the court because the original was lost). Too often, however, lawyers charge excessive fees and incur unnecessary expenses. Professional advisers who are unscrupulous or inept can take a simple estate and run up fees exceeding those charged by a capable advisers for a complex estate.

Case Study: Bad Bob Jones, Esq., prepared a will for Mr. Lawrence, an elderly New Jersey man. Bad Bob named himself as executor. The only relative and beneficiary of the estate was a daughter, Randi, living in California. When Mr. Lawrence died, Bad Bob began to serve as executor, but he quickly redrew the lines between executor and beneficiary and regularly helped himself to estate assets. Five years after the investigation began, the identification of stolen assets continues. Five years! Bad Bob far exceeded tolerable bounds by paying his own home mortgage out of the estate, paying himself personally as well as his law firm, and failing to maintain proper records. The court estimated that the fees for the estate should

have been $40,000 (that itself being high for what appeared to be a sim-
ple $500,000 estate), yet the first wave of investigation revealed more
than $120,000 of payments; more continue to be found. When called on
the carpet, Bad Bob refused to cooperate with the court, denied everything, and missed court dates. That was probably his undoing. Bad Bob
might one day find himself in jail. Sadly, too many unscrupulous attorneys get away with lesser abuses with little or no consequences.

How can you protect your future inheritance from depredation by
overeager professional advisers? This chapter gives you practical suggestions for helping your parents protect themselves. Protection is
important. Randi, in the preceding case study, will never receive all
the assets to which she is entitled. She will never be fully compen-
sated for the court costs and years of aggravation. She was still for-
tunate, however, because Bob had obtained a bond for serving as
executor. Thus, the independent bonding company became liable to
reimburse the estate for much of the losses. Many beneficiaries are
not so lucky. The pilfered funds are dissipated long before they can
be found, and court and other costs of obtaining retribution usually
out weigh the losses.

Shady probate practices in business are as old as Methuselah.

Celebrity Case Study: Billy Joel, Elton John, and MC Hammer: Their
millions were mismanaged, causing them to file for bankruptcy at the
peak of their careers. If these stars can be taken, so can your parents!

Case Study: The *New Jersey Record News* reported on December 27,
2001, that an attorney who was appointed executor was alleged to have
paid $23,000 from the estate's account for his personal home mortgage.

WHO IS THE HEIR, ANYHOW?

Some lawyers and other professionals involved with estate planning
and probate might view your future inheritance as their personal
retirement fund. To maximize the monies you will receive in the future, you need to understand how to protect yourself and your loved
ones now.

Case Study: A longtime attorney, with what appeared to be a respectable reputation, had prepared a will. The will itself was complete malpractice. No contingent beneficiary was named (i.e., if the one person named to receive assets had died, the estate would have been distributed through intestacy; the will would have been worthless). No tax planning was done, which ultimately would cost the family 50 percent of the money involved (i.e., 50 percent of what was left after the lawyer finished pillaging the estate). This situation could have been avoided through a simple trust, or even by the naming of a successor beneficiary. The attorney did take great care, however, to name his daughter as executrix. The daughter then appointed the father as attorney to represent the estate. The two of them took fees in excess of 7 percent of the estate, plus extras. The executrix then hired her sister-in-law as the broker to sell the decedent's house. All told, the lawyer's family took more than 12 percent of the estate. Their combined fees were about 20 times what the hourly cost would have been to do the little work they did! Sound bad? It was worse.

They did almost nothing properly. They withheld distributing estate assets for more than two and a half years although it was hard to identify any reason for the delay except to increase their fees. All of the decedent's securities were liquidated and the money placed in CDs at low interest rates for the entire period. During this time period, the country experienced one of the greatest bull markets in history. The family lost out on it all but regularly incurred bank charges and other avoidable expenses. The bills for legal services and for services purportedly provided by the executrix were so contrived as to be silly. Does this sound bad enough yet? Well, there is more.

When the heir took them to court for mishandling of the estate's assets, the court not only failed to demand accountability (gotta protect the old boy's club), it permitted the attorney to bill the estate for his time in court (he was there solely because the heir was objecting to the attorney's family pillaging the decedent's estate). The attorney sat in the court waiting for the case to be called for three hours, all of which he billed to the estate. He could have brought other work to do while waiting, but that would have been too fair. So he sat and did nothing, while his clock ticked at the expense of the family.

DO NOT TRUST A LION IN SHEEP'S CLOTHING: CLERGY, TRUSTEES, AND MORE

Those willing to steal your parents' assets, and your inheritance, come in all shapes, sizes, and professions. Often, seemingly innocuous individuals who are being paid or who volunteer to assist you often become a hindrance instead of a help. Whereas most people are well aware of this risk in their daily activities, they may be less vigilant when dealing with professionals, fiduciaries, and religious leaders.

Celebrity Case Study: An individual executor squandered the estate of Doris Duke, the famous tobacco heiress, until the court finally terminated him in favor of an institutional trustee.

Celebrity Case Study: Groucho Marx was disabled by a stroke and hip surgery in 1977. His companion/manager, Erin Fleming, fought against Groucho's three children to control both Groucho and his assets. After he died, the battle over his estate lasted for six years. Groucho's three children as well as his three ex-wives ended up receiving almost nothing from his estate.

It is shocking how often even clergy have been involved in unscrupulous schemes. Although a charitable cause may benefit a worthy organization, you should never be parted from your money before you know all the facts of the matter. Separating someone from his or her assets under false pretenses constitutes fraud whether it is perpetrated by your friendly neighborhood con artist or your trusted family religious adviser.

Case Study: To understand the following case study, you need to review some background regarding charitable planning. Any individuals (e.g., your parents) can set up a charitable remainder trust (CRT) and give all of their assets to the trust. In return, they will receive a monthly check for life. A similar but less complex technique can be used for your parents' home. They can deed their home to a charity and create a life estate, retaining the right to live there for life. They will qualify for a charitable contribution deduction for income tax purposes today, and on their death, the charity will get the home. But what happens if they need their principal? What happens when you, their heir, discover that you will never again visit the house that your parents lived in, your beloved childhood home?

Superficially, it looked like a great plan. The clergyman had convinced the frail elderly widow to give all of her appreciated assets to a CRT. The widow's primary asset was her home. If she gave it to the charitable trust now, the particular charity would be assured of getting it. An attorney on the religious organization's board of directors had conveniently prepared all of the documents for the widow's signature. To be sure her heirs (nieces and nephews) could not successfully challenge her having given all of her assets to charity, the attorney requested another attorney active with the charity to represent the widow when she signed the documents. After all, if she had her own legal representation, then

---

how could the natural heirs claim it was not her wish to do it? The plan would have gone through except that the second attorney, unlike the first, had a few scruples and refused to permit the widow to jeopardize her financial well-being. He stopped the widow from unwittingly disinheriting her nieces and nephews and giving away her only sure source of income in case of dire need. The heirs, in turn, escaped the pain of having shady practices and questionable religious leaders destroy their aunt's financial security and last wishes for bequests.

The wolves can come in all kinds of sheep's clothing. The following examples refer to the exploitation of children's earnings, but they teach the same lesson: Mismanagement destroys assets. For one child athletic star, the wolf came dressed as her parents (look who wanted to "inherit" more!).

Celebrity Case Study: When Dominique Moceanu was 17 years old, she sued her parents for her independence, accusing them of frittering away her earnings and robbing her of her childhood as they pressured her to succeed. When she ran away from home, Moceanu said her parents had even threatened to fire her beloved Romanian coach and have the woman deported. At the time of her suit, Dominique was quoted in the *Houston Chronicle*, "They haven't been working since 1996. Where does their income come from? Me."

Celebrity Case Study: When Jena Malone was a 14-year-old actress with film credits including Kevin Costner's *For Love of the Game* and Susan Sarandon's *Stepmom,* she filed a lawsuit against her mother. She claimed in court papers that her mother had lived off of her income and had mismanaged more than one million dollars of the teenager's earnings, draining her college fund and neglecting to pay $20,000 in back taxes.

Celebrity Case Study: When Jackie Coogan, child actor and namesake of the "Coogan Law," turned 21, he expected to receive the estimated four million dollars he had earned. Because his mother refused to cooperate in releasing the funds to him, he was forced to sue his mother and stepfather for his earnings through the assets of Jackie Coogan Productions, Inc. The suit dragged on in the courts for months, and the settlement was nowhere near the promised fortune. The assets of the company had dwindled to $252,000, of which Jackie received half. The adults who were supposed to be protecting the working child's finances had heedlessly spent the rest of the money. These improprieties led to the 1939 passage of California's Child Actors Bill (Cal. Jurisprudence 36-1).

SO MOM'S WILL SAYS YOU HAVE TO HIRE THE LAW FIRM OF DEWEY, CHEATEM & HOWE

Is there a reason your parents have named a lawyer who wrote their wills as the executor? In many cases, the only reason is that the attorney suggested and drafted the clause. Sometimes, the elderly or infirm are misled to believe that it is necessary to name the attorney preparing the will.

Encourage your parents to ask why their wills contain self-serving statements requiring you, as an heir and executor, to hire a specific law firm. Not only might such a clause be a lawyer's obvious attempt to secure business, generally it cannot be enforced in a court of law. You are always free to hire whomever you desire. If the attorney is a longtime friend, adviser, or confidant, that might explain the situation. Might. But in the earlier example in this chapter, Bad Bob, according to the newspaper accounts, knew Mr. Lawrence "as a friend."

SELECTING A LAWYER TO PROTECT YOUR PARENTS' INTERESTS AND THEIR ESTATE

How should your parents go about retaining a lawyer? They should hire a specialist. If their estate is large and they need tax planning, they should hire a tax attorney who specializes in estate planning. If their estate is small and their major focus is saving their limited assets from nursing home costs, then an attorney who specializes in elder law planning is necessary. They should obtain references, check the attorney out online (or let you do it for them), ask other professionals for referrals, and ask questions. Here are a few signs to watch for:

- Specialists tend to charge more than general practitioners, but tailor documents to achieve your parents' precise goals. Some attorneys mass-produce generic documents that are barely tailored to your parents' situation, but they may still be expensive.

- Qualified estate planners will generally offer several optional planning ideas for most of the concerns your parents raise.

There is almost always more than one way to handle estate planning. Even if the attorney believes a particular approach is best, he can explain other options and why they are not appropriate. There is no one-size-fits-all estate plan.

- Your parents should be wary of any attorney known for, and advocating, a single approach to estate planning. A living trust expert is probably a huckster and not a qualified expert.

- No qualified attorney can quote a price without understanding some general information about the size of your parents' estate. Is their estate large enough to warrant tax planning and if so how much? Is the estate small enough, along with other factors, to suggest elder law planning? The planning, and hence costs, can differ considerably. Some basic family information is necessary as well as a rudimentary understanding of your parents' goals and objectives. Some parents and benefactors want to pursue their lifestyle and simply leave whatever is left to heirs unencumbered. Other parents want to take aggressive efforts to maximize bequests. Still others want to control in great detail a beneficiary's use of money. No expert can estimate a fee without knowing these particulars.

- If the attorney permits you, as a potential heir, to attend all meetings and the will signing, there is definitely a problem. You should be asked to leave at some point during the meetings (assuming your parents invite you to attend). The attorney needs to be certain that you are not unduly influencing your parents to make a bequest to you. You should not be in the room for any portion of the will signing for the same reason. A good attorney might even suggest or insist that your parents make arrangements to get to the attorney's office for the will signing without your assistance. These factors might all become important if there is ever a will challenge.

- The best way for your parents, or any other layperson to assure they have a qualified estate-planning expert is to have a meeting (or if costs are too significant) a telephone conference, with the attorney, their accountant, and their financial planner. Usually it will soon become obvious if one of the professionals is unsatisfactory.

SELECTING A LAWYER WHO WILL PROTECT THE HEIRS' INTERESTS

Once your parents have passed away, how should you retain a lawyer for their estate? First, the person charged with making that decision is the executor named in the will (or if there is a living trust, but no will, the trustee). There are often warning signs if your parents' estate is being taken advantage of. How can you be sure that your parents' assets are properly handled to preserve the maximum amount for you, the rightful heir? How do you structure payments to the lawyers in a way that mitigates their ability to rip you off?

Inquire about the proportion of the firm's work that is concentrated in estates and probate. Do they have the staff, or relationships with other professionals, to handle unique issues that may arise? If the estate owns real estate or is facing litigation, does the firm have the specialized skills or relationships with other firms that can provide them? It is not necessary for any firm to have all the expertise, as long as it can coordinate other professionals involved. You are better off with a firm that acknowledges its limitations, than with a firm that puffs its capabilities to handle anything. What professional credentials do the attorneys have? Do they lecture, write, or take other steps to keep current?

Does the firm have various layers of staff at different billing rates? Many probate matters are routine and can be handled by a beginning level associate, or a paraprofessional, or even a skilled secretary, at a fraction of the cost of a senior lawyer. On the other hand, some probate tax and legal issues are extraordinarily complex and should only be addressed by an experienced attorney. Thus, a broad range of staff is probably in your best interest. There is no reason to pay $350, or more, an hour for a routine matter. Whereas, if you have a complex business valuation issue that is certain to provoke an IRS audit, a senior and experienced estate practitioner should handle that aspect of your parents' estate.

Are you comfortable with their billing practices? Legal fees can be a significant source of probate costs. Will the firm work with you to minimize fees by involving you in administrative or other work? Or when you inquire, do you get the impression that the firm wants to handle all aspects of the estate?

Planning Tip: For a detailed discussion of the roles and criteria for hiring the many different professionals that service an estate, see: Shenkman, *Complete Probate Guide* (John Wiley & Sons, Inc.).

FIDUCIARIES ARE SUPPOSED TO BE TRUSTWORTHY

Who are the executors and/or trustees of the estate and what roles do they play? If a bank is named, what is its function? The term *fiduciary* means a position of trust. A fiduciary duty is a responsibility of care. The executor or trustee is charged with exercising certain care in carrying out the requirements and intent of your parent's will (and any trusts formed in the will). The will (or trust) is the legal document that governs the relationship of the executor (trustee) to the estate assets and to you and the other beneficiaries. This duty of care is imposed under the will and state law. In addition, court cases of your parent's estate also create certain obligations and duties on the executor and trustee. These obligations and responsibilities are intended to protect the beneficiaries, but you and the other beneficiaries need to monitor the proceedings. Beneficiaries should receive replies to questions, be informed in writing of major events, receive releases to sign before any distributions, be entitled to a copy of the will and to an informal or formal accounting of the estate's finances.

FIGHTING CITY HALL

Challenging the abuses illustrated in the examples in this chapter is usually expensive. Because there is no assurance that the court will see the situation in the same light as you and the other beneficiaries, a challenge could be a costly and fruitless exercise. The result, invariably, is that unethical professionals can pillage your parents' estate if you do not protect yourself and the other beneficiaries. Vigilance is the key.

Is this abuse widespread? Real wide—say open sesame! An elderly person with no family nearby is the most susceptible to such abuse. And do not rely on the legal system or courts policing this problem. Sometimes they cover it up. The "old boys' network" continues to function efficiently in some places, thank you. Cover-ups are not common, but not common does not guarantee your protection. If you suspect a problem, get the advice of another experienced professional early on. Do not wait for things to magically work out. Express your concerns in writing. If your concerns are unfounded, the professionals and fiduciaries will be able to clarify the matters involved. For the best protection, have a team—an accountant, attorney, financial planner, and executor—each can keep an eye on the other.

If it is not too late, find a new lawyer, accountant, or trustee. If it is too late to preempt the problem, it may be possible to file a lawsuit to recoup losses caused by unethical or illegal business practices. But the abuse can work the other way too. Some litigators will play on your emotions to pursue frivolous claims. Be sure you're reaching the real problems, not emotions.

WATCHING THE COOKIE JAR

Whenever anyone recommends a professional, institution, or even a layperson to your parents while they are developing their estate plan—or to you and other heirs while you are handling your parents' estate—it behooves you to check out their credentials and reputation. An expeditious Internet search of their name and any related litigation can immediately tell you and your loved ones if this individual is someone who can be trusted. Additionally, a hasty mental computation of the percentage of the total estate that will be eaten up in fees may raise a red flag that someone is trying to take advantage of you or your loved ones.

Lawyers, accountants, and financial planners may act from a position of trust, but that does not mean you should trust them unequivocally. Whereas it is foolish to create problems where they do not exist, it is wise to be alert and to protect those you love from danger when traversing an area that may be so full of risk.

LESSONS TO LEARN

Before people learned not to trust used-car sales pitches, someone had to trust one and get burned. The same holds true of any professional selling a service, or a "friend" named as executor. If your parents, or you as executor, visit a professional who tells you that a costly procedure is essential (possibly performed by a particular expert or that same professional), if it doesn't make sense and the professional can't explain why it's necessary, an alarm should always signal in your head. Likewise, having a team: lawyers, accountants, and financial planners all telling you or a member of your family what to do, your family will be better protected. Checks and balances are key. If you're uncomfortable, your best bet is to seek out a second opinion.

13 DEALING WITH WILL CONTESTS AND LAWSUITS

Your brother and sister got their fair share, why didn't you? Did it happen because your brother and sister were in the hospital room the week before mom died while you were stuck in Timbuktu on a business trip? Did your elder sister, who cared for your mother during her last months, secrete all of her assets so that little would be left for you? Did your dad's girlfriend seduce him just to get his estate at your expense?

Family feuds of the famous regularly appear in the media. James Brown was recently embroiled in a million dollar lawsuit with his two daughters, Denna Brown Thomas and Yamma Brown Lumar, over the right to royalties from his songs.

How do you challenge a will? What are the five ways to best attack a will? When should you not?

Celebrity Case Study: Gene Roddenberry's daughter, Dawn, was disinherited after she ignored her father's instructions not to contest his will. The will asserted that anyone who contested the contents would automatically forfeit any share of the estate. By challenging the will, Dawn forfeited hundreds of millions of dollars even though she withdrew her suit the day it was due to go to court. Her brother, who was executor, brought suit against her on behalf of the estate asserting that she had forfeited her claim when she filed the suit and the court agreed.

So the girlfriend has your dad on videotape before he died explaining why you were left out of the will; how can you attack the videotape to win your case? If you are able to settle before the court date, how do you protect yourself in a properly handled settlement agreement?

Case Study: A classic bequest that commonly causes problems is the family vacation home or residential rental property. This goes wrong so often, and so badly, that no one with real estate should ignore it. Here is a typical scenario. Mom and Dad bought a rental/vacation home at the lake. It has four apartments. They assumed that on their deaths their children would rent it when not using it, and share the use of it in a fair way. After all, for the past 20 years everything had worked like a charm. Mom and Dad overlooked that the "charm" was that they were alive to dictate terms. They overlooked that selfish behavior by any child could jeopardize the other children's inheritance. Before Mom and Dad died—on their request and without any reasonable analysis of the possible problems or their real goals—their attorney had written their will leaving the vacation home to their three children. Following the parents' deaths, their oldest son moved into the vacation home occupying two of the four apartments, leaving the other two rented. As a part owner, he did not feel he had to pay rent. Two years later, his siblings, in exasperation, hired an attorney to deal with the situation.

Even in less extreme cases, who decides when to sell the family farm or vacation home? If the roof goes bad, who pays? Should all the heirs pony up equally? What if one of your siblings uses the property more? What if your brother is wealthy and you are not? Who should pay? What happens if you pay and your sibling does not? Needless to say the key in all these conflicts is to remain on speaking terms with your siblings while protecting what is yours.

HELP YOUR PARENTS SAFEGUARD THEIR WILL
AGAINST ATTACK

Planning to address a will challenge should begin with your parents' first estate-planning meeting, not after a lawsuit has been filed following their death. Prevent angry relatives from challenging your parents' new will in court by having your parents sign another will that their attorney draws up a few months after the new will. Whenever your parents properly sign a new will, all previous wills are generally revoked. But relatives who feel they were unfairly treated in the new document may try to invalidate the new will when your parents die, claiming your parents were not in their right mind when they signed it, or that the person receiving most of their estate (you) unduly influenced them.

Expect your parents' new will to be challenged if they leave a disproportionate amount to one beneficiary. For example, if your parents leave most of their estate to you, but have two children, chances are good that the other child will challenge the new will's validity.

Whenever your parents create a new will with a significantly changed distribution plan, especially one that is not equal, encourage them to consult with an experienced estate planner about signing a similar will a few months later. To differentiate the two wills, they should add some changes that demonstrate they reconsidered the will but have not changed the provisions in question. Your parents might add bequests of charitable gifts—a few thousand dollars to the local library, for example—to their newest will. This addition might help demonstrate to a court that your parents reconsidered their will but remained consistent in their intentions concerning their children.

Also, suggest to your parents that they discuss saving their previous wills with their estate attorney. These documents will help the attorney prove to the court that your parents' most recent intentions were genuine. Several similar wills over a long time period will show a court that they did not write up a new will or change their intentions on a whim. Having similar wills makes it more difficult for disgruntled beneficiaries to invalidate them. Even if the court throws out your parents' latest will, the beneficiaries would have to go through the whole legal process to challenge the previous one and the one before that. This could be a lengthy and costly legal process. Plus, it becomes difficult for a disgruntled heir to demonstrate that your parents were mentally incompetent to make rational decisions concerning their estate if a considerable amount of time elapsed between similar wills.

HOW TO ATTACK A VIDEOTAPED WILL SIGNING

Many people assume that if their parent or benefactor is elderly or infirm that their will-signing ceremony should be videotaped to demonstrate competency and compliance with state law will-signing requirements. Instead of making this assumption, encourage your parents to discuss this carefully with their estate planner. The answer is not simple or clear. The result may depend on how the law in your parents' state of residence views a videotape of a will signing. Your parents also run a real risk with this approach. A videotape can work to your disadvantage. It can highlight in bold any errors that the attorney or others involved in the process made. The disgruntled beneficiaries can hire forensic psychologists to review and analyze the tape, frame by frame, to identify to the court nuances of your parent's conduct that suggest a problem of competency, or uncertainty. "That flinch when asked if she wishes to leave her entire estate to the gardener, suggests she was being coerced. . . ."

EMOTIONS, NOT JUST MONEY, CREATE PROBLEMS WITH OTHER HEIRS

Estate planning is a highly emotional process. Although most estate planners focus on tax savings, the emotional issues inevitably surface and have to be addressed. The reaction of children to wealth, or perceived differences in treatment, can have a tremendous impact on a family.

Parents often have distribution schemes that favor a particular child, or even pit one child against another—whether on purpose or through an oversight. It is essential to address this potential problem with your parents at the earliest possible moment. It happens often enough that you have to try to be cognizant of what is developing, and with your own professional adviser review alternative suggestions. Try to be objective and to help the family as a whole to avoid detrimental emotional factors.

Case Study: Clarence had two daughters and wanted to leave most of his estate to the younger daughter, and have the younger daughter serve as trustee for any moneys given to the older daughter. This scenario is almost guaranteed to be problematic, if not destructive for the family.

It is imperative from a family perspective to address the impact of such a plan. Why are the parents planning their estate in this manner? Is it because of hurt and disappointment they feel as parents? Do they think it is a reasonable plan to address the needs of their children? If someone can help them to stand back and recognize that the decision is not in the best interest of their family, they may be willing to consider alternative suggestions.

The father in the preceding example, may be so full of his own emotions that he does not see that he is pitting sister against sister. A professional estate-planning team can help explain to him that the requested dispositive scheme may fracture the family by drawing battle lines between the children. There is no way that kind of estate plan can work to the advantage of either the sibling managing the funds or the sibling whose funds will be managed. In that kind of situation, all roads lead to a courtroom and expensive legal fees.

LETTER OF INSTRUCTION

It can sometimes be useful for parents to communicate their desires and objectives for provisions in their will. These clarifications, which often are inappropriate to include in a legal document, sometimes suffice to address the hurt feelings or other emotions of confused or angry heirs who feel shorted. Thus, one step in averting a will lawsuit might be for your parents to write a detailed letter to their executor, trustees, heirs, and others.

Their instructions as to how personal jewelry should be distributed could be included. Since this can change frequently, it is often too costly and difficult to continually amend a will to address personal property. Funeral and burial instructions can be described in this letter. This is important since a will is often not available in time to provide this information.

A copy of this letter can be kept in your parents' safe deposit box, a copy given to their executor, and a copy kept with the attorney holding their original will.

The sample letter in this chapter lists some of the points your parents might wish to address. Because of its highly personal nature, a detailed form letter would not be of much help. Encourage your parents to take the time to address the issues important to you.

Caution: If you expect your parents' wills to be challenged, recommend to your parents that they discuss and disclose any letters of instruction to their estate-planning attorney. The attorney might review the letters and advise changes, or suggest other actions. The person challenging the will could use an unartfully drafted letter to demonstrate an ulterior motive, confusion, and so on. Always encourage your parents to get professional advice to avoid undoing the benefits of the rest of their plan.

HANDLING THE PROBLEM OF THE DOT-COM SIBLING

Careful handling of heirs with vastly different lifestyles and financial situations might avert a future will challenge. Suppose that parents have two children. One child is a dot-com multimillionaire, and the other one is a divorced schoolteacher barely making ends meet. What should the parents do? You cannot argue that they are wrong in wanting to give the child in greater need more help. But then will the dot-com kid be hurt? The old adage, "Damned if you do, and damned if you don't" comes to mind.

Case Study: Sally and Harold have two children. Their son is a struggling artist trying to make ends meet. Their daughter is an unmarried successful executive, with a sizable stock option portfolio. Sally and Harold realize their son needs more help, so in their wills they each leave, following the deaths of the last of Sally and Harold, 60 percent of their estate to their son, and 40 percent to their daughter. The decision was agonizing, because they love both children and want what is best for everyone. They want both children to be happy, but they know that their son needs the extra help. Sally died. All of her money is distributed to Harold (and a Bypass Trust for Harold) under her will. When the daughter receives a copy of her mother's will, however, she is furious.

Figure 13.1   Sample Letter of Instruction

Parent-name
Parent-address

June 2, 2009
Mr. Executor-name
123 Main Avenue
Anytown, Some State

RE: *Letter of Instructions*

Dear Executor:

This letter addresses a number of important issues. It is not binding
legally, but it is my hope that you will be morally bound to carry out
its instructions.

1. *Care of Grandchildren.*
   - Upbringing:
   - Type of Home:
   - Education:
   - Summer Camp:
   - Extra Learning Experiences:

2. *Financial Provisions for Children.*
   - Work:
   - Religious Milestones:
   - Wedding:

3. *Burial and Funeral Details.*

4. *Distribution of Personal Property.*

Sincerely,

_____

Parent-name

She verbally abuses her frail father, Harold, and eventually she begins to physically intimidate him. Panic stricken, and tormented by the possibility of the children's relationships being destroyed over money, he revises his will equalizing the bequests. Unfortunately, the damage has been done. The siblings will never get along. The relationship between the daughter and father will also never be the same.

There are several possible solutions to address this type of problem. They all, however, start with the most important first step, which estate planning too often tends to ignore. Everyone involved in this emotional decision is human, with pride, needs, and feelings. Even if you are at war with your parents and/or siblings, you must acknowledge and respect them. Try to help your parents work through the planning stages of their estate in a manner that creates the least friction, and, when possible, stimulates healing.

In some, perhaps even in many circumstances, open and frank discussions with your parents about their concerns, goals, and worries may solve the problem. In the preceding example, if Sally and Harold's daughter had been brought into the estate-planning discussions and told frankly that her brother needed financial help, it might have avoided much angst and bitterness. How? The openness and regard the parents would have shown for her feelings by bringing her into the discussion may have been enough.

Another approach is for your parents to equalize their heirs, but to handle the wealthy and poorer heirs' bequests in different ways. For example, the poorer sibling may be poorer as a result of being a spendthrift, being irresponsible, not focusing on investments, and so on. Perhaps then the answer is not in dividing assets differently, but instead, in controlling the less astute sibling's assets for his or her benefit. This can be done in a constructive and positive way, or at least in a way less likely to assure the family's destruction.

Celebrity Case Study: Jay A. Pritzker, the wealthy Chicago patriarch, held a meeting to discuss the distribution of the Pritzker billions in assets to family members. The success of this was highlighted in a *New York Times* headline "Knives Drawn for a $15 Billion Family Pie"! Liesel Pritzker, age 18, is suing the family, claiming her trust funds were emptied to benefit other members of the family.

In other situations, it is really an issue of less financial resources, not irresponsibility. Parents can address this in many ways that are

less offensive, and less blatant, than simply distributing more to the
needy sibling.

Case Study: Larry Jones had two children, Rich Daughter and Poor
Son. If Larry were to give more money to Poor Son, he might alienate the
affections of Rich Daughter. His bigger concern was simply that "stuff
happens." What if Rich Daughter's stock options should become worthless, or she should develop a major uninsured health problem? What if he
were to give more assets to Poor Son and Poor Son thereafter would win
a lottery or sell one of his paintings and become wealthy? The problem
with the simplistic approach is that it can create disaster if the circumstances change. Instead, Larry divided his estate into three equal parts.
He gave one equal part to each child. The third equal part was to be held
in a trust for everyone. On the face of it, this approach looked equal for
both children. Reality is that if circumstances did not change, Poor Son's
children would get far more, if not all, of the monies in the trust. Importantly, there was no statement that one child was to be favored over
the other. It was not even implied. And if circumstances were to reverse
in the future and the formerly Rich Daughter needed help, the flexibility was built into the plan to make that happen as well.

A sample clause can illustrate how such a trust could be implemented in your parents' estate plan:

Sample Language: The Executor shall pay to my Trustee, in trust an
amount equal to one-third (⅓) of my residuary estate. The Trustee, shall
hold the amount determined in this provision, in trust, to be held in a single trust for all of my Children (my Children are Rich Daughter and Poor
Son only) and Grandchildren to be disposed of as follows:
   The Trustee is hereby directed to manage, invest, and reinvest the
same, to collect the income thereof, and to pay over the net income
and/or principal of the Trust to or for the benefit of such one or more
of my Children and Grandchildren living from time to time, to such extent, in such amount and proportions, and at such time or times as the
Trustee shall determine in accordance with the Standard for Payment,
below. I suggest, but do not require, that the trustee consider the different economic circumstances of my Children when making distribution decisions. Any net income not so paid over or applied shall be
accumulated, and added to the Trust Estate at least annually and
thereafter shall be held, administered, and disposed of as a part of the
Trust Estate.
   This Trust shall terminate upon the first to occur of the following
events: (i) Upon the youngest of my Grandchildren living upon my death
reaching the age of Thirty-Five (35) years; or (ii) Upon the death of my
youngest Grandchild living at any time if my other Grandchildren living
shall all have then reached the age of Thirty-Five (35) years; or (iii) Upon
the death of the last to die of all my Grandchildren if none of them shall
reach the age of Thirty-Five (35) years.

> Upon the termination of this Trust, the Trustee shall transfer, and pay over the principal of the Trust to my then living Grandchildren in equal shares (per capita and not per stirpes), provided, however, that if a Grandchild is not then living but has then living issue the share to which such deceased Grandchild would have been entitled had such Grandchild then been living shall be paid to the issue of such Grandchild, per stirpes, outright and free of trust for any of my Grandchildren or more remote descendants who are then over age Thirty-Five (35), or in trust for any of my Grandchildren or more remote descendants who are then under age Thirty-Five (35) in accordance with the trust for persons under age Thirty-Five (35) [elsewhere in the will].

ENCOURAGE YOUR PARENTS TO PICK FIDUCIARIES CAREFULLY

When Larry (in the previous example) gave one-third of his estate to each child and the remaining third to a trust for both children and their descendants, who should have been in charge of that trust? If Larry named his two children jointly (i.e., to serve as cotrustees) it might have worked if both were responsible, fair, and not influenced by others (such as their respective spouses). However, conflict would have been inherent in the plan because one pot of money, the trust, was available for distribution to each child and that child's children. In many, perhaps most, cases naming the children to be in charge of that type of decision could be an invitation to disaster.

If your parents want your inheritance to be well managed while minimizing friction between you and your siblings, they have to select a trustee, or group of trustees, who can make the tough decisions, show independence, and minimize if not avoid, sibling rivalry. This might be a family friend, or a bank or trust company. Perhaps you and your siblings could serve, with the family friend, bank, or trust company being the trustee to break ties.

SHOULD YOUR PARENTS USE AN "IN TERROREM" PROVISION IN THEIR WILL?

If your parents expect a disgruntled heir to sue, they should discuss with their attorney the pros and cons of including what is called an *In Terrorem* provision in their wills. This provision provides that anyone challenging the will should not be entitled to any inheritance under the will. Depending on state law and the circumstances of your parents' estate, this provision may not be upheld in court.

Sample Clause: If any beneficiary under my Will in any manner, directly or indirectly, contests this will or any of its provisions, any share or interest in my estate given to the contesting beneficiary under my Will is revoked and shall be disposed of in the same manner provided herein as if the contesting beneficiary and his or her issue had predeceased me.

WILL CHALLENGES

Lawsuits challenging wills are burgeoning, and could undermine your inheritance. Alternatively, a will challenge might be the only way for you to secure the inheritance you were cheated out of. The large values of estate transfers of wealth that are now occurring stimulate lawsuits, just because of the dollars involved. Society has changed. The Cleaver family is no longer. The increasing complexity of many family structures—blended families, nontraditional families, second, third, and later marriages, make the prospect of a will challenge more likely. If American society still reflected the *Leave It to Beaver* family that many politicians extol, wills would be simple. On Ward's death, all to June. On June's death half to Wally and half to Beaver. Simple. Done in a half-hour episode. But not particularly common.

Demographic changes compounded by the litigious nature of many baby boomers who are the beneficiaries of these large wealth transfers assures that estate litigators will be busy for decades. If you are a beneficiary whose siblings, mom's new beau, or others, have shut out of a will, you need to understand when you can challenge a will to protect your rights. If you are serving as an executor, or are simply a beneficiary under Aunt Edna's will, you should be familiar with some of the more common will challenges by others so you can protect the estate and your inheritance.

Hurt feelings can trigger a will challenge. "Why didn't Uncle Joe give me as much as my brother?" When a beneficiary receives less than expected, a will challenge may result. If a parent disinherits a child, that child might seek to challenge the will. Whether the challenge is primarily to assuage the hurt of a will clause confirming a parent's lack of love ("For reasons best known to me, I leave nothing to my son John"), or for the money, a challenge is nevertheless more likely.

In many instances, a will challenge is the result of problems with the will itself. The document may not have been signed with the proper formality required by state law. It may have lacked the requisite language in the document or not had the proper number of witnesses, or the witnesses may have been disqualified. For example, all of the witnesses may have been beneficiaries. These are the reasons this book has consistently advised you to have your parents hire a specialist, even if the cost is greater, than to use an attorney who concentrates on house closings or automobile accident cases.

In some instances, there might have actually been fraud or duress when your parent signed the will. Fraud could have occurred if the will signed was not the one your parent intended (a switch was intentionally made). Duress could have occurred if your burly older brother intimidated mom to sign a will leaving him most of her estate when mom did not really want to sign. If your dad was suffering from Alzheimer's disease and did not sufficiently understand what he was signing, a challenge may result.

Why challenge a will? If you succeed in challenging the will, you may be able to convince the court to write your name in the will where it was arguably forgotten. For example, your three cousins were listed as sharing equally in a $600,000 distribution. Your name was not listed. Perhaps the testator, your uncle, merely forgot your name. Perhaps your estranged cousins conspired against you by influencing your uncle to leave your name out of the will so that their shares would be larger. You may want to challenge the will to assure an inheritance.

What happens if your siblings challenge your parent's will and succeed? In most situations, the executor will probably try to negotiate a settlement with them, sign an agreement settling all disagreements, obtain a release, and get their consent to the will being admitted, in order to complete probate. This can save a fortune of time and expense, not to mention personal angst. Settling, even if it requires paying tens of thousands of dollars to your hated half-brother, may also be advantageous for all when compared with the costs of litigation. Your parent's executor might push for a settlement if he thinks that it will be less costly than the estate attorney's estimated likely costs of fighting the lawsuit.

If you are the executor, be certain to discuss with a probate litigation attorney whether you should obtain the approval of any or all of the beneficiaries or other people affected by the outcome of the suit and settlement. You do not want to later be sued by the beneficiaries you thought you were protecting with the settlement. In other cases, if the will challenge is successful, the entire will may be thrown out and you may no longer be able to serve as executor. If the will is disregarded, and your parent had signed a will prior to the will thrown out in the will challenge, that next most recently signed prior will may be reinstated. Where there was no prior will, it will be as if your parent had died without any will (intestate). Then state law will dictate who receives how much of your parent's estate.

If a person would inherit under the state law intestacy statute, but the will gave him or her nothing, then a successful will challenge could provide a windfall. This is sadly the motivation behind many will challenges.

On what basis can someone challenge a will? One of the most common justifications for a will challenge is the mental incompetence of the person signing the will. If your parent did not have a sufficient frame of mind to understand and sign the will, it cannot be valid. The second typical basis for challenging a will is undue influence. This is when someone coerces or even forces your parent to sign a will. These two reasons are often, but not always, used together when a potential heir attacks a will. Although your parent might have been incompetent but not subject to undue influence, usually mental incapacity makes a person more likely to fall prey to undue influence.

How does the challenger prove undue influence? The initial burden of proof is on the person challenging the will. This means the challenger must prove it occurred. However, the courts understand full well that undue influence often occurs in secrecy. Few people, unless they are on the *Jerry Springer Show*, are going to advertise that they are threatening old Uncle Steve if he does not add them to his will. The threats are more typically on Uncle Steve's yacht where the nearest witness is farther away than screams can carry. This is why many courts allow a shift of burden of proof if the person challenging the will can demonstrate that a confidential relationship existed between your parent and the person exercising the undue influence under suspicious circumstances. A confidential relationship exists if your parent was dependent on the person exercising the undue influence. For example, Nephew Tom threatened housebound Aunt Jane that he would stop doing food shopping for her unless his share under her will was increased. Shifting the burden of proving the case is important because the person who has the burden to prove the case is more likely to lose.

How do you defend the estate and the will against a challenge? First, do not try without competent legal assistance. A probate attorney or estate planner may not have the expertise. You want an attorney who specializes in probate or litigation, with considerable experience in estate litigation. Often, this will be a specialist other than the specific attorney who has assisted you with planning and probate matters.

If the will challenge is based on the decedent not having sufficient mental capacity, to protect the integrity of the will you will have to prove that your parent had sufficient capacity. Competency means that mom understood the nature and extent of her assets. Did she know what she owned? Did mom understand the natural objects of her bounty? This usually includes family members. This does not mean that mom had to name family members as beneficiaries, but she must have understood who her family members were and that she was not naming them. Mom should have understood that the purpose of her signing the paper in front of her was to execute her last will. She must have understood that by executing the will she was directing where her assets were to be distributed following her death.

Competency of your parent can be demonstrated through witness testimony. What did the lawyer who supervised the will ask your parent at the will signing? What did your parent answer? What was the recollection of the witnesses to the will? Did the lawyer prepare a memorandum to the file or other notes demonstrating your parent's mental state and condition? It may be worthwhile to poll the people who had regular daily or weekly contact with your parent for their thoughts, observations, and opinions about your parent's mental state, at or about the time period when the will was signed. Try to develop a description and picture about your parent and his life. What people were important in your parent's life? What motivated your parent to favor you over another beneficiary? How can you demonstrate the relationship your parent had with the persons who were left out of the will or not favored in the will? Was your parent under the care of a physician? If so, the physician who treated your parent might be in the best position to testify about the your parent's competency. The physician may have seen your parent on a regular basis and may have asked a series of relatively common questions on medical history, lifestyle, and so on. If mom was taking medication, the physician may have asked numerous questions to be certain that she was handling the medication physically and to assure that she was taking the medication at the appropriate times and in the appropriate quantities. This can be persuasive proof in a competency test. The competency determination is at the time the will was signed. Even if mom was not competent sometime after she signed the will, as long as it can be demonstrated that she was competent when signing it, the will can sustain the challenge. It is not uncommon for a person to have a lucid interval of competence between periods of incompetence. However, it can be difficult to prove this.

If you are faced with a will contest or other estate litigation—no matter which side of the fence you are on—the best bet in most cases is to settle rather than go through full-blown litigation. An illustrative settlement agreement appears in the For Your Notebook section.

LESSONS TO LEARN

There are literally millions of reasons one of your parents' heirs may have inherited more than the others. If you are the heir who is left out in the cold, you have several options. Your first choice is simply to sue. Although that may satisfy your outraged ego, it might not be the best course of action as it is expensive and it will surely strain whatever future relations you may have with your fellow heirs. Determining whether this is the appropriate next step may require a determination of why you were left out. Did the named heirs have the opportunity to exert undue influence on your parents before they died? Were there last-minute changes in the will that cannot be explained away by any means other than foul play? Were you estranged from your parents? Is it possible that there was no time after reconciling for them to change their will? If the answer to any of these questions is yes, you may seriously want to consider hiring a lawyer to cut you a slice of the pie. On the other hand, trying to understand why your parents might have validly wished to divvy up their estate as prescribed may save you a lot of money in legal fees and a few close family relationships.

Reasons other than estrangement or foul play might spur your parents to divide their estate on a less than equal basis. Often, estate plans center around your parents' perceptions of who needs more and who can provide for themselves. If you can discuss these concerns with your parents while they are still alive, you may save yourself much heartache later. Open and frank discourse can allow you to reconcile any differences you and your parents may have, as well as protect your inheritance by providing your parents with alternative methods to assist their financially less secure children. Alternatively, if you are the financially less secure child, you may be able to convince your parents of your greater need so they can address it in their estate plan through trusts or outright bequests.

FOR YOUR NOTEBOOK

SAMPLE SETTLEMENT AGREEMENT

Settlement Agreement

State of SomeState
Surrogate's Court
County of Big
- -X
                                                    :
Accounting of Tina Trophy as Executrix   :   Agreement Settling
of the   :   Account
                                                    :
Last Will and Testament of   :
                                                    :
        Father P. BigBucks,   :
                                                    :   File No. _____
        Deceased.   :
- -X

AGREEMENT made as of the 9th day of March 2005, by and among Tina Trophy BigBucks as Executrix of the Last Will and Testament of Father P. BigBucks, deceased (in such capacity, the "Executrix"); Tom Jones as trustee of the Father BigBucks Family Trust ("Bypass Trust"); Tina Trophy BigBucks, Nancy Niece, Daughter Big-Bucks, and Ina Inheritor (collectively, the "Beneficiaries").

RECITALS

1. **WHEREAS,** Father P. BigBucks (the "Decedent") died on August 13, 2003, a resident of, and domiciled in, the County of Bergen, State of SomeState.

2. **WHEREAS,** The Decedent's Will was admitted to probate and Letters Testamentary were issued to the Executrix by the Surrogate's court, County of Bergen, State of SomeState on January 4, 2004.

3. **WHEREAS,** No formal objections to the probate of the Decedent's Last Will and Testament dated June 4, 2001 (the "Will") were filed, however, each party hereto has and raises objections to the provisions therein, as set forth herein below.

4. **WHEREAS,** This Agreement Settling Account ("Settlement") reflects the settlement of all claims by all parties hereto against each other concerning the Decedent's estate (the "Estate"), the Bypass Trust, each other with respect to the Estate and Bypass Trust (the "Business Interests").

5. **WHEREAS,** Pursuant to Will, Ina Inheritor did not receive any bequest.

6. **WHEREAS,** The Executrix wishes to render an account of her acts and proceedings as such Executrix from the date of death to the closing and final distribution of the Estate (the "Accounting Period"); to make final distribution of the Estate in the manner hereinafter provided; and to be discharged by the Beneficiaries and all Parties hereto of and from any and all liability for the Executrix's actions with respect to the Estate, the Bypass Trust, and the Businesses, during the Accounting Period and in making such final distribution.

7. **WHEREAS,** The Beneficiaries and other Parties hereto wish to avoid the expense and delay that would attend the judicial settlement of such an account, and have requested the Executrix to submit to them an account (the "Account") of the Executrix's acts and proceedings for the Accounting Period in the form of the Schedules annexed hereto, which Schedules all Parties hereto have and hereby do accept as complete, accurate, and reflective of the settlement herein made.

8. **WHEREAS,** The Parties hereto hereby accept, in lieu of a judicial settlement of the Account, or any formal accounting, the Settlement herein reflected and the releases and indemnities hereinafter provided.

9. **WHEREAS,** The Executrix has submitted the Account to each of the Beneficiaries and other Parties hereto, and each of the Beneficiaries and other Parties hereto has examined the Account and is satisfied that the Account contains in all respects a full, complete, and true statement of all of the acts and proceedings of the Executrix in connection with the administration of the Estate during the Accounting Period,

and that there is no error or omission in the Account to the prejudice of any of the Beneficiaries.

10. **WHEREAS,** All of the individual Parties hereto are of full age and sound mind and are fully advised of their rights in the premises, and each entity which is a Party hereto has full right and authority to make the agreement and accept the Settlement herein.

NOW, THEREFORE, in consideration of the foregoing premises, specifically incorporated herein by reference and the mutual covenants and agreements herein contained, and of the agreement by the Executrix, at the request of the Beneficiaries and other Parties, to render the Account in the form annexed hereto without requiring the preparation of an account in form that would permit it to be judicially settled and without requiring a judicial settlement of the Account at this time, and of other good and valuable consideration, receipt of which is hereby acknowledged:

a. Each of the Beneficiaries and other Parties hereto does hereby acknowledge and agree that the Account is in all respects just, true, proper and correct and that it contains a full disclosure of all of the acts and proceedings of the Executrix in connection with the administration of the Estate during the Accounting Period, the funding of the Bypass Trust, the operation and distribution of the Businesses, the interpretation and application of the Will, and all other matters relating directly or indirectly to the Will, the Bypass Trust, the Businesses, the Estate, and the affairs of the Decedent.

b. Each of the Beneficiaries and other Parties hereto does hereby ratify, approve and confirm the Account and each and every one of the acts, proceedings, collections, and disbursements set forth therein, and waives the right to enforce the judicial settlement of the Account.

c. Each of the Beneficiaries hereto does hereby consent to the following:

(1) The payment of Larry Lawyer unpaid legal fees and disbursements.

(2) The payment of the sum of $10,000 to Tina Trophy BigBucks, which constitutes Executrix's commissions.

(3) The waiver of trustee commissions to the Trustee of the Bypass Trust.

d. Each of the Beneficiaries does hereby acknowledge receipt from the Executrix of the final distribution of the property due each Beneficiary as set forth in the manner provided herein and in the Account.

e. Each of the Beneficiaries does hereby remise, release, and forever discharge the Executrix, individually and as such Executrix, of and from any and all, and all manner of, action and actions, cause and causes of action, suits, debts, dues, sums of money, accounts, reckonings, bonds, bills, specialties, covenants, contracts, controversies, agreements, promises, variances, trespasses, damages, judgments, incidents, executions, claims, and demands whatever, whether in law or in equity, which she or he ever had, now has or shall or may have for, upon, or by reason of any act, omission, collection, disbursement, cause, matter or thing whatsoever, recited, contained, appearing or set forth in the Account or in this Agreement Settling Account, or reasonably to be inferred from anything therein or herein contained, or for, upon or by reason of anything done or omitted to be done by the Executrix in the administration of, or otherwise in connection with the Estate, or in making final distribution of the property of the Estate remaining in the Executrix' hand and of the income, if any, received therefrom subsequent to the Accounting Period in the manner provided herein and in the Account.

f. Each of the Beneficiaries agrees to, and does hereby, indemnify and save harmless the Executrix, individually and as such Executrix, from any and all liabilities, damages, losses, charges, fees, costs, and expenses of whatever kind or nature (including reasonable counsel fees) not to exceed, however, an amount equal to the value of the property distributed to each Beneficiary, which the Executrix shall at any time sustain or incur by reason of any objection, demand, or claim of whatever kind or nature made or asserted against the Executrix by anyone for, upon, or by reason of any action, omission, collection, disbursement, cause, matter or thing whatsoever recited, contained, appearing or set forth in the Account or in this Agreement Settling Account, or reasonably to be inferred from anything therein or herein contained, or for, upon or by reason of anything done or omitted to be done by the Executrix in the administration of, or otherwise in connection with, the Estate, or in making final distribution of the property of the Estate remaining in the Executrix's hand and of the income, if any, received therefrom subsequent to the Accounting Period in the manner provided herein and in the Account.

g. The parties hereto agree that the Executrix may at any time, if the Executrix in their sole and absolute discretion shall deem it advisable to do so, and without notice to any party hereto, either (a) record or file this Agreement Settling Account and/or the Account in accordance with the provisions of any statute, law or rule of court of the State of SomeState or of any other State as an instrument settling the account of the Executrix for the Accounting Period or (b) institute or conduct legal proceedings to obtain a judicial settlement of the Account, if in the sole discretion of the Executrix, they shall deem it advisable to do so, and in either event, each of the Beneficiaries does hereby waive the issuance and service of process and does hereby consent that a decree judicially settling the Account be made, settled, and entered without any notice to them.

h. Each of the Beneficiaries shall, and does hereby, certify that she or he has heretofore made no sale, mortgage, pledge, assignment, gift, or other transfer of her or his right, title, and interest in and to the Estate.

i. The Executrix warrant and agree, at the Beneficiaries' request, to execute such other documents and instruments and take all such actions as shall be necessary and proper to effect the final disposition of the property in the manner provided herein and in the Account.

j. In consideration of the distribution to the Beneficiaries of all amounts due to the Beneficiaries as provided in the Will, the Beneficiaries agree to repay to the Executrix for the benefit of the Estate, any amounts which may be required to satisfy taxes or other obligations of the Estate which may hereafter become payable, including, but not limited to counsel fees and other administration expenses, not to exceed, however, an amount equal to the value of the property distributed to each Beneficiary.

k. The parties hereto agree that the provisions of this Agreement Settling Account shall be binding upon and shall inure to the benefit of the respective heirs, legatees, legal representatives, successors, and assigns of the parties hereto.

l. The parties hereto agree that this Agreement Settling Account (a) constitutes the entire understanding among the parties, (b) may be executed in one or more counterparts, the aggregate of which shall be deemed to constitute the original thereof, (c) cannot be changed without a duly acknowledged writing, and (d) shall be construed in accordance with the Law of the State of SomeState.

IN WITNESS WHEREOF, each of the parties hereto has executed this Agreement Settling Account, all as of the day and year first above written.

Tina Trophy BigBucks, Executrix and
Beneficiary and Bypass Trust Trustee

Nancy Niece, Remainder Beneficiary

Daughter BigBucks, Remainder
         Beneficiary, Bypass Trust Co
         Trustee, manager of Businesses

14 PREVENTING YOUR EX-SPOUSE FROM RUNNING OFF WITH YOUR INHERITED ASSETS

With almost half of all marriages ending in divorce, caution is in order if your parents plan on bequeathing assets to you, especially a family business or rental property. If they simply give assets outright to you on their death, you may (as is the norm) mix those assets with other assets you own with your spouse. In the event of a divorce, you may end up splitting those commingled assets 50/50 (or what is left after legal fees) with your ex. Not the result you or your parents want.

Losing money is bad enough, but what about eventually dealing with an ex-husband in the family business? Or your ex-wife owning stock in a family business she has never worked in? Dealing with a friendly divorce (although pundits say there is no such thing) is hard enough. Dealing with a messy divorce is even harder. If you add the trauma of later having to deal with your ex-spouse on a daily basis at your family place of business, it can be more than most people can reasonably handle. Planning can help prevent that kind of stressful situation. Inheriting more does not simply mean putting your parents' house in order. Often it means seeing to your own, as well.

If you have or expect an inheritance or large gifts, hire a matrimonial attorney to address planning risks. If you are not yet married, the matrimonial attorney can coordinate the planning with your estate planner to minimize the risk of losing the assets your parents give or bequeath to you. This planning might include establishing trusts to segregate and control the assets. If you have not yet received the gifts or inheritance, you might be able to persuade your parent to give or bequeath the assets in trust for your benefit, instead of giving or bequeathing the asset to you directly. In all cases, action is required.

SIGNING A PRENUPTIAL AGREEMENT TO RETAIN BENEFICIARY STATUS

Some parents, distraught over the financial devastation of divorce, have endeavored to assure that an heir will execute a prenuptial agreement before marriage by incorporating *in Terrorem* provisions into their wills and trusts. Such clauses mandate that if you fail to sign a prenuptial agreement, you will lose your status as a distributee under their will or trust, or face a more restrictive standard for receiving distributions (e.g., ascertainable standard instead of comfort and welfare). If your parents have taken this approach, you may have no choice.

PRENUPTIAL AGREEMENTS

The prenuptial agreement is the first line of defense in dividing up personal and marital assets. Such agreements have been the subject of much press for the rich and famous (e.g., Michael Jackson and Lisa Marie Presley's minute-long marriage and J-Lo's two-minute marriage). In planning to inherit more, three very distinct uses of prenuptial agreements are necessary:

1. If your parent remarries, they should sign a prenuptial agreement to protect their assets in the event their marriage ends in

divorce, and to control what will happen to their assets if they die while married to their new spouse.

2. To protect your inherited assets from your spouse.
3. To protect a family business from a sibling's divorce.

A prenuptial agreement addresses what will happen if your parent's second or your future marriage ends in separation or divorce. Since most concepts apply similarly to your parent's remarriage or your marriage, the discussion will be in the context of your situation. Its goal is to limit what your ex-spouse can expect from you economically. If you anticipate, or already have, a large gift or inheritance, the prenuptial agreement might provide that these assets, and the income from them, are to be expressly excluded from consideration in a divorce, or that the amount will be limited as agreed. Prenuptial agreements are commonly used where the two parties to the marriage have very different economic situations. It is also advised for second and later marriages when either you or your new spouse has financial obligations predating the marriage. The problem is that in many states a divorce court might, even informally, consider what you own in reaching its conclusion.

The rules differ from state to state, so specific legal advice from a matrimonial or family law attorney is essential. For a prenuptial agreement to be valid:

- You and your prospective spouse should each be represented by an independent attorney.

- The agreement should be signed in advance of the marriage (not on the way down the aisle—the longer before the marriage the better).

- The agreement should be signed, witnessed, and notarized with the same formality used for a real estate deed.

- You and your prospective spouse must make full and clear disclosures of what you each own and owe. It is often best, and may even be required in your state, to attach detailed balance sheets to the agreement. If you have a large inheritance, it should be identified in the agreement and clearly segregated in an account indicating that it is inherited. State law varies, but the more that you disclose the more likely that the agreement from your perspective should be respected. If you will not disclose everything, have your future spouse waive the right to the disclosures acknowledging that she was not informed of everything. Be certain that your attorney advises you as to the impact of not fully disclosing the validity of the agreement. You might change your mind.

- The agreement should be fair and reasonable. These terms are impossible to define, so you should take any steps possible to demonstrate why the agreement was fair or reasonable. If you have a huge inheritance you want to keep separate, the fact that your future spouse has an income adequate to support her might be helpful.

- Steps should be taken to corroborate that your future spouse was not signing under duress, because of fraud, and that you were not overreaching.

The prenuptial agreement should endeavor to address all legal, tax, and financial issues that might be relevant. These include the law that will govern the agreement (which state). What alimony or support rights will your spouse have in the event of divorce? Is your future spouse releasing any of her rights to support or property settlement in the event of a divorce? Are you obligated to leave anything to your new spouse in your will, or is she partly or entirely waiving what she would be entitled to under state law? You might wish to include specific language about keeping assets separate to limit creditors' claims on your estate, especially a creditor of your future spouse.

POSTNUPTIAL AGREEMENTS

Postnuptial agreements are the next line of protection for personal assets in a marriage. They do not have the same protective value in most cases as a prenuptial agreement because they are being signed during the course of the marriage. However, if a large gift or inheritance is coming your way, it might well be worthwhile.

Planning Tip: If you are uncomfortable telling your spouse that you need a postnuptial agreement, have your folks insist on it before the gift; let them be the bad guys.

Just because you did not think to have your spouse sign a prenuptial agreement does not mean you cannot try to protect your future gifts or inheritance. Throughout the course of your marriage, earnings may fluctuate wildly and a spouse will often receive special bequests from deceased loved ones. Even if you have been married for 30 years and everything seems peachy, consider having a lawyer draw up an agreement between you and your spouse that any assets you receive as an inheritance and the income therefrom shall remain yours alone and will not become a marital asset. Even if inherited assets are considered immune from matrimonial claims under your state's laws, a written acknowledgment can be a useful additional safeguard. For example, such an acknowledgment may avoid a fight during a later divorce over which assets are inherited.

If a postnuptial agreement is to be entered into, are you planning on giving assets to your spouse? Review with your matrimonial attorney what you need to do for the agreement to have validity.

A common reason for a postnuptial agreement is to protect a family business by having your spouse opt out of receiving business interests from your family in exchange for your typically giving her other nonbusiness assets.

PROTECTING SEPARATE ASSETS FROM YOUR EX-SPOUSE

Assets that you received as gifts or inheritances are separate property that your ex-spouse should not reach as long as you retain the separate identity of these assets, and do not transmute them into marital property (the extent and requirements for this will depend on state law). Keep any gift or inheritance separate. If the amounts are moderate, set up a special brokerage or bank account to hold solely these separate assets. If the amounts involved are large, consider setting up a special revocable living trust as an accounting entity to keep gifts or inherited property separate. If you have separate property and your ex-spouse contributed to its appreciation (e.g., she helped you pick the stocks, she ran the computer program that helped you select the asset allocation model) that appreciation may become marital, warns Amy J. Amundsen, Esq., of Memphis, Tennessee.

If you have separate property, save the documents demonstrating that you received it as separate property. If you can, ask your parents, or your aunt, or whoever else gave you gifts, to provide you with a copy of the checks. If the amounts were more substantial, obtain copies of the gift tax returns from your parents or whoever made the gifts. For inheritance, try to obtain a copy of the federal estate tax return that demonstrates what you received. If the estate was smaller than the amount required to file a federal estate tax return, obtain a copy of a state tax filing. Many states have inheritance or other taxes that are assessed at levels much lower than the federal estate tax. If these are not available, try to obtain a copy of the will and any releases signed when assets were distributed. These items can all help to confirm the separate nature of the assets.

If your marriage was relatively short lived, some assets you owned before the marriage may be held outside the settlement. Review this with your attorney since the laws will differ from state to state and will depend heavily on the facts involved.

You have to be careful how you handle separate assets. In one case, the husband, Joe, used separate trust fund assets to directly pay from the trust for personal expenses, from vacations to a new sports car for the wife. Later, the husband transferred cash from his business to the trust to replace the monies previously spent. The amount of marital expenses funded from the trust, and the frequent commingling of marital assets (i.e., business earnings) with the separate property in the husband's trust resulted in the court finding that the trust assets had been so commingled, and the independence of the separate property so totally disregarded, that the entire trust was treated as a marital asset.

GETTING A RECALCITRANT SIBLING TO SIGN A PRENUPTIAL AGREEMENT

If you do not want to risk your parents' hard-earned business assets being distributed to an ex-son/daughter-in-law, consider advising your parents to bequeath their assets in a manner that excludes any child who has not signed a prenuptial or postnuptial agreement. No agreement, no inheritance. This is rough stuff and likely to cause a lot of heartache . . . but maybe not. Your sibling can say to his or her beloved, "Look, I trust you and don't need a prenuptial agreement. But mom and dad will exclude me from my inheritance if I don't sign one!" Your parents may just take the burden off your sibling so that he or she can insist on what they may have actually believed was reasonable. This could also give you a bargaining chip in dealing with your own spouse when discussing pre- and postnuptial agreements. Be sure to check with a matrimonial attorney in your state before trying this technique.

HOW TO PROTECT STOCK IN YOUR FAMILY BUSINESS FROM AN EX-SON-IN-LAW

In many cases, the soon-to-be-married couple will not sign a comprehensive prenuptial agreement, however advisable from a legal, tax, and financial standpoint. In some of these situations, when a family business is involved, the family may be concerned about protecting the stock in the family business from attack in a divorce. If this concern is sufficiently strong, the family may insist that the soon-to-be-married family member who owns stock (or partnership or other family business interests) sign at least a limited agreement to protect the family business. Other steps are also important to protect the family business. There should be a comprehensive shareholders' (partnership or operating) agreement between all of the owners. This agreement should delineate the restrictions on transfer, control issues, and so on. Some attorneys even have the new spouse or the son/daughter-in-law execute a copy of the entity's agreement (e.g., shareholders' agreement for a corporation) in the limited capacity of stating they agree to the nontransfer provisions. Discuss this issue with both your corporate and matrimonial attorneys.

Sample Form: For a sample form, see www.laweasy.com, Divorce Forms.

Consider with your corporate attorney what provisions should be in the entity's documents as well. If gifts of stock in a family business are to be made, consider making the gifts into trusts for the benefit of the donee, instead of directly to the donee. If spouses are to receive the economic benefit of shares, consider using inter vivos marital trusts such as an inter vivos qualified terminable interest property trust (QTIP).

DOES YOUR OR YOUR PARENT'S PARTNER HAVE A CLAIM ON YOUR INHERITANCE?

There are $5.5 million people living together who are not married. This figure has grown 72 percent in the past decade, according to a recent issue of *Money* magazine. The demographic trend is increasing. This includes not only same-sex partners but many elderly who choose for financial or personal reasons not to marry. In fact, this trend cuts across all socioeconomic levels. If you or your parent is in this group, consult a family lawyer about whether you or your parent should have a contractual arrangement governing the legal, economic, and perhaps other aspects of your relationship to protect your inherited assets. Because the concepts are identical, whether it is your partner or your parent's partner, the rest of the discussion will be presented as if it is your partner that is involved.

Partners who live together without the formality of a marriage do not have many legal protections that married couples have. These include common-law rights of dower and curtesy, the statutory right of election against an estate, the estate and gift tax marital deduction, and forms of joint ownership (tenancy by the entirety). The law is generally less clear about how to apply the rights between nonmarried partners. The day after you are married, you have a statutory right to equitable distribution just for having walked down the aisle. But this is not true in a relationship where you have merely cohabited with a partner, even for decades. "To protect yourself or your parent, an agreement endeavors to fill in these gaps," cautions Charles Abut, Esq., a matrimonial practitioner in Fort Lee, New Jersey.

A living-together agreement may contemplate that the parties may (or may not) decide to marry. The prenuptial agreement, in contrast, is based on the parties' intent to eventually marry, and to memorialize their wishes for the dissolution of that pending marriage. If you have to seek enforcement of the living-together agreement, state laws vary considerably, and courts may consider a host of concerns.

One issue is whether you, as the economically powerful partner because of a large inheritance, will be effective in protecting the growth of those assets in the future. The dependent partner, in contrast, may not be viewed by a court as being in an arm's-length position to negotiate the agreement with you.

The living-together agreement attempts to establish you and your partner's economic, legal, and other ties during and after dissolution of your relationship. In many states, there is little direct case law to provide guidance as to how courts will treat these contracts.

You should inquire whether the concept of palimony is recognized in the law of your state. Depending on your state's laws, the courts might determine that your unmarried partner has the theoretical legal right to financial support from you.

Consider the following points in working with a lawyer to draft a living-together agreement:

- Wills and trusts must address a range of issues. Who inherits what? These include all the normal will questions any person must address. A contractual agreement (stipulation) as to how wills will be addressed is advisable. The gift or estate tax marital deduction is not available for living-together couples, so planning becomes more important than for married couples in many instances. If the estate may be taxable, planning that is more sophisticated than a bypass will is necessary.

- Acquisition of real and personal property should be set forth in detail. Who pays which expenses? Who keeps the property if the relationship terminates? How is the property titled?

- Life insurance should be addressed, assuming that you and your partner have an "insurable interest." It behooves you to address life insurance amounts, coverages, and viatical settlement provisions. These may provide for prepayments in the event of a terminal illness. An insurance trust (ILIT) is even more important for nonmarried couples to minimize estate tax in the absence of a marital deduction and protect assets for the intended heirs.

- Disability insurance might make sense. Address sharing of expenses. The issue of who can pay if one is disabled is critical. Will you be obligated to use inherited assets to support your partner?

- Benefits will not automatically be afforded to a partner. This might require obtaining private retirement, insurance, and other arrangements. These should be addressed in an agreement. Failing to do so may deplete your assets, including inherited assets. If it is your parent, a failure to plan may jeopardize your inheritance.

TRUST IN TRUSTS

The safest approach for your parents in protecting assets from future divorces of their children is to gift or bequeath assets in trust and never directly to the child. This approach, however, may limit your own access to your inheritance and is not 100 percent guaranteed. Although unlikely to force any distribution of separate gift or inherited assets, some state laws may consider trust assets or income as available to you, when planning the overall divorce settlement terms. This option is not perfect, but it is still safer than putting the assets in an heir's hands, and certainly much safer than the commingling of assets by that heir with his or her spouse.

Remember that not every heir must be treated identically under your parents' will, and if protection for you from an ex is important, consider advising your parents about some of the following alternatives:

- Your parents should name someone independent as a trustee of a trust they establish under their will to protect your assets, or at least cotrustee with you. Do not name you as the only trustee of your own trust.

- Your parents should not include any mandatory requirements to distribute money from your trust. Do not give you (the intended heir) the right to demand principal from the trust (this is technically often in the form of what is referred to as a "5 and 5 power"). Leave distributions solely to the discretion of a trustee other than your sibling.

- Follow all formalities and be sure the trustee does so as well. If you and your family ignore the formalities of the trust (e.g., separate bank account, record keeping, filing tax return), do not expect the courts to respect the trust either.

Another option to consider in addition to, or instead of, advising your parents to set up a trust for you, is to have them set up trusts for your children. Have your parents make gifts of funds to the trusts instead of to you or your children directly. It may provide a bit more security through the uncertainty of the divorce process. This may protect the funds from a situation of a divorce court ordering a distribution favorable to your ex, and then saddling you with the additional responsibility of funding a substantial portion of college costs from other resources.

Although all the devices previously outlined for protection from an ex-spouse can protect you, they may limit your access to your inheritance—often severely.

LESSONS TO LEARN

Your ability to inherit more does not depend solely on the choices and legal maneuvers of your parents. There are many things you can do today to maximize your inheritance of tomorrow. The most necessary step is separating your inherited assets from those that you share with your spouse, and you should do this from the inception. Whether you use a prenuptial agreement, a postnuptial agreement, or convince your parents to establish trusts instead of giving outright bequests, the sooner you address this all-important issue the less able your spouse will be to take your inheritance from you in the event of a divorce. Advising your parents about the uses of trusts can also protect a family business from your siblings' ex-spouses.

15 INHERIT THE BEST WAY POSSIBLE—A LIFETIME TRUST

Maximizing your inheritance is not only about getting the most dollars. It is about finding the best way to get them. Is there a better way to get them? Absolutely. With your parents' cooperation, you can receive your inheritance in a way that will protect it for your benefit so you can maximize what you have. With the proper use of perpetual or dynasty trusts, your inheritance will never be subject to a gift, estate, or generation skipping transfer tax again, no matter how wealthy you become and no matter what the government does with the gift and estate tax rules. By leaving money in a trust for your benefit instead of leaving it directly to you, your parents can protect the money you inherit from a future spouse, through divorce, malpractice claims, lawsuits, and other things that go bump in the night. With a little extra planning, a trust can even minimize estate income tax on your money for decades to come.

This chapter outlines this magical planning and some of the key terms you want in the trust so that you will have reasonable control over the assets while obtaining all these additional benefits. For the family that plans together, the potential benefits are tremendous. This chapter explains the distribution provisions to put in such a trust so that you can get at the money but your creditors cannot easily reach it.

BENEFITS OF DYNASTY TRUSTS

Dynasty trusts can be thought of as self-funded trusts since you can be the one contributing assets to, or funding, the trust. Yet you remain a beneficiary. Your parents can make gifts or bequests for you to the same trust. These trusts are often called perpetual trusts because they can continue forever. They also are known as domestic asset protection trusts because they can protect your assets without the need to move the trust to an offshore tax haven jurisdiction such as the Cook Islands. For the sake of simplicity, they are referred to in this book as *dynasty trusts* because the combination of all these benefits is the development of a dynasty trust for your family.

Planning Tip: Throughout this book, dynasty trusts are described as a key planning tool. Given the uncertainty of what Congress might do next, why not secure tax benefits for as long as possible, instead of waiting to see what the next Congress will serve up? A dynasty trust, especially a domestic asset protection dynasty trust as Alaska and Delaware law can provide, is potentially the most powerful tool to address this planning uncertainty.

A dynasty trust can not only benefit you, but your parents can apply the same planning concept for their benefit as well. A dynasty trust can remove assets from your parents' estates as well as their spouses' estates. It may also protect your parents' assets from their creditors. These assets can be maintained in perpetuity outside the GST, estate, and gift tax systems. Keep in mind that dynasty trusts must be formed in a state that has eliminated the rule against perpetuities. This is a legal concept that in general terms limited the duration for which a trust could last. If the assets of the trust are to be available to your parents in their lifetimes, then a further restriction is that the state selected for the trust must permit them to make a completed gift to a trust, such that its assets are protected from their creditors, yet still can be distributed to them. Alaska and Delaware are the two most popular states for these trusts.

Although the assets in a dynasty trust could be available to either your parents or their spouses, and even their children, ideally assets that are not really needed should stay in the dynasty trust (to avoid wasting the asset protection and the tax protection afforded by the allocation of estate tax exclusion and GST exemption). Any family members specified, including your parents, can reach the assets, but the longer they remain in trust the greater the eventual tax benefits. Why remove them unless they are needed since distributions that are not spent may become subject to estate and GST tax in the future? Thus, the ideal is to continue to grow the dynasty trust outside the estate and transfer tax systems for the eventual use of grandchildren and future heirs. The leverage in multigenerational tax savings can be tremendous.

These funds also can serve as a last resort or safety net for your parents if a malpractice or other claim somehow destroys their asset base.

Caution: Your parent retaining the right to be a discretionary beneficiary of a dynasty trust could cause the IRS to challenge the position that the assets of the dynasty trust are not taxable in your parent's estate. It could also be a basis for a malpractice claimant or other plaintiff to argue that they should be able to reach the assets in the dynasty trust to satisfy claims. The laws concerning dynasty trusts are relatively new and, compared with insurance trusts and other more common, long-used techniques, unproven. You must evaluate these risks with your parents and their advisers before proceeding.

A common technique when funding dynasty trusts is to make gifts to the trust with leveraging techniques to maximize the tax benefits. This can be done with the intentionally defective irrevocable trust (IDIT) technique described earlier in this book or, more simply, by transferring noncontrolling interests in family limited partnerships (FLPs) or limited liability companies (LLCs), valued with discounts for lack of control and marketability.

STRUCTURE AND OPERATION

A common approach used to structure a dynasty trust is to name an Alaska or Delaware (or more recently Rhode Island or Nevada) bank or trust company to serve as cotrustee. Having a cotrustee licensed and operating in Alaska or Delaware not only provides objective and professional management, but from a legal perspective creates a substantial connection (nexus) to that state. This can support the position your parents will have to take that the favorable laws of that state will apply to them.

The assets transferred to the dynasty trust can include cash and marketable securities. It is often advisable to have some assets such as cash or securities deposited directly in an institution in Alaska or Delaware. The bulk of the assets transferred to a dynasty trust are more typically interests in a closely held FLP or LLC to leverage the discounts for tax purposes. The FLP or LLC also provides your parents, and ultimately you, with greater control and asset protection.

Example: Marc, age 67, is an anesthesiologist and concerned about malpractice claims and maximizing his children's eventual inheritance. He forms a dynasty trust in Alaska in 2001. The trust is to benefit Marc, his children, and all future descendants. Marc transfers $100,000 of cash and marketable securities to the trust, investing them in the Alaska bank or trust company that he has selected to serve as cotrustee. This further supports his nexus to Alaska and the application of Alaska law.

Marc maintains a substantial $3 million brokerage account with a trusted financial adviser. He does not want to lose investment control over his portfolio or the assistance of his adviser. He transfers $2.2 million of his securities portfolio to a family limited liability company he formed on the advice of his attorney in 2001. Marc did not transfer the remaining $800,000 based on his attorney's advice that he must retain reasonable assets for living expenses and emergencies in his own name. Marc then gifts, in 2002 when the exclusion increased to $1 million, a 40 percent interest in the equity of the LLC to the dynasty trust. This 40 percent interest is valued at $650,000 [$2.2 million × 40 percent less discounts for lack of control and marketability]. He also gifts $11,000 in value of the LLC to each child and grandchild.

Marc remains manager of the LLC and thus has some reasonable measure of control. Further, his trusted financial adviser continues to advise him concerning investments on most of his portfolio.

If Marc, in this example, were married, the transfers could have been increased with proper planning to utilize the exclusion available to him and his spouse.

Marc's children and other heirs are beneficiaries of the dynasty trust and part owners of the LLC. The control that Marc retains is likely an important factor encouraging him to make these gifts.

Your parent would allocate the generation skipping transfer tax exemption to protect the assets so transferred. This technique, however, could also be combined with the IDIT.

In 2002–2003, your parent will be able to contribute up to $1 million (and if married, your parent and spouse can contribute up to $2 million) to a dynasty trust without gift, estate, or GST tax. These amounts will increase substantially if the estate tax exclusion and GST exemption increases, as enacted in the 2001 Tax Act, are allowed to occur. In fact, by 2009 one will be able to gift $3.5 million to a dynasty trust. All of these figures can be increased substantially with leveraging techniques.

There is substantial uncertainty about estate tax and related laws. The result is that it is probably wise to grab the tax benefits while they are available. So if the exclusion increases, encourage your parents to gift more to a dynasty trust. The dynasty trust is ideal in that the estate and GST benefits can be preserved forever. It is also ideal in that few taxpayers are comfortable making irrevocable gifts that they can never benefit from. The dynasty trust, if it proves sustainable when attacked in future years, is the best of all planning scenarios since your parents can secure their tax benefit, yet remain a beneficiary of the trust. This fact should entice your parents to gift far greater amounts out of their estates.

The post-2001 Tax Act system retains, as explained earlier, a maximum lifetime gift tax exclusion of $1 million. The maximum funding of a dynasty trust while your parent is alive (e.g., up to the $1 million maximum) and again at death (perhaps with the remainder of their estate) will enable you and other heirs to avoid all gift and estate taxes when you pass these assets to your heirs, including appreciation. The knowledge that future generations can realize huge tax savings encourages many parents to consider this type of planning.

What if the estate tax is actually repealed? Congress will only have the income tax to raise revenues. The dynasty trust provides a valuable income tax planning tool as well. The states where your dynasty trusts located are unlikely to charge state level income tax. Over many years, the compounded benefits of these tax savings can be substantial. Further, a trustee of a dynasty trust with a broad discretionary distribution power under the dynasty trust agreement can distribute funds to any beneficiary. This will draw out taxable income to the beneficiaries receiving such distributions. The result is that the trustee will have some latitude to sprinkle taxable income to the beneficiaries in the lowest income tax brackets. As the Congress seeks to raise revenues in future years, the income tax may be the way.

LESSONS TO LEARN

A dynasty trust, whether formed now to reduce estate taxes and protect your parents' assets, or funded at their death to protect you and their other descendants, should become a far more popular planning tool. Ignoring its uses and advantages would be foolish. Not only can it protect your inheritance, by emphasizing lawsuit protection, professional management, and state income tax savings for your parents, it can also build your parents' confidence that you are trying to assist them. Highlighting that this particular kind of trust provides them with full access to all their funds at all times can help convince them you are out to help, not out for what you can get.

16 SAFEGUARDING YOUR INHERITANCE

This final chapter highlights the answers to the problem presented in Chapter 1: What are the most important steps to maximize your inheritance? While all the information that has preceded this chapter is important, if you are working within strict time constraints, at least make sure you take the six steps outlined in the following pages.

When planning each step, adhere to these principles:

- *Help your parents simplify and organize.*
- *Think holistically.* It is about life, not just money.
- *Plan.* Recipes are good for cakes, not estate plans. Tailor every step to your family's unique needs, personalities, and phobias.
- *Document.* Yes, Virginia, lawyers and accountants need to earn a living too.
- *Follow through.* The best of intentions, if not implemented, will achieve nothing.
- *Start again.* Remember the famous quote about the best-laid plans of mice and tax attorneys. . . .

KEY STEPS TO PROTECT YOUR INHERITANCE

Six steps are necessary to protect your inheritance. If you miss any single step, you may have taken great strides to protect your parents, and your inheritance, but you have surely failed in certain areas and, depending on which step you skipped, wasted much of that precious time you spent helping your parents with their planning.

Although the six steps are simple to outline, they are complex to complete. By following all of the steps, however, you should effectively protect your inheritance.

Step 1: Just the Facts Ma'am: Sergeant Joe Friday Had It Right

Preparing a periodic summary balance sheet that highlights your parents' financial picture is one of the most important steps in helping them analyze their personal financial status to determine what business, tax, and legal actions are necessary. Basic financial information is critical to their planning and your inheritance. At least once every several years, or following any significant event, your parents should analyze their assets and personal circumstances to be sure their plan will accomplish their (and your) objectives, and to identify changes that they must make to keep their planning on track.

When your parents fill in the balance sheet shown in this chapter, they do not need to provide excessive detail. The primary goal is to look at the "big picture." Focusing on detailed asset allocations, the specific stocks your parents own, and so on, is important, but it can obscure larger and more important issues. Once your parents have completed this process, they should review the balance sheet with their professional advisers periodically to obtain input and confirmation of the steps in their plan.

Even the best estate plan will be of limited value if your parents have not organized, simplified, and obtained control over their assets. For most people, the key is to consolidate asset holdings. This can help immeasurably in achieving better investment returns and lower risk, since you can better identify your parents' asset allocation mix. You will minimize probate expenses and delays since there will be less paperwork to handle. It will also help you protect your parents and yourself in the event of disability, advanced age, or other emergencies in your parents' lives.

They should make a list of every asset or account that they hold. For each asset, your parents should ask if they have a reason for owning it. If not, they should consolidate or divest. For example, small bank accounts at a local branch in your parents' old neighborhood should be closed out. A small $5,000 real estate investment in another state can create substantial liability exposure and ancillary probate. Is it really worth keeping? Do your parents really need CDs in four banks? Can't they consolidate them at one brokerage firm where the insurance limits provide adequate protection? If they have nominal holdings in several small stocks or bonds, do they really need them? They might make their situation easier by putting these securities in street name or even selling individual securities and buying index funds or mutual funds. Remember, when simple works, simple is better.

Over the years, people tend to accumulate a proliferation of bank accounts, brokerage accounts, mutual funds, and stocks and bonds, the reasons for which have long ago been forgotten. Your parents are probably no exception.

In the event of disability, it will be burdensome to identify and track dividend and interest payments, to marshal assets to assure proper cash flow, and so forth. At death, attorney's fees dramatically magnify probate costs. Time delays are exacerbated as trustees and lawyers attempt to identify and gain control over these assets. Using a living trust will not avoid this since assets will still have to be valued for tax purposes and distributed to heirs. Simplifying your parents' financial picture will help assure that their living trust program will do everything they want and you need.

Discuss with your parents how they are going to manage their investments, pay bills, and handle daily affairs if they become disabled. If something happens to them, on whom will they rely to help care for financial matters? You? Another of their children? Friends? A distant cousin with whom they have almost no contact? If they are ill or disabled, they will have to depend on someone to help them.

Step 2: Think Holistically

Estate planning is about your parents in their entirety. It means meeting personal wishes, religious objectives, investment objectives, goals for charitable giving, and personal feelings for a spouse (whether or not your parent). You need to respect their philosophy as to how much, how, and when children or other heirs should inherit. Assuring that they have adequate insurance protection might require consideration of long-term-care insurance, Medicaid, and other elder care issues. When you treat your parents as "whole" persons by planning holistically, they will be far more comfortable addressing indirectly (and perhaps even directly) your inheritance.

In very few situations will a parent be comfortable with a head-on discussion about saving taxes on your inheritance. Focus on them first. Focus on how planning will keep them in control, protect them and their assets, and achieve their goals. You will benefit more.

Step 3: Develop an Estate-Planning Team and a Plan

Help and encourage your parents to develop an estate-planning team. This is one of the most crucial steps to inheriting more. Life is complex. Proper estate planning requires the participation of many areas of expertise. If you really want to help your parents as well as yourself, the team approach is best.

Your parents' team should include a lawyer, possibly one who specializes in elder law, an accountant, an investment or financial planner, an insurance expert, your parents, and, if your parents are willing, yourself. If you have the time and your parents' assets are sufficient, the team can include appropriate specialists and consultants in particular fields of law and investment.

If your parents are on a tight budget, the key professionals can fill multiple slots on the team, or meet by telephone conference instead of face to face.

The team approach assures better decisions and gives your parents an important check and balance on each professional. If any particular professional is not up to speed or is not focusing on your parents' best interests, the other professionals may identify this deficit long before you or your parents, as laypersons, notice the problems.

Step 4: Have Your Parents Get Their Documents in Order

Your parents need to have certain key documents drawn up to ensure a smooth transition in ownership of their assets. Not only must they be drawn up properly, but they also must be stored in a safe place that is accessible to you whenever they may be needed.

One of the most important documents is a will. It should set out as clearly as possible your parents' intent for the distribution of each of their assets. The will should name an executor and on the death of your parents, that executor should be provided with a separate list of all assets, their locations, the intended recipients, and an appropriate tax minimization scheme.

Other key documents are a properly crafted power of attorney and living will. As they implicate your parents' care in life as well as asset distribution after death, these documents should be accessible at any time of day or night. A lawyer should draw them up so that all eventualities are addressed and nothing of import is inadvertently overlooked. Living wills, in particular, should address medical care, religious concerns, and general instructions for medical professionals and family members.

Insurance documents should not be overlooked. These policies—whether for life, medical, long-term care, or any other kind of insurance—are what will ensure health care and appropriate living facilities for your parents' in their lifetimes.

Beneficiary designation forms should be reviewed and current.

Step 5: Follow Through on the Plan

It is not enough for your parents and the members of their team to discuss what needs to be done. Active participation in the

implementation of the plan is necessary as well. To protect your inheritance, you must ensure that in addition to your parents' having
the proper documents drawn up and signing them as soon as possible, they purchase any required insurance. Assets must be titled
properly and should be consolidated and investment strategies
changed, as the plan may require. If your parents own a house and
carry proper casualty insurance, perhaps you should also put an
alarm system in place to protect your parents.

Be proactive. Your mantra should be "follow up." Why? Because
all the planning in the world means nothing if the plan never comes
to fruition. So often taxpayers with the best of plans and intentions
die with draft wills and memos telling them what to do, but nothing has been done.

Step 6: Start Again: Life Throws Curves, so You Have to Monitor, Reevaluate, and Update

Even if you think you have planned until you can plan no more,
reevaluate every few years and begin planning again. All it takes is
one major purchase or sale, illness, family reconciliation, or fight to
throw off the entire plan. Periodic reevaluation is necessary to ensure that no important detail is being missed.

THE BALANCE SHEET AND STRATEGIC PLAN

The Importance of the Snapshot Balance Sheet

The following pages can help you guide and encourage your parents
in organizing a Snapshot Balance Sheet that provides an overview
of your parents' current financial picture. It is vitally important to
have such a perspective to identify planning opportunities or to update an estate plan. The summary balance sheet serves a different
purpose than the detailed financial, insurance, and related data
many planners and computer software programs focus on. While a
detailed financial analysis is always important when making specific

investment, insurance, and related decisions (remember the devil is in the details), the big picture is the key to planning.

The Snapshot Balance Sheet, in contrast to the more typical detailed analysis, will help your parents and their advisers use totals of various asset categories to analyze their overall estate, financial, and tax picture and identify appropriate estate-planning techniques to minimize tax. Both levels of analysis are essential to best protect yourself, your parents' assets, and those people you are concerned about. The detailed analysis, however, will require your parents' coordination with other advisers, as discussed in earlier chapters. See Figure 16.1 for a sample Snapshot Balance Sheet.

Tips for Completing the Snapshot Balance Sheet

Tailor It to Your Parents' Situation. Flexibility and creativity are necessary to complete the Snapshot Balance Sheet in a way that best reflects your parents' personal and unique circumstances. Remember, an overview is the goal. The objective is not to cram every detail onto a single page. Too much detail might obscure global issues. If the categories or columns do not work, modify them as you see best. As much as possible, however, use the general format provided. If you need help, call your estate planner or, alternatively, have your financial planner assist you in preparing the Snapshot Balance Sheet at a meeting.

Issues. Any questions, assumptions, or important points should be noted in detailed schedules following the Snapshot Balance Sheet (or in attachments to those schedules). To alert advisers to the additional notations or information, indicate in the "Planning Comments" column, "See page 00."

Round Up. Simplify. List dollars in thousands (i.e., "000s" omitted). Rounding is fine (e.g., use "350" for a house that was recently appraised at $347,000). It is simple, clean, and makes the analysis easier. The goal is to obtain a snapshot of your parents' financial status, not the details.

Combine.   Combine similar assets on one line. For this planning tool, whether your parents have four brokerage accounts or three mutual funds is unimportant as long as the assets are owned the same way (e.g., jointly with a spouse). A total, by category, may suffice. Although, if they have too many accounts, consolidation is an important planning step.

Pension/Retirement Assets.   List pension and retirement assets in the "Pension Assets" column (don't list the same items in other columns). These assets are segregated to help identify nonpension assets for funding an applicable exclusion (credit shelter) trust before having to use retirement plan assets. Retirement/IRA assets also require special attention in planning. Beneficiary designations (who will inherit the assets) affect the actual distribution of assets, the timing of distributions to your parents and heirs (minimum distributions), income tax consequences, and estate tax consequences. Review these with your accountant and financial planner. If your parents change custodians, they should be sure to execute new beneficiary designation forms.

Real Estate.   For real estate assets, you may wish to note in the margin if they are located outside the state where your parents reside. This highlights the issue of ancillary probate, which may warrant planning to minimize or eliminate ownership structure (by your parents alone, partnership, tenants in common, etc.).

Community Property.   If your parents live in a community property state, you may need to use a chart with a column for community property. At minimum, identify with an asterisk any property that is community property. Other special rules may apply, and you may need to request the assistance of counsel in the particular community property state.

Miscellaneous Points.   In the "Planning Comments" column, note any special or important considerations. These may include beneficiary designations (e.g., for insurance, IRA, other retirement assets, annuity, brokerage account); liabilities or contingencies (e.g.,

Figure 16.1 Snapshot Balance Sheet

Date: _____

(The following chart should be completed in pencil to facilitate updating and corrections. A photocopy can then be made to create a permanent record.)

Asset Category	Owned by Your Father	Mother	Jointly Owned by Parents	Pension/ Retirement Assets	Total by Category	Planning Comments
Cash	$	$	$	$	$	
CDs						
Marketable securities						
Mutual funds						
House net of mortgage						
Vacation home net of mortgage						
Other real estate investments net						
Annuities						
IRAs						
Other pension/retirement						
Closely held business net						
Possible inheritances						
Possible claims/losses						
Liabilities						
Life Insurance: [ ] Death Values: [ ] CSV						
Total estimated net worth	$	$	$	$		

a law suit filed by a tenant because of an injury at your parents' vacation home); location of an asset in another state or country; the name of co-owners of an asset (other than your parents); the face value of insurance. Your parents' estate planner may use the "Planning Comments" to summarize key planning steps they might wish to consider.

Using the Inherit More Balance Sheet

Once the Snapshot Balance Sheet is completed, your parents' estate planner, financial planner, accountant, and other professionals can use it to help develop an overall plan. Too often planning becomes so focused on details that important general planning issues are overlooked. Use the following tips, as well as a consultation with your professional advisers, to evaluate your parents' financial, tax, legal, estate, insurance, and other needs. The details are important, but start big first.

Update Regularly.   Basic current financial information is critical to estate, financial, asset protection, insurance, and other planning. At least once every several years, or following any significant event, your parents should analyze their assets, liabilities, and other key data, to be sure that the estate plan will accomplish their objectives, and take advantage of tax and other planning opportunities.

Consolidate.   If your parents have too many different accounts and assets, consolidate assets to simplify planning, make their estate more manageable in the event of disability, and minimize probate fees. If your parents consolidate, watch out for transfer costs, the triggering of taxable income, or capital gains on selling certain funds or assets.

Plan to Use Your Applicable Exclusion.   If both of your parents are alive and married, they may wish to take advantage of the $1 million (2002) applicable exclusion amount (increasing to $3.5 million in 2009) available to every taxpayer. This is the amount that they can bequeath without an estate tax. After 2009, the estate tax is scheduled to be repealed and modified carryover basis rules will apply. This means that there will be no estate tax, but your parents' heirs may have the same low tax basis (investment) in assets they inherit that your parents had. However, the estate tax is scheduled to be reinstated in 2011. These changes, compounded by the uncertainty as to whether they will occur, make planning complex. Frequent review and analysis of the plan and documents is essential. Assets are often bequeathed (directly or via the surviving spouse disclaiming assets) to a trust formed under the will of the first spouse to die. This is a trust designed to benefit the surviving spouse (and often other heirs) while assuring that the assets in that trust are not taxed in the surviving spouse's estate. This is called a *Bypass Trust* since the assets avoid, or bypass, taxation in the surviving spouse's estate.

Title (Own) Assets Properly. How your parents own their assets (title) can be critical in determining whether assets can be reached by their creditors, including nursing home costs. It may also be advisable to divide ownership of assets between your parents so that each estate can fund an applicable exclusion trust (no matter which parent dies first). Joint ownership of assets, pay on death/in trust for accounts, beneficiary designations, and other techniques can defeat this planning opportunity because on death those assets pass automatically to the joint owner and cannot pass through a will (or revocable living trust) to the Bypass Trust. Without the use of specialized beneficiary designation documents, assets such as pensions, IRAs, insurance, annuities, and some brokerage accounts may not be available to fund a Bypass Trust. It may be possible to use disclaimers (a formal process of refusing an inheritance so the assets pass as if your parent were not alive) to salvage this type of planning. Disclaimers, however, are complex and should generally not be counted on except as a last resort. Even if the estate tax is repealed, assets will have to be divided to take maximum advantage of the modified carryover basis rules, protect assets from creditors, and serve other planning purposes.

Plan for Nonprobate Assets. Your parents can minimize the assets in their estate subject to probate if they wish. This can be done by using a revocable living trust and properly owning assets, and by careful use of beneficiary designations. However, they have to co-ordinate the ownership of assets with their documents and plan. For many people, most of their estate may pass outside their will (i.e., outside probate). Insurance may be paid to a named beneficiary, IRA accounts will be paid to the designated beneficiaries of those plans, a house may be owned jointly, and so on. Your parents must evaluate these matters to be certain that their goals are being met. Their planner may need to help them restructure assets to better fund the Bypass Trusts, take advantage of the modified basis step-up rules after 2009, and so on. This often may require changing assets from one spouse to another. In doing so, however, caution is essential. If the recipient spouse is not a United States citizen, there is no unlimited marital deduction; thus, a tax could be incurred on the transfers. Pension and retirement assets, as well as professional practices and businesses subject to transfer restrictions, may not be appropriate to transfer. Changing ownership (title) can affect the risk of claimants reaching an asset, probate procedures necessary to transfer the asset, and other important attributes.

Evaluate Tax Leveraging Techniques. If your parents wish to leave assets of more than $1 million (2002) to a Bypass Trust, or to anyone other than a spouse, special tax planning may be necessary to leverage benefits. A common tax leveraging technique is to make gifts to a Grantor Retained Annuity Trust (GRAT). These are trusts to which your parents transfer assets but retain an annual (or more frequent) annuity payment. After a specified number of years, their heirs (not grandchildren) will own the assets. This technique can help leverage the value of large gifts. Compare this technique to a note sale to a defective grantor trust. If your parents have a valuable house, they may want to consider a qualified personal residence trust (QPRT) to transfer the value of a primary residence and/or vacation home to their children (not grandchildren) in a tax-advantaged manner. They retain the right to live in the residence for a specified number of years, after which their children would own the house and the parents would rent it. Even if their estate will not be taxed, a QPRT can be an effective technique to assure the transfer of a family vacation home or farm to the next generation.

Consider Multigenerational Planning.   For larger estates, additional decisions and financial information may be necessary to plan for the generation skipping transfer (GST) tax and the GST exemption (the amount your parents can bequeath to future generations free of the GST tax). The GST exemption can require the use of trusts, filing of gift tax returns to allocate GST exemption, and so on. Because the rules for allocating the GST exemption are so complex, your parents should review these requirements with their accountant every year. An increasingly common planning technique to take advantage of this type of planning is to set up a trust to continue in perpetuity. This is often called a dynasty trust (see Chapter 15).

Asset Protection Steps May Be Warranted.   Identify asset protection concerns that may affect your parents. Do they own real estate or a business that is not organized as a corporation, limited partnership (LP), or limited liability company (LLC)? Their advisers may recommend an LLC or LP format as part of their overall plan. These entities can limit liability. If the asset is mortgaged real estate, lender, tenant, and other approvals may be required. Also, your parents and their advisers should consider title and casualty insurance, transfer taxes, and recording fees when making a transfer. Does the spouse or partner with the greatest risk (e.g., malpractice, business) own too many assets? Your parent may consider transferring certain assets to their spouse or partner who is less at risk. Consider costs, legal constraints, and so on, of any such transfers.

Use FLPs, LLCs, and Other Entities.   If your parents have substantial security, real estate, and/or business holdings, they may want to consider consolidating some of these assets into a family limited partnership (FLP) or a limited liability company (LLC) to fund complex tax-oriented trusts, facilitate making annual gifts, secure valuation discounts for lack of control or marketability (thus reducing gift and estate taxes), and protect the assets from claims. If your parents have a business, have they considered succession planning issues? Is the business properly organized in entity format (LP, LLC, S corporation, etc.) to protect them against liability? Have they structured the business to try to qualify for discounts for the lack of marketability, lack of control, or other discounts for estate purposes? Have your parents properly structured their assets to minimize liability exposure and risk? Are real estate investment properties and business interests segregated into different legal entities (such as limited liability companies)?

Review Property Insurance Coverage.   Do your parents have adequate property and casualty insurance for all assets? A common error is not purchasing business liability insurance and assuming your parents' homeowner's policy covers it. Request written confirmation from your agent. If they do not have adequate personal excess liability (also called "umbrella") insurance, your parents' estate, and your inheritance, could be in serious jeopardy if a large claim succeeds. Periodically, your parents should have their insurance agent provide them with a summary of all coverage and review its adequacy.

Income Tax Planning Must Be Coordinated with Estate Planning. Your parents and their advisers should consider the cost or tax basis for assets. This can affect income and estate tax planning. It is often not possible to note this level of detail on the Snapshot Balance Sheet. However, generally, if they have an asset that has appreciated substantially over what they paid for it, holding that asset until death will usually eliminate all predeath capital gains (before 2010 when the modified carryover basis rules become effective). If they gift the asset to you and other heirs, they will continue to have their low purchase price as their tax basis. If they sell the asset, the excess of what they receive over this basis figure will generally be taxable.

Evaluate Investment Allocations and Planning.   Are your parents' investments reasonably allocated to various classes considering their entire personal financial profile? Do they have adequate liquidity? Should lines of credit, disability insurance, deductibles on

Figure 16.2 Inherit More Balance Sheet

Balance Sheet Item	Question/Concern	Planning Conclusion	Action to Take
1.			
2.			
3.			
4.			
5.			
6.			
7.			

property and casualty insurance, or other steps be taken in light of their liquidity position?

After your parents complete their Snapshot Balance Sheet and review the preceding points, they (hopefully with your assistance) should list questions to discuss with their professional advisers. You can then note additional planning points, or items your parents should follow up on, on your Inherit More Balance Sheet (see Figure 16.2).

LESSONS TO LEARN

Inheriting more is not only possible, it can almost be assured with proper planning. This chapter has highlighted six key steps to help you inherit more, all while helping your parents achieve greater financial security.

Index

AARP, 109
Abut, Charles, 54, 245
Accelerated death benefits, 80–82
Accounting professionals. *See*
    Professional/legal fees
Advisors. *See* Fiduciary(ies)
Affinity group fraud, 105
Alley, Kirstie, 50
Amundsen, Amy J., 242
Applicable exclusion trust. *See* Bypass
    trust
Art. *See* Personal property
Asset(s), 85–110. *See also* Investment(s);
    Personal property; Real estate
    finding/identifying, 147–162
        contacting parents' former employers
            about continuing benefits,
            161–162
        contacting state, 159–160
        reviewing property insurance
            policies for listed/scheduled
            property, 160
        sleuthing with income tax return,
            148–158
    hard to divide, 137–146 (*see also*
        Home[s]; Personal property)
    nonprobate (planning), 266
    protection of, 267
        from creditors, 70, 79, 133
        encouraging parents to prepare a
            budget, 90–91
        management of money, 89–90
        scams that prey on the elderly,
            102–109
    separate, 241–242
ATM/pay phone sales (scam), 105

Baby boomers, 1, 8
Baksa, Richard, 36
Balance sheets, 260–270
    strategic planning ("inherit-more"),
        264–270
        applicable exclusion, 264–265
        asset ownership, 265
        asset protection steps, 267
        consolidating, 264
        evaluating investment allocations/
            planning, 268–270

evaluating tax leveraging techniques,
    266–267
income tax planning, 268
multigenerational planning, 267
nonprobate assets, 266
property insurance coverage, 268
template, 269
updating regularly, 264
using FLPs, LLCs, and other
    entities, 267–268
Bank accounts:
    beneficiary designations for, 130
    issues affecting various types of,
        132–133
    junior taxpayer, 130
    parent taxpayer, payable on death to
        junior taxpayer (POD), 132
    parent taxpayer and junior taxpayer,
        132
    parent taxpayer and junior taxpayer,
        jointly, with right of survivorship,
        131–132
    parent taxpayer in trust for junior
        taxpayer, 130–131
Beneficiary(ies):
    bank accounts, 130
    designation forms, 134, 259
    insurance, 266
    IRA accounts, 266
    nonprobate assets, 266
    power of attorney for changing, 174
    signing prenuptial agreement to retain
        status as, 238
Bonds, Barry, 125
Bono, Sonny, 178
Broker(s), 16–17, 109
Brokerage accounts, 113–114
Brown, James, 215
Buddhism, 23, 36–39
Budget, 90–91
Burger, Warren, 164, 170
Burial/funeral wishes, 20–26
Bypass trust:
    celebrity case study, 178
    dividing title to assets to facilitate
        funding of, 155–156
    investment considerations, 101–102
    life insurance and, 72–73

Bypass trust *(Continued)*
  ownership forms, 129, 155–156
  taxes and, 196, 265, 266

Capital gains, 99
Carvel, Tom, 170
Catastrophic illness insurance, 187
Certificates of deposit (CDs):
  "callable" (scam), 107–108
  joint tenants with the right of
    survivorship (case study), 4–5
Charitable giving:
  donor advised fund, 44–45
  by heirs, 42–43
  helping parents plan for, 42
  options for, 43–44
  registration and tax-exempt status,
    109
  religions and, 30, 34, 38, 39–40
  talking to your parents about, 42–46
Charitable lead trust (CLT), 45–46
Charitable remainder trust (CRT), 150,
  206–207
Cher, 178
Christian (Eastern) Orthodox issues and
  estate planning, 27–31
College:
  cost of, 1–2, 8–9
  gifts for and gift tax, 193–194
  savings plans, 194
Community property, 125–129, 156,
  262
Conflict, theories of, 9
Consolidation, 86–89, 264
Coogan, Jackie, 207
Corporations, 124, 157–158
Credit card bills, 158–159
Creditors, protecting assets from, 70,
  79, 133
Cruise, Tom, 48

Death:
  definition of, 29, 31
  life support issues, 38, 40
  personal wishes about, 21–22
  simultaneous (both parents), 118
Disability:
  consolidation and, 87
  insurance, 82, 246
  living trust, 176–177
  living wills, 17, 40
  power of attorney and, 174 *(see also*
    Power of attorney)
  remarriage and, 49–50
Disclaimer/renunciation, 19–20
Diversification:
  importance of, 97–99
  stock market meltdown, 92–93

work sheet to determine parents'
  investment goals, 98
Dividend income, 150–151, 155–157
Dividend reinvestment plans (DRIPs),
  156
Divorce/remarriage. *See* Marriage/
  divorce
Documents/paperwork, 163–180, 259
  essential documents, 166–178, 259
    beneficiary designation forms, 259
    durable power of attorney, 173–175,
      259 *(see also* Power of attorney)
    insurance, 259 *(see also* Insurance)
    safest approach, 175–178 *(see also*
      Living trusts)
    wills, 166–173, 259 *(see also* Wills)
  guardianship, 165–166
  importance of, 163, 259
  what happens without essential legal
    documents, 163–166
  worksheet/checklist, 179
Duke, Doris, 170–171, 206
Durable power of attorney. *See* Power of
  attorney
Dynasty trust, 249–254

Educational institutions, and gift tax,
  193–194. *See also* College
Elder law planning, 182–183, 186–187
Estate planning:
  essential documents *(see* Documents/
    paperwork)
  inheritance planning *vs.*, 2–3
  scaring your parents into action,
    197–198
  team, 258–259 *(see also* Fiduciary[ies])
Estate tax, 190, 195–202, 253
  deductions, expenses, and credits, 200
  exclusions, 194–195, 200, 264–265
  life insurance and, 172
  need for understanding of, 195–196
  taking advantage of special valuation
    rules, 198–200
  title/ownership form, 117–118
  who pays, 201–202
Exclusions, 194–195, 200, 264–265
Executor or personal administrator, 140.
  See also Fiduciary(ies)
Exercise: self-assessment (helping parents
  through aging process), 10–12
Ex-spouse, protecting inheritance from,
  237–248. *See also* Marriage/divorce

Family(ies):
  business owned by, 243–244
  hybrid *(see* Marriage/divorce,
    remarriage [parent's])
  median net worth, 8

Family limited partnerships (FLPs), 76–77, 199, 251, 252, 267–268
Fiduciary(ies). *See also* Professional/legal fees:
  communicating investment goals to, 97
  estate planning team, 258–259
  executor or personal administrator, 140
  gathering key data for, 114–117
  mismanagement, 203–213
  selection of, 168–169, 224
  trustworthiness of, 211
First to die, and community property, 126
Fleming, Erin, 206
Forbes, Malcolm, 172
Forensic accountant, 148
Funeral/burial wishes, 20–26

Gender differences, approaches to estate planning, 18–20
Generation skipping transfer (GST) tax:
  defined, 190
  multigenerational planning, 267
  trusts and, 62, 196, 251, 253
Generation skipping trust (GST), 79
Gift(s):
  annual, 6
  complete/incomplete, 131, 191–192
  life insurance, 70
  made within three years before death, 198
  power of attorney and, 174
  tax laws encouraging, 55
  Totten Trust, 131
Gift tax, 190, 191–195, 200
Goldberg, Gary, 90, 167
Gordon, Jeff, 48
Grantor retained annuity trust (GRAT), 70–71, 150–151, 196, 266
Grantor retained interest trust (GRIT), 196
Greenbaum, Gary, 99
Gross return, 99
Guardianship, 165–166
Guggenheim, Benjamin, 91

Hall, Jerry, 50
HALT, 109
Health care proxy, 17, 164
Heirs:
  emotions creating problems with, 218–219
  ownership of life insurance policies by, 76
  siblings with unequal financial situations, 220–224
Hidden assets. *See* Asset(s), finding/identifying

Hinduism and estate planning, 39–42
Holistic thinking, 258
Home(s):
  bequeathing, 143–145
  case of missing family apartment, 7–8
  insurance, 83–84
  mortgages, 153–154, 155
  vacation, 143, 145–146, 216
Honigfeld, Howard, 114
Hopko, Thomas, 28
Hughes, Howard, 168

Income tax:
  planning, 189–190, 268
  trap of joint ownership, 120, 198
Income tax return (using parents' to find assets), 148–158
  Form 1040—the basic income tax return, 150–151
  obtaining a copy, 148–149
  Schedule A—itemized deductions, 151–155
    home mortgage and interest deductions, 153–154
    home mortgage interest, 155
    interest deductions generally, 154
    medical/dental expenses, 151–152
    other expenses—safe deposit box, 155
    personal property taxes, 153
    real estate taxes, 152–153
    state/local taxes, 152
  Schedule B—interest and dividend income, 155–156
  Schedule E—rental real estate and businesses, 157–158
  sleuthing with parent's tax return, 149
Income *vs.* total return, investing for, 99–102
Inheritance planning:
  vs. estate planning, 2–3
  key steps (six) to protect your inheritance, 255–260
  principles, 255
  talking to your parents, 15–46
    about charitable giving, 42–46
    choosing discussion topics that give comfort, 15
    gender approaches to estate planning, 18–20
    about personal wishes, 20–26
    about religious issues, 26–42
    showing your parents that you want to protect them, 16–18
    when to begin, 16
  using "inherit-more" balance sheet, 264–270
    applicable exclusion, 264–265

Income tax return (using parents' to find
  assets) *(Continued)*
  asset ownership, 265
  asset protection steps may be
    warranted, 267
  consolidating, 264
  evaluating investment allocations/
    planning, 268–270
  evaluating tax leveraging techniques,
    266–267
  income tax planning, 268
  multigenerational planning, 267
  nonprobate assets, 266
  property insurance coverage, 268
  template, 269
  updating regularly, 264
  using FLPs, LLCs, and other
    entities, 267–268
  using snapshot balance sheet, 260–264
  what does inheriting more mean to
    you, 8–12
Insurable interest, 246
Insurance, 69–84
  accelerated death benefits, 80–82
  beneficiaries (nonprobate assets), 266
  catastrophic illness, 187
  disability, 82
  documents, 259
  homeowners, 83–84
  life, 69–80
    amount needed, 71–72
    estate taxes and, 172
    family partnership ownership of,
      76–77
    heir ownership of, 76
    key facts, 69
    options for, 72–73
    ownership of, 75–80
    reasons for, 70–71
    second-to-die insurance, 74
    term, 74
    transfers to trust within three years
      before death, 198
    trust, 77–80, 198, 246
    types of, 73–75
    variable, 74
  long-term care, 17, 72, 82, 181,
    186–187
  misuse of (scams), 104
  property and casualty, 83, 160, 268
  riders/floaters (fine art/jewelry), 84
  second-to-die, 74
  tax return information (asset
    identification), 150, 160
  terminally ill patients, 80–82
  umbrella or personal excess liability
    coverage, 84
  viatical agreements, 80–82

Intentionally defective irrevocable trust
  (IDIT), 192, 251, 252
Interest deductions, 154
Interest income, 155–156
Internet fraud (scams), 106–107
In Terrorem (no-contest provision), 172,
  224–225
Investment(s):
  asset allocation, 93–97
    evaluating, 268–270
    work sheet, 95–96
  broker(s), 16–17, 109
  brokerage accounts (ownership),
    113–114
  communicating goals to a fiduciary,
    97
  considerations for bypass trusts,
    101–102
  considerations for QTIPs, 101–102
  consolidation, 86–89, 264
  diversification, 97–99
  evaluating, 268–270
  flim-flam scams, 102–109
  goal work sheet, 98
  income *vs.* total return, 99–102
  longer life spans and, 92
  maximizing returns, 88
  protecting, as parents age, 87–88
  seminars, 109
  stock market, 16–17, 92–93
IRA accounts, named beneficiary, 266
Irrevocable life insurance trust (ILIT),
  77–80, 246
Islam and estate planning, 32–36

Jachter, Chaim, 31
Jackson, Michael, 238
Jackson, Shoeless Joe, 140
Jagger, Mick, 50
Jewelry. *See* Personal property
Jewish issues and estate planning, 31–32
Joint ownership, 118–129
  common-law definition, 118
  community property, 125–129, 156,
    262
  corporation, 124
  estate and gift tax consequences of,
    120–123
  income tax trap, 120, 198
  joint title as will substitute, 118–119
  life estates, 124
  limited liability company (LLC), 124
  partnership, 124
  qualifying for unlimited marital
    deduction and, 61
  tenancy:
    in common, 124, 129–133
    by the entirety, 128–129

tenancy, joint:
case study, 111–112
converting to tenants in common, 124
distinguishing from other forms of ownership, 119–120
severing, 123–124
vs. tenancy by the entirety, 128–129
types of property, 123
time shares, 124
types of, 124
what language to use, 119

Kanumalla, Venkat, 39
Kidman, Nicole, 48

Lafferty, Bernard, 170–171
Lawyers, selecting, 208–211
Letter of instruction, 219–221
Liberace, 21
Life estates, 56–58, 61, 124
Life insurance. *See* Insurance, life
Life spans, 92
Life support issues, 38, 40
Lifetime exclusion. *See* Exclusions
Lifetime trust. *See* Dynasty trust
Limited liability company (LLC), 124, 251, 252, 267–268
Limited partnership (LP), 267
Living-together agreements, 54–55, 244–246
Living trusts, 17, 141, 166, 175–178
Living wills, 17, 40
Long-term care insurance, 17, 72, 82, 181, 186–187
Look-back rule, 185–186
Lopez, Jennifer, 125, 238
Lumar, Yamma Brown, 215

Magness, Bob, 172
Malik, Muhammad Farooq, 33
Malone, Jena, 207
Marriage/divorce:
ex-spouse, protecting inheritance from, 237–248
getting recalcitrant sibling to sign prenuptial agreement, 243
postnuptial agreements, 240–241
prenuptial agreements, 238–240, 243
protecting separate assets from, 241–242
protecting stock in family business, 243–244
signing prenuptial agreement to retain beneficiary status, 238
trusts, 246–247

property:
community, 125–129, 156, 262
ownership (*see* Joint ownership)
separate, 127
tenancy by the entirety, 128–129
remarriage (parent's), 25, 47–68, 196
burial issues, 25
case histories illustrating problems with hybrid families, 52–53
celebrity case history (Anna Nicole Smith), 51–52
life estate recommended (for second wife), 56–58
prenuptial agreements, 53–54
problem with typical estate plan, 47–51
trusts to protect your inheritance, 58–60
what if father's new wife wants more money in her name, 55
spousal/marital trusts (*see* Qualified terminal interest property [QTIP] [marital trusts])
spousal right of election, 63–66
defined, 63
waiver, 65–66, 68
typical entitlement of surviving spouse, 64–65
unlimited marital deduction, 60–62, 74
Marshall, J. Howard, 51
Marshall, Pierce, 51
Marx, Groucho, 206
Median family net worth, 8
Medicaid. *See* Nursing home costs
Medical/dental expenses, 151–152
Mismanagement, 203–213
Moceanu, Dominique, 207
Modern portfolio theory, 94
Monroe, Marilyn, 167
Mortgage, 124, 153–154, 155

Net return, 99
No-contest provision (In Terrorem), 172, 224–225
Notarization, 167
Nursing home costs, 17, 181–187
elder law planning, 182–183, 186–187
long-term care insurance, 17, 72, 82, 181, 186–187
Medicaid, 184–186, 197
rules differing from state to state, 183–184
veterans benefits paying, 181

Organ donations, 29, 32, 38
Ownership/title, 111–135, 265
bank accounts (*see* Bank accounts)
beneficiary designation forms, 134

Ownership/title *(Continued)*
  brokerage accounts, 113–114
  community property considerations,
    125–129
  determining how your parents own
    assets, 113–114
  estate tax planning in traditional
    family unit, 117–118
  gathering key data for parents'
    advisers, 114–117
  jointly held property (*see* Joint
    ownership)
  personal assets (jewelry/art/antiques),
    114
  real estate, 113
  safe-deposit box, 133–134
  stocks/bonds, 113
  tenancy by the entirety, 128–129
  title (definition/importance of),
    111–113
  U.S. savings bonds, 134

Paperwork. *See* Documents/paperwork
Parents, dialogue with, 15–46
  about charitable giving, 42–46
  choosing discussion topics that give
    comfort, 15
  gender approaches to estate planning,
    18–20
  about personal wishes, 20–26
  about religious issues, 26–42
  showing your parents that you want to
    protect them, 16–18
  when to begin, 16
Partition, 123
Partner, domestic (living-together
    agreements), 54–55, 244–246
Partnerships:
  FLPs (family limited partnerships),
    251, 252, 267–268
  income/loss from (tax return
    information), 157–158
  ownership of life insurance policies,
    76–77
  taxes and, 199
  types of joint ownership, 124, 267–168
Pay phones and ATM sales (scams), 105
Pension/retirement assets, 262, 266
Perpetual trust. *See* Dynasty trust
Personal excess liability coverage, 84
Personal property:
  insurance (riders/floaters), 84
  joint tenancy and, 123
  letter of instruction, 219–220
  living trusts and, 141
  ownership, 114
  safe-deposit box, 133–134

Personal wishes, honoring, 20–26
  burying expensive assets with body, 25
  costs of requests, 24
  how death will come, 21–22
  problems implementing requests,
    24–26
  unusual requests, 22–24
Planning team, developing, 258–259
Ponzi/pyramid schemes (scams), 107
Postnuptial agreements, 240–241
Power of attorney, 17, 148–149,
    163–164, 173–175, 176
  accessibility of document, 259
  appointing agent separately *vs.*
    together, 173
  getting copy of income tax returns,
    148–149
  and living trust (not mutually
    exclusive), 176
  need for, 17
  special *vs.* general, 173
  springing, 174
  what happens when missing, 163–164
Preminger, Eve, 170–171
Prenuptial agreements, 238–240
  asset ownership and, 114–115
  community property laws and,
    125–126, 127
  getting recalcitrant sibling to sign,
    243
  protecting stock in family business,
    243–244
  before remarriage, 53–54
  validity requirements, 239–240
Presley, Elvis, 169
Presley, Lisa Marie, 169, 238
Prime bank schemes (scams), 108–109
Pritzker, Jay A., 222
Pritzker, Liesel, 222
Probate:
  assets not under, 266
  minimizing problems, 88
  estate (*vs.* taxable estate), 197
Professional/legal fees, 203–213. *See
    also* Fiduciary(ies)
  checking credentials, 212–213
  court challenges, 211–212
  fiduciaries and trustworthiness, 211
  "lion in sheep's clothing," 205–207
  wills and designation of law firms,
    208
Promissory notes (scams), 105–106
Property and casualty insurance, 83

QDOT, 116, 196
Qualified personal residence trust
    (QPRT), 196, 266–267

Qualified terminable interest property
    (QTIP) (marital trusts):
celebrity case studies, 172, 178
first-to-die, 74–75
investment considerations, 101–102
payment of estate tax, 196, 201–202
remarriage and, 48–49, 55
requirements, 60–62
pros/cons, 62–63
spousal right of election and, 64, 65

Real estate:
case of missing family apartment, 7–8
community property and, 126
home(s):
    bequeathing, 143–145
    case of missing family apartment,
        7–8
    insurance, 83–84
    mortgages, 153–154, 155
    vacation, 143, 145–146, 216
joint tenancy, 123
life estates, 56–58
living-together agreements and, 246
ownership forms, 113, 126
rental property, 145–146, 157–158,
    216
snapshot balance sheet, 262
taxes, 152–153
valuation, and estate taxes, 199
Real return, 100
Recent widow/widower scam, 103–104
Regis, John, 192
Religion and estate planning, 26–42,
    177
Buddhism, 36–39
Christian (Eastern) Orthodox issues,
    27–31
Hinduism, 39–42
Islam, 32–36
Jewish issues, 31–32
Remarriage. See Marriage/divorce
Rental property, 145–146, 157–158,
    216
Renunciation, 19–20
Revocable living trusts, 17, 141, 166,
    175–178
Right of election, spousal, 63–66, 68
Robbie, Joe, 171–172
Roddenberry, Gene, 215

Safe-deposit box, 133–134, 155, 158
Savings bonds, 134
Scams that prey on the elderly, 102–109
affinity group fraud, 105
"callable" CDs, 107–108
Internet fraud, 106–107

investment seminars, 109
pay phone and ATM sales, 105
Ponzi/pyramid schemes, 107
prime bank schemes, 108–109
promissory notes, 105–106
recent widow/widower scam, 103–104
unlicensed individuals selling
    securities, 104–105
viatical settlements, 108
Web sites, 102
Second-to-die insurance, 74
Settlement agreement, sample, 231–236
Significant other, parent's, 54–55,
    244–246
Simultaneous death, two parents, 118
Smith, Anna Nicole, 51–52
Snapshot balance sheet. See Balance
    sheets
Spouses. See Marriage/divorce
Springing power of attorney, 174
State inheritance taxes, 190
Stevenson, Parker, 50
Stock(s)/stock market. See also
    Investment(s):
aggressive brokers, 16–17
certificates, and title, 113
meltdown, 92–93
Strasberg, Lee, 167

Tax(es), 189–202
allocation clause, 201
basis, 115
estate tax, 190, 195–202, 253
    deductions, expenses, and credits, 200
    exclusions, 194–195, 200, 264–265
    impact of poor planning, 5–7
    vs. inheritance taxes assessed in many
        states, 190
    joint ownership and, 120–123
    life insurance and, 70, 71, 172
    prepayment, 71
    rates, 200
    taking advantage of special valuation
        rules, 198–200
    title/ownership form and, 117–118
    understanding of essential for proper
        planning, 195–196
    using to scare parents into estate-
        planning action, 197–198
    who pays (tax allocation clause),
        201–202
evaluating leveraging techniques,
    266–267
generation skipping transfer (GST):
    defined, 190
    multigenerational planning, 267
    trusts and, 62, 196, 251, 253

Tax(es) *(Continued)*
  gift tax, 190, 191–195
    exclusions and tax rates, 200
    incomplete gifts as intentional
      planning technique, 192
    joint ownership and, 120–123
    requirement that gift be complete
      (to be taxable), 191–192
    tax benefits for avoiding/
      minimizing, 192–193
    transfers that trigger, 191
  income tax:
    planning, 189–190, 268
    trap of joint ownership, 120, 198
  information about (on parents' tax
    return), 151, 152–153
  investment return and, 100
  transfer taxes, three kinds, 190–191
  wills and, 171–172
Taxable estate *vs.* probate estate, 197
Team, estate planning, 258–259
Teitelbaum, Stanley, 2, 9
Teitelbaum, Sylvia, 19, 20
Tenancy. *See also* Joint ownership:
  in common, 124, 129–133
  by the entirety, 128–129
  joint:
    case study, 111–112
    converting to tenants in common,
      124
    distinguishing from other forms of
      ownership, 119–120
    severing, 123–124
    vs. tenancy by the entirety, 128–129
    types of property, 123
Term life insurance, 74
Thomas, Denna Brown, 215
Time shares, 124
Title, importance of, 111–113. *See also*
  Ownership/title
Total return, 99–102
Totten Trust, 131
Transfer taxes, three kinds, 190–191. *See
  also* Estate tax; Generation-skipping
  transfer (GST) tax; Gift tax
Trusts, 58–63
  applicable exclusion amount (*see* Bypass
    trust)
  bypass (*see* Bypass trust)
  credit shelter (*see* Bypass trust)
  dynasty, 249–254
  estate tax and, 20
  ex-spouses and, 246–247
  generation skipping trust (GST), 79

  insurance, 77–80, 198, 246
  investment considerations, 101
  living, 17, 141, 166, 175–178
  living-together agreements and, 245
  marital trust, 60–63
  protecting your inheritance with,
    58–60
  setting up family trust, 59–60
  Totten, 131
  two common types of, 59

Umbrella or personal excess liability
  coverage, 84
Unclaimed funds, office of, 160
Unlicensed individuals selling securities
  (scams), 104–105

Vacation homes, 143, 145–146, 216
Vanderbilt family, 56
Variable life insurance, 74
Veterans benefits, and nursing home
  costs, 181
Viatical insurance, 80–82, 108
Videotaped will signing, 218

Waiver, spousal right of election, 65–66,
  68
Wall, Ginita, 127
Welch, Jack, 49
Williams, Ted, 26
Wills, 164–174, 215–236
  absence of, 164–165
  asset ownership and, 116–117,
    118–119
  basics, 167–168
  challenges to:
    defending against, 225–229
    safeguarding against, 209, 216–217
  changes/versions, 217
  fiduciary selection, 168–169, 224
  heirs/sibling with vastly different
    lifestyles and financial situations,
    220–224
  importance of, 164–165, 259
  joint title as substitute for, 118–119
  letter of instruction, 219–221
  living-together agreements and, 245
  no-contest provision (In Terrorem),
    172, 224–225
  notarization, 167
  sample settlement agreement, 231–236
  state differences, 167
  taxes and, 171–172
  videotaped signing of, 218